In Your Best Interest

The Ultimate Guide To The Canadian Bond Market

W.H. "Hank" Cunningham

16

EasyRead Large

RHYW

Copyright Page from the Original Book

Copy editor: Allison Hirst
Design: Courtney Horner

Library and Archives Canada Cataloguing in Publication

Cunningham, W. H.
In your best interest [electronic resource] : the ultimate guide to the Canadian bond market / by W.H. "Hank" Cunningham. -- 3rd. ed.

Type of computer file: Electronic document issued in PDF format
Also issued in print format.
ISBN 978-1-55488-890-0

1. Bond market--Canada. 2. Bonds--Canada.
3. Fixed-income securities--Canada. I. Title.

HG5154.C85 2012b 332.63'230971 C2011-903810-2

1 2 3 4 5 16 15 14 13 12

Conseil des Arts du Canada Canada Council for the Arts Canadä ONTARIO ARTS COUNCIL CONSEIL DES ARTS DE L'ONTARIO

We acknowledge the support of the **Canada Council for the Arts** and the **Ontario Arts Council** for our publishing program. We also acknowledge the financial support of the **Government of Canada** through the **Canada Book Fund** and **Livres Canada Books**, and the **Government of Ontario** through the **Ontario Book Publishing Tax Credit** and the **Ontario Media Development Corporation**.

Printed and bound in Canada.
www.dundurn.com

Dundurn
3 Church Street, Suite 500
Toronto, Ontario, Canada
M5E 1M2

Gazelle Book Services Limited
White Cross Mills
High Town, Lancaster, England
LA1 4XS

Dundurn
2250 Military Road
Tonawanda, NY
U.S.A. 14150

TABLE OF CONTENTS

PRAISE FOR IN YOUR BEST INTEREST

"*(In Your Best Interest)* is full of excellent information and advice that's presented in a smart and highly readable format. If you want to learn more about the fixed-income markets and how they really work, Hank's book is a must read!"

—Debra A. Hewson, President and CEO, Odlum Brown Limited

"I've always been impressed by Hank's knowledge of the bond market."

—Mark Bunting, host of *Market Call Tonight,* BNN

"Wise, justifiably opinionated, and clearly written—accessible to the ordinary investor."

—Thomas Kierans, Chair of the Social Sciences and Humanities Research Council and a Senior Fellow of Massey College at the University of Toronto

"Hank Cunningham is a widely acknowledged authority on Canadian fixed-income investing."

—Robert C. Caldwell, Managing Director (BFS), Macquarie
Private Wealth Inc.

"In my opinion, it is the essential guide for anyone interested in learning about our fixed income markets and in particular the Canadian bond market."

—Bob Moore, investor

Author's Note

This book contains numerous numbers, tables, charts, graphs, and calculations. While the author has made every effort to provide accurate information at the time of publishing, neither the publisher nor the author assumes any responsibility for errors or for changes that occur after publishing.

This edition is dedicated to my daughter Valerie

ACKNOWLEDGEMENTS

Besides reiterating my acknowledgements to Lyman MacInnis, his son Alan, and Stuart Henry in inspiring the first edition, I would like to extend my gratitude to several other people. First, I would like to thank Odlum Brown Limited for giving me the opportunity to work with them. I owe a special thanks to Debra Hewson, the CEO of Odlum Brown, for her support.

In addition, there are many individuals who have contributed to this edition either directly or indirectly. Among these are Jeremy Fleming, Robin Hanlon, Peter McRae, **Murray Leith, Tom Kierans, Stephanie Rio-**pelle, and Kevin Prins.

Through my website and from media appearances, I have had the pleasure of speaking with many individuals who have contributed solid suggestions for this edition. It is heartwarming to know that my book has struck a chord with people who are interested enough to offer me ideas to make it a better book. Thanks to all of you.

Finally, I wish to acknowledge the love and support that my daughter Valerie has provided me, always.

INTRODUCTION

Welcome to the third edition of *In Your Best Interest.* In this edition, I have added a lot of new content, including a chapter on Exchange Trade Funds (ETFs), a new section on forecasting interest rates, and beefed-up sections on preferred shares, convertible bonds, and real return bonds (RRBs). I have also included an update on Canada's ABCP fiasco and what has happened in the income trust sector.

The core principles of this book remain unchanged; individual investors, through a laddered portfolio of individual interest-bearing bonds or zero coupon bonds, are able to preserve their principal while obtaining satisfactory returns. The events of the past three years certainly underscore the importance of maintaining well-balanced portfolios with the fixed-income portion designed to avoid the four biggest risks to fixed-income portfolios:

1. Maturity risk (also known as reinvestment risk)
2. Credit risk
3. Inflation
4. Currency

All of these factors can be mitigated using a laddered approach; I have long favoured ladders with maturities from one to ten years. This allows investors to capture the extra yield available in the six-to ten-year maturities, while at the same time the average term of the portfolio is only just over five years. Ten-year maturities allow for greater credit selection while a steady parade of maturities ensures that, should inflation become a problem, money will be available for reinvestment at higher yields.

Most Canadians will retire in Canada and will need Canadian dollar income. It is imprudent, in my view, to diversify a fixed-income portfolio out of the Canadian dollar, since, with today's low nominal yields, a small adverse currency move can wipe out any extra yield. The explosion in ETFs has not swayed my view on owning individual bonds; there is such a bewildering array of choices that investors end up guessing again. I think that specialty ETFs such as high-yield or emerging-market bond funds might have a role to play, but for regular investing, I prefer individual bonds and GICs. While it is true that ETFs have lower fees than do mutual funds and are designed to merely track an index, they share the same major fault that mutual funds do: they never mature and you don't know what their future value will be.

CREDIT CRUNCH

Lehman Brothers bankrupt, Bear Stearns sold for peanuts, Merrill Lynch absorbed by Bank of America! Who could have guessed that these icons would disappear and that hundreds of billions of dollars would be needed to prop up many other institutions, including the likes of General Motors? This was all triggered by the subprime fiasco and the accompanying collapse in the underlying derivatives. The housing market entered the biggest swoon since the Great Depression and it remains severely depressed today. In turn, this is having an adverse effect on the employment market, as many jobs go unfilled as the mobility of labour is severely hampered by the weakness in the housing market.

Nevertheless, a global economic recovery did get underway but has proven to be a halting, sub-normal one. To be sure, the emerging market countries of China, India, Singapore, Brazil, and others have displayed solid growth. However, we are experiencing a rolling sovereign debt crisis in Europe which, so far, has focused on Ireland, Greece, Portugal, Spain, and Italy. It shows no signs of ending.

It is a curiosity of this cycle, particularly in the United States, that both the corporate and the consumer sectors have conducted serious deleveraging while the U.S. government has had to undergo the indignity of a credit rating downgrade as the politicos in Washington seem unable to put together any meaningful fiscal package.

During this time, monetary stimulus has been extremely accommodative with short-term interest rates near zero and the yield curve very steep. This is producing problems for investors as money is earning a negative real return. While some market anomalies have corrected, there still remain some interesting issues for investors. U.S. ten-year government bonds yield under 2 percent while a significant percentage of the S&P 500 stock market index yields more than 3 percent. Corporate profits remain healthy and dividends are safe and likely to increase.

What are investors to do?

The temptation is to reach for extra yield; long-term yields are significantly higher than shorter-term yields, while high-yield or junk bonds offer tempting returns. For those of you with ladders, particularly one-to ten-year ladders, I recommend that you stay the course and keep reinvesting in the longest maturity of your ladder. This is not the time to be managing your ladders. There is a place for high-yield bonds in portfolios, but for this purpose I recommend high-yield ETFs for their diversification, yield, and currency protection.

For those tempted to nab some of those high-yielding Euro-area issues, I advise caution, as there is both currency and sovereign risk involved. To invest in international bonds, again the road to follow is ETFs, and I have added significant material on ETFs to this edition.

This book is entitled *In Your Best Interest* for good reason. The investment business fails most individual investors by selling them products inappropriate for their circumstances. The basic tenets of fixed-income investing remain the same:

1. Keep what you start with.

2. Earn a return on it.

What else has happened since the second edition is that I joined Odlum Brown Limited as their fixed-income strategist. Odlum's history began in 1923, and in my opinion, it is one of the finest brokerage houses in Canada. Based in Vancouver, they focus on research and strategy for their individual clients. They do not underwrite securities nor do they trade as principal. Thus, they offer objective investment advice, untainted by the natural conflicts of dealing with underwriting products. I am very proud to be associated with them.

This is not an "I told you so" book. The principles I espouse here are applicable at any stage of an economic or market cycle. Investors have learned that they cannot rely solely on equity markets for their retirement needs. The principles of preservation of capital and returns on that capital have returned to the forefront of investing, and as retirement draws nearer, investors are starting to realize that fixed-income investments should constitute a healthy percentage of their portfolios. The principles explained in this book may be applied at any time and in any investment cycle, by investors of any age. I could have written this in the middle of the bubble and it would have carried the same message: individual investors, by adopting and employing simple principles, can produce solid returns via investing in high-quality individual fixed-income securities. What this equity-market volatility has underscored is the need for investors to invest their savings in the different categories of investments appropriate to their ages and circumstances. This mixture of investments is more commonly labelled the "asset mix." The most common categories in which to invest your money are bank deposits (cash), treasury bills, common equities (stocks), real estate, GICs, and bonds. Within each category, you can deploy your money in different ways. Within common equities, for example, you could invest in solid, dividend-paying banks and utilities or in aggressive, high-growth, high-risk technology stocks. In the bond market, you could buy Canada Savings Bonds, corporate bonds, or high-yield or "junk" bonds.

Generally, the younger you are, the more you will invest in equities and real estate. As you age and enter your peak savings years, with an empty nest and no mortgage, your thoughts begin to move toward building an adequate retirement pot to provide you with enough income. This is the time when your asset mix should become more skewed to individual fixed-income securities whose income stream and future value are known, away from the more volatile and unpredictable equity securities. You will still have some equities, but they will more than likely be conservative, dividend-paying ones. This is not a time for fixed-income mutual funds or ETFs, as their future value and income level are uncertain. But more on this later.

Accentuating the importance of this asset mix is demography. The baby boom is in or entering its peak earnings years. As people age and their assets grow, they want more personal attention and individualized solutions for their investment needs. This partly explains why mutual funds are falling from favour and why there has been a marked growth in individually managed portfolios, investment counsellors, and in self-directed individual portfolios. Simply put, mutual funds or ETFs cannot differentiate one investor from another and thus cannot offer any specific solutions. Recent scandals have further increased investors' distrust.

One analogy from a book about demographics and the financial markets[1] explains that mutual funds of today are akin to the cheap beer of university days. While we may drink less today, we want the beer to be high quality, or perhaps we now prefer a fine wine. Translating this to investment terms, we become fussier and desire individually managed portfolios and more personal attention. This analogy is particularly appropriate for the fixed-income markets, where bond mutual funds or ETFs are just not appropriate for

1 The Pig and the Python, David Cork.

retirement planning in that returns, income, and future values are all uncertain.

I will show you how to achieve solid, certain returns by focusing on a specific strategy and on specific securities. The laddering strategy involves investing monies in fixed-income investments of different but evenly spaced maturities. This strategy has stood the test of time, and it will continue to do so. It has outperformed, and will continue to outperform, the majority of bond mutual funds whose managers charge too much for merely average performance. The laddered approach takes the guesswork out of the direction of interest rates and allows investors to own individual fixed-income securities with a defined income stream and a known future value. In addition, there are very valuable, retail-investor-friendly investment products called zero coupon or "strip" bonds that are excellent retirement planning tools; they provide investors with the precise future nominal value of their money. These strip bonds, when combined with the laddered approach, are ideal for RRSPs. I have also come to the view that real return bonds (RRBs) deserve to be included in your RRSPs. Currently, however, RRBs are very expensive and I do not recommend them. There is a section devoted to an analysis of these bonds in Chapter 5.

For taxable income needs, I again recommend the laddered approach, but using interest-bearing provincial and corporate bonds for their higher yield. Mutual bond funds and ETFs, you may have noticed, are not part of this strategy. In this edition, I have expanded the product section considerably, added a chapter on preferred shares, included an updated analysis of online fixed-income trading, and have expanded many portions, including bond market transparency. Exchange Traded Funds (ETFs) have proliferated in the past two years, offering investors far more cost-effective choices in fixed-income markets. I have included an in-depth discussion of the fixed-income ETF choices facing investors.

By demystifying the fixed-income market and by educating you in all of its aspects, I will show you how to meet your income and retirement needs and make the retail fixed-income market less expensive, less formidable, more accessible, and more efficient. In other words, I want to make you wealthier. That could mean increasing your net worth and your income, making your retirement portfolio bigger, or allowing you to retire sooner. To accomplish this, I will examine the bond market, what it is, how it functions, and explain the various individual products. As well, I will point out sound strategies to follow that have worked for others.

The prime reason I am in this business is to make my individual investors better off by offering them excellent advice. A high percentage of investment advisors (IAs), however, merely sell products and do not focus on their clients' needs. Thus, it is in your best interest to not only learn about the fixed-income markets and how they work but also to select an IA who can help you to satisfy your needs. Even without finding the right IA, you can still do it yourself using an online bond-trading account. (Later in the book I have included an analysis of available sites.) After reading this book, you will be able to buy and sell individual bonds, know how to choose the appropriate ones, how to build your own portfolio, and where you can find a good IA.

The following sections are included in the book: what the bond market is, how it functions, the various products, how to use this market profitably, winning strategies, how to find and choose an IA, the mathematics of bonds, the concept of duration, how to forecast interest rates, bonds for the speculator, retirement planning (RRSPs and RRIFs), reinvestment risk, preferred shares and bond mutual funds, and GICs versus individual fixed-income products. There are separate chapters for zero coupon bonds and for the laddered approach, as they represent the cornerstones for your retirement needs. In addition, there is an expanded section on real return bonds (RRBs) and an expanded products chapter, separating conventional bonds from structured products. As an added bonus, you will know which way bond prices go when interest rates fall! I should point out here that all the various terms that are explained within the body of the book are also defined in the glossary located on page 223 at the end of the book.

Someone asked me the other day about how the bond market worked. I have been asked that question countless times, but this time, without a lot of forethought, I blurted out: "It is all about relationships." After I said it, I realized that I had tripped over the most concise and accurate description of how the bond market actually functions: relationships. Your success in the fixed-income market will be directly related to your relationship with your IA. Therefore, I spend some time discussing how to find a suitable one. That IA must have an excellent relationship with the trading desk of his or her firm. And that trading desk must have a strong relationship with all the IAs of that firm, as well as with the various counterparties it trades with. Thus, I stress the value of finding that right IA, one who will provide you with a good financial relationship and who knows how to build a relationship with the bond-trading desk of his or her firm. You may not have to worry about this if you are simply opening an online trading account. Perhaps the best of all worlds is to find an IA with fixed-income expertise and combine that with an online account. This would offer you the flexibility you need to do it yourself.

In addition—and this is vital to your understanding of the fixed-income markets—almost all bonds trade in relation to another bond. Most bonds do not trade every day, so they are priced in relation to a bond that does. You will discover that bond prices change all the time, all day long, as the actively traded bonds (dubbed "benchmarks") change in price. Other factors that can affect your returns are the relationship between short-term yields and long-term yields (the "yield curve"), the yield relationship among developed countries, the relationship between supply and demand in the different sectors of the market, and the relationship between today's prices and yields and historical prices. This, in turn, permits you to conduct technical analyses, which can be of great help in timing purchases and sales. I urge you to study all these relationships, as they are vital to understanding this gigantic, practically invisible market.

In this book I will also share with you some of my personal thoughts, experiences, and anecdotes from a lifetime in the securities business. I have held a wide variety of positions, including research analyst, institutional bond trader, institutional salesman, zero coupon specialist, portfolio manager (for two prominent financial organizations, Standard Life and Investors Group), and global bond trader (for CIBC). Since 1988, I have built and managed three fixed-income trading departments (Dean Witter Canada, First Marathon Securities, and Blackmont Capital), whose mission was (and still is) the provision of competitive pricing on a complete array of fixed-income products combined with top-notch service to investment advisors and their individual clients. Since April 2009, I have been associated with Odlum Brown Limited as their fixed-income strategist, and I have found it to be rewarding to work with their investment advisors and clients to enhance their returns. I have also enjoyed my repeat engagements with BNN as they recognize the need and demand for education in the world of fixed-income.

I will briefly explain the wholesale or institutional business and point out its relevance to the retail market for fixed-income securities; its dominance and structure go a long way in explaining why the retail fixed-income investor has difficulty finding good service and prices.

Another important reason for this difficulty is the poor education of both IAs and their clients. I am a leading proponent of making fixed-income markets more visible or transparent to the investing public by electronically distributing a wealth of prices and offerings on an extensive array of constantly re-priced fixed-income products, solely with the retail investor in mind. (I use the term *transparency* to mean the ease with which individual investors can gain access to information and prices for fixed-income securities. Fixed-income trades would be reported post-trade for everyone to see.) These quotations are now made available through IAs or directly to private clients via electronic connection with various vendors such as GMarkets, Reuters, or Bloomberg. The larger investment dealers offer bonds online to their internal sales forces and their discount brokers via their own private legacy systems. In addition, CBID Perimeter (CBID) offers real-time quotes on a variety of government and corporate bonds on their website: w ww.canadianfixedincome.caIn addition, www.canadian bondindices.com offers a wealth of information for individuals and www.canpxonline.com features live prices on benchmark bonds.

There are several initiatives underway in the realm of transparency. The net result will be broader visibility and availability of real-time bond pricing for individuals. Also, these online systems come with tools to make it easier for individuals to implement their strategies. I will talk more about transparency later.

Like all markets, the bond market is undergoing a transformation. With the return to deficits at all levels of government, there are a lot more government bonds to choose from. Corporations, on the other hand, have exhibited considerable discipline and have not had to use the bond market as frequently as before the recession. The result has been a considerable narrowing of the yield spread between government and corporate bonds, with the attendant superior performance of corporate bonds. The amount of money invested by individuals in Canada in fixed-income investments totals approximately $793 billion. Approximately 58 percent of this total is in GICs. Bond mutual funds amount to $106 billion, ETFs $11 billion, while investments in individual fixed-income products total $218 billion. It is my belief, and a central theme of this book, that a large percentage of this money will find its way into individual fixed-income products, which, combined with safety of principal, offer greater yield than do bank deposits and GICs. Simply put, bond mutual funds charge too much in fees and produce average returns with uncertain future value. GICs are too short-term for long-term planning and are illiquid. Individual bonds offer a defined income stream, a known future value, liquidity, plus the flexibility to accommodate individual circumstances.

Now, let us begin the process of providing you with the information and tools to help you make financial decisions in your best interest.

CHAPTER 1

What Is a Bond, What Is the Bond Market, and How Does It All Work?

WHAT IS A BOND ANYWAY?

A bond is a piece of paper (well, a computer blip these days) that "bonds" borrowers and lenders. The borrower rents money from the lender and agrees to pay a certain rate of interest for the rental, normally at prearranged times, typically every six months. Thus, a bond is the original amount of the loan plus a series of rental cheques or interest payments. Eventually, the lease is up and the landlord gets the property (capital) back and can re-lease it or hold on to it.

Here is the anatomy of an actual bond, the Canada 3.5 percent due June 1, 2020. For purposes of illustration, we will assume a principal value of $100,000. In other words, $100,000 is the amount that the lender will receive back at maturity. I will use this bond in different chapters of the book. This is a benchmark issue, with $13.1 billion outstanding. This bond pays interest semi-annually, so we may display the internal workings of this bond as follows:

the interest payments are the principal value ($100,000) times the coupon rate (3.50 percent) divided by 2, since the interest is paid twice a year. Therefore, each payment is $1,750.

BENCHMARK BONDS

A benchmark bond is an actively traded bond that is used to determine the prices of less actively traded bonds. The media report benchmark prices so that the investing public can see the direction of bond prices. As well, issuers of new bonds use them as reference points to price their issues. The Bank of Canada regularly adds to existing benchmark issues at the key maturity dates: two, five, ten, and thirty years. This contributes to a smoothly functioning marketplace. Investment dealers also use these benchmark bonds to hedge market risk.

DATE	INTEREST	FACE VALUE
December 1, 2011	$ 1,750	
June 1, 2012	$ 1,750	
December 1, 2012	$ 1,750	
June 1, 2013	$ 1,750	
December 1, 2013	$ 1,750	
June 1, 2014	$ 1,750	
December 1, 2014	$ 1,750	
June 1, 2015	$ 1,750	
December 1, 2015	$ 1,750	
June 1, 2016	$ 1,750	
December 1, 2016	$ 1,750	
June 1, 2017	$ 1,750	
December 1, 2017	$ 1,750	
June 1, 2018	$ 1,750	
December 1, 2018	$ 1,750	
June 1, 2019	$ 1,750	
December 1, 2019	$ 1,750	
June 1, 2020	$ 1,750	
June 1, 2020		$100,000
	$ 31,500	
Total	**$131,500**	

So, an investor who bought and held this bond until maturity, without reinvesting any of the interest payments, would have received a total of $131,500.

If the investor held this bond inside an RRSP or held it in a taxable account but did not need the interest, each of these interest payments would need to be reinvested. I am introducing the concept of reinvestment at this stage, as it is a very important component of bond yields. Bond yield calculators assume that each interest payment will be reinvested at the purchase yield, clearly not a real world assumption, but it does provide consistency, as all bonds are measured the same way. Don't worry; we will examine all of this later in more detail.

At one time, investors in bonds received beautiful lithographed letter-sized pieces of paper as evidence that they had made this loan. Today, most of these physical pieces of paper have disappeared, replaced by the "book-based" system, whereby the Central Depository for Securities (CDS) maintains the records of who owns what. Your evidence of ownership is the contract you receive from your financial institution and your monthly statements.

Most bonds are issued with a coupon rate, which is the rate of interest investors will be paid. How is this rate determined? It is a product of the length of time to the maturity date, the general level of interest rates, and the creditworthiness of the borrower. Unlike a mortgage, which is a specific relationship between an individual and a lender, there may be hundreds of holders of the same bond, as individual bond issues may range from $15 million to $20 billion.

WHAT IS THE FIXED-INCOME MARKET, AND HOW DOES IT OPERATE?

The fixed-income market, or bond market, operates in what we call an "over-the-counter" manner. To understand what this means, let us first examine how the equity market functions. When investors purchase, say, one hundred shares of TransCanada PipeLines, they purchase them from other investors who are selling the shares at the same price. These trades take place on a public stock exchange, where prices are clearly visible. Both the buyers and the sellers pay a fee (or commission) to their respective IAs. The financial institutions (for example, investment dealers or brokers), hereafter called FIs, merely facilitate this transfer from the buyer to the seller; they do not assume any principal position and thus do not risk their principal or capital. Therefore, retail equity transactions are called agency transactions, since the FIs merely act as agents.

The bond market functions in an entirely different fashion. There is no visible public market, and almost every trade is done on a principal basis and is quote-driven. That is, the FI's bond traders are using the firms' capital to maintain inventories and make markets in the broad spectrum of fixed-income securities.

Consider TransCanada PipeLines for a moment. It has one class of common shares with 699 million shares outstanding as of March 14, 2011, with a market capitalization of $27 billion. At the same time, it had 62 bond issues outstanding, of all different sizes, maturities, and characteristics, ranging in maturity from 2011 to 2067 and in coupon from 3.40 to 12.20 percent, having a combined face value of $16.9 billion. Many of them are held in large percentages by the investing institutions, rendering them illiquid. Very few of these issues trade every day, so if you are interested in investing in one of them, your IA will ask the retail bond-trading desk, which will likely not have them and will turn to the wholesale bond-trading group, which will then attempt to make a market for that particular bond.

It is somewhat like a grocery store or convenience store. To help individual investors, retail fixed-income departments stock their shelves with inventories of the various bond and money market products. There are special sales at times, and of course the investment dealers will showcase the products that they want you to buy. When inventories run out or become low, the retailers go to the institutional department to get restocked. As retailers have all kinds of costs—communications, technology, salaries, rent, and financing the inventories, to name a few—prices are marked up from the institutional price. I can tell you that the price markups are very small at most investment dealers. As with grocery stores, you can comparison shop by opening accounts at different investment dealers or discount brokers. Recently, I conducted a survey of online bond trading at the five major dealers to further assist you in your do-it-yourself dealings. You will find the details on page 58.

Quotations for bonds often confuse investors. The base denomination for bonds (other than stripped bonds) is $1,000. This is called the "face," "book," or "par" value. It is the principal amount that you invest and will receive back at maturity. We quote bonds on a percentage of face value. When you see a bond quotation, it may be, for example, $98. This means that the bond is trading at 98 percent of the face value. In other words, the $1,000 bond is worth $980.

As well, bonds (except for stripped bonds) trade with accrued interest attached. The value of that accrued interest is not included in the price. The seller of the bond that you are buying expects, and deserves, to receive the interest accruing from the last interest payment. The buyer pays that accrued interest in addition to the purchase price. This is because the new owner of the bond will receive the full interest payment when it is eventually paid, even though he or she is entitled to only the interest accruing from the date of purchase to the settlement date of the sale.

Assume, for example, that you sold a bond, there were three months before the next payment, and you did *not* receive the accrued interest. The next owner of the bond would then receive the full six months' interest payment when it came due. Therefore, the next owner's money earned double for that period and yours earned nothing! Since it is impractical and inconvenient to wait until the payment is received before selling the bond, the interest owing to the seller is calculated and paid by the new owner on the settlement date.

Let us re-examine the above example: a bond paying 4 percent semiannually with a face value of $10,000 is sold at 98 percent of face value with 90 days of accrued interest owing to the vendor. The seller of the bond receives $9,800 of the original principal plus the accrued interest owed from the last payment date. If this bond had been held for a full year, the investor would have received $400 in interest (4 percent of $10,000). We divide $400 by the number of days in a year to calculate how much interest accrues daily: $1.09589 accrued per day. Now we take this number and multiply by 90 to arrive at how much accrued interest is owed to the seller: $98.63 of accrued interest. Therefore the seller receives the $9,800 plus the $98.63 of accrued interest for a total of $9,898.63.

BID, ASK, OFFER

The terms bid, ask, and offer create some confusion. When you are selling a bond, the investment dealer provides you with a bid. If you are buying, you need to know what the

dealer is asking for the bonds or where he offers it. It becomes confusing when you say that you want an offer for these bonds. That could mean that you want a bid. Stick to bid and ask.

So, what happens to the buyer? Assuming the buyer pays the same percentage of face value, he or she pays exactly the same as the vendor receives. In the real world, the two prices will not be the same as a result of commissions being charged. The accrued interest will be the same. As we recall, the bond market functions as a principal market where the investment dealers make markets in bonds using their firm's capital. Thus, there will be a difference in the "bid," what a trader is willing to pay for a bond, and the "ask," which is the price at which a trader is willing to sell. As well, the IA needs to make a living, so he or she takes the bid or ask price from the trader (depending on whether the client is selling or buying), subtracts or adds the commission, and then gives the client a net price. Note that no commission is added or deducted in a fee-based account.

Getting back to the buyer: when the next interest payment is due, the buyer will receive the full six-month payment ($200). Subtracting the $98.63 interest previously paid, the buyer has netted $101.37 of accrued interest for the period that he or she has owned the bond. Should this new owner keep the bond through successive payment dates, he or she would receive the full $200 each six months until the bond is sold or it matures.

Also, you will notice that prices for bonds range from discounts, say $90 (or 90 percent of face value), to premiums, such as $110 (or 110 percent of face value). Why is this? Interest rates move up and down, and bond prices move inversely to yields. (Not a week goes by without someone asking me which way bond prices go when yields go up. They go down. Bond prices and yields move in opposite directions, and you will understand why when you read the chapter Basic Math.)

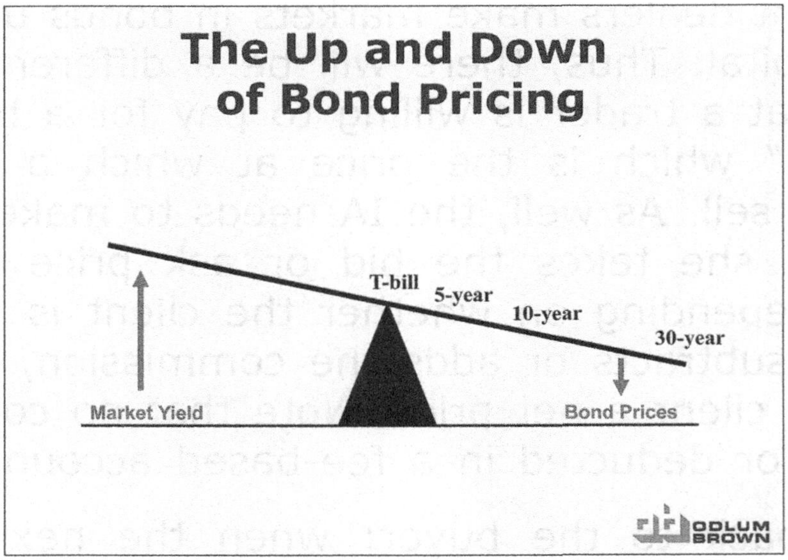

This is to put them in line with currently issued bonds. If the price on our Canada 3.5 percent bond due June 1, 2020, was exactly $100, then its yield to maturity would be 3.5 percent. If market yields moved to 6

percent, no one would buy this bond at 3.5 percent, so we adjust its market price to $83, which equates to a yield to maturity of 6 percent. Conversely, if yields fell to 2 percent for this maturity, this bond would be re-priced to $112.13. We will examine in detail how these prices are actually calculated in the chapter Basic Math. Don't worry.

Individual quotations on bonds (bids and asks) are not readily visible, although there are determined attempts underway to increase the transparency of the bond market. Online or discount brokers have offerings of fixed-income securities, while in the case of FIs, the IAs can see their firms' inventories displayed electronically from their internal systems and can relay these to their customers. In addition, there are three public sites with up-to-date bond prices on a reasonable cross-section of the bond market:

- www.canadianfixedincome.ca provides free access to a broad list of bond prices. Further, individual investors may subscribe to Bondview, which offers a more complete view of the marketplace, for $19.95 per month.
- www.canpxonline.caoffers hourly updates on benchmark Government of Canada bonds. Eventually, they plan to introduce Canada's equivalent to the U.S. Trace system whereby all corporate bond trades will be displayed with a time delay.

- www.canadianbondindices.com offers a plethora of information on fixed-income markets, including live updates, some trading volume statistics, as well as performance numbers.

There are daily quotations in newspapers and more extensive lists in the weekend press, but they are not all-inclusive; they typically represent institutional pricing (greater than $1 million in size), and they are just a snapshot at a certain point in time. While they are useful indicators of where bond prices were, bond prices will be different when you attempt to buy or sell, since they fluctuate far more than investors (and IAs) realize. In any event, retail investors will not be able to transact at these prices for two basic reasons: first, they are dealing in retail quantities; second, since the bond market is a principal market, as we now know, a bond trades on a net basis (that is, with no visible commission added).

Let us consider that there might be a different (i.e., higher) price for a retail fixed-income transaction by individual investors than for a wholesale purchase by a giant financial institution. Returning to our grocery shopping analogy, individuals normally find the shelves adequately stocked for their relatively small purchases. If the store did not maintain adequate inventories, the management would have to shuttle back and forth from the wholesale warehouse. The warehouse sells in bulk quantities, so the store manager must decide how much to buy, balancing the needs of the customers with the prices for different quantities of merchandise. After adding the merchandise to the shelves, the manager now raises the wholesale price to retail to account for various factors such as heat, lighting, salaries, insurance, spoilage, and taxes.

A retail fixed-income department operates in a similar fashion. I do not run to the wholesale, or institutional, market for every $10,000 worth of bonds that I sell. Instead, I will sell them "short" (that is, sell now and buy later), or I might suggest another bond that I do have in inventory. In practice, I buy in bulk various fixed-income products from the wholesale market and add them to my "shelves," which I call my inventory. Once I do that, I incur market risk, which I offset by hedging. Hedging involves neutralizing market risk so that I do not incur capital gains or losses as the market prices change. I also incur yield-curve risk and credit risk. I also maintain state-of-the-art computer and communication equipment. As well, there are the other basic costs, such as remuneration! Also, since most bonds do not trade every day, I resort to "matrix" pricing to at least provide a quotation. How do I do that? I do that by comparing one of those bonds to an actively traded benchmark issue, such as a Government of Canada bond of similar maturity, and adding a yield spread to that bond based on where I know or believe that they have been trading recently. I then compute a price. It is as if I know there are some TransCanada PipeLines (TRP) bonds down in the factory, but rather than keep you waiting, I price them and sell them to you now and go buy them later because I know what my relative cost will be. If I know that the "factory" contains none of what I am asked to sell, I will search everywhere for them or, more likely, suggest a similar bond.

Even given all this, the markups from the wholesale fixed-income market to the retail market are amazingly small, meaning that individual investors can be well served by the fixed-income market.

This type of pricing is necessary since, and returning to the TRP example, there may be just one class of common shares outstanding, but there could be sixty or so different bond issues of different maturities, sizes, and features. There is just not enough liquidity to display a bid and an ask all the time in the same fashion as the equity market. The FI "makes a market" in the various instruments, willing to be long or short to accommodate investor interest. In addition, governments of all types borrow money in the bond market, and, of course, they do not have any common shares to trade!

TRANSFER PRICE

The transfer price is the price at which the fixed-income trading department transfers it to the IAs. To get paid, they must add a commission to this price in the case of an investor purchase, unless the transaction is in a fee-based account.

The bottom line is that the bond market functions as a clearing house between borrowers and lenders. For IAs to earn a living, in the case of client purchases, they raise the ask price received from the bond department and get paid the differential as a commission. Again, this does not occur in the case of fee-based accounts. This is not visible to the investor, although this may soon change. I will talk about initiatives in this area in the transparency discussion. The opposite occurs when clients sell, with IAs deducting from the bond desk's bid to create a commission. This is referred to as a "haircut" in the business, as you've just had a trimming!

Furthermore, the less-liquid bonds, such as corporates and zero coupons, are most frequently quoted on a matrix basis. Since many of these instruments do not trade every day, they are priced in reference to an instrument that does. For the most part, Government of Canada bonds of different key maturities constitute the benchmarks by which other securities are priced. While I have included more on benchmarks later, I think it is important to mention them now, as the majority of fixed-income securities offered to investors are priced in relation to them.

The Bank of Canada is committed to building up very large and therefore liquid benchmark issues at the key maturities: two, three, five, ten, and thirty years. They are vital not only in pricing bids and offerings, but also in pricing new provincial and corporate issues when they come to market. The benchmarks form a valuable base level from which other bonds may be valued. For example, let us take a provincial bond: the Province of British Columbia 3.70 percent due December 18, 2020. It is valued by the market at 74 basis points above the relevant benchmark, the Canada 3.5 percent due June 1, 2020. (1 percent is divided into 100 pieces, each of which is called a basis point. In this case, the B.C. bonds at 74 basis points higher in yield than the Canadas are 74/100 of 1 percent higher. You will encounter the term "basis points" frequently throughout the book.) To trade these, a trader will observe where the Canadas are trading, add the 74 basis points to the benchmark yield, and then calculate the price for the B.C. bond. Let us say that the Canada 3.5 percent June 1, 2020, is trading at $102.49 to yield 3.1 percent. Now we add the 74 basis point spread and arrive at a yield of 3.84 percent for the B.C.s, which produces a price of $98.87.

Thus, as the liquid, actively traded benchmark issues change in price and yield, so do all the matrixed bonds. The yield spread between the benchmarks and these bonds fluctuates in reaction to supply and demand factors, changes in the yield curve, and changing credit risk perceptions.

The role of investment dealers, then, is to make markets in a wide-ranging list of bonds, bidding for bonds for which there are no apparent buyers or short-selling bonds where they are not sure there are sellers. FIs sell bonds short all the time, either to accommodate demand when they know there will be a seller of the same bond soon, or to hedge long positions (quantities of bonds that they already own). They may also short-sell bonds if they think they have become expensive compared with some other bond. Thus, they are a buffer between the differing needs of a cross-section of bond market participants. These longs and shorts are all held in the dealers' inventories, which are typically segregated by type (money market, short-term Canadas, mid-term Canadas, long-term Canadas, provincials, strips, and corporates). The dealers hedge these inventories with offsetting transactions in the benchmark issues (or in the futures market) to eliminate or reduce market risk. Bond trading volumes are enormous, averaging approximately five times the daily amount of equity trading (approximately $38.4 billion). Why is this? First of all, the amount of bonds outstanding is huge, exceeding $1.9 trillion in Canada.

Corporations and governments issue bonds all the time for various reasons, such as rolling over maturing debt, paying off bank lines, funding deficits, and building new factories. Investors of all kinds (governments, pension funds, mutual funds, trust companies, life insurance companies, foreign investors, and individual investors) all have varying fixed-income needs, and these needs change over time. Some of these investors trade for speculative reasons; others think they can outsmart their peers by aggressive trading; while still others merely match the term of their assets and liabilities. In addition, new issues come to market that may be more attractive than bonds already owned. As well, bonds mature, making money available for reinvestment, or as they shorten in term over time, investors may wish to sell them in order to buy ones with a longer term to maturity.

COMPOSITION OF CANADIAN FIXED-INCOME MARKET (as of December 31, 2010, $ billions)

Money Market (less than one year)		
Treasury Bills	Federal	$ 174.90
	Provincial	$ 41.70
Bankers Acceptances		$ 45.80
Commercial Paper		$ 53.20
Total Money Market		$ 315.60
Bond Market		
Federal Government Bonds	Domestic	$ 404.30
	Foreign	$ 5.70
Provincial and Municipal Bonds	Domestic	$ 406.20
	Foreign	$ 118.30
Corporate Bonds	Domestic	$ 797.50
	Foreign	$ 247.60
Total Bonds		$ 1978.60
Grand Total		**$2,294.20**

Source: Bank of Canada

TRADING VOLUME FIRST QUARTER 2011 DAILY AVERAGE ($billions)

Money Market	
Government Treasury Bills	$ 7.33
Bankers' Acceptances	$ 5.74
Commercial Paper	$ 8.28
Total Money Market	$21.35
Bond Market	
Canadas	$29.36
Crown Corporates, Provincials, and Municipals	$ 6.78
Corporates	$ 1.99
Strip Bonds	$ 0.29
Total Bonds	$38.42
Grand Total	**$59.81**

Source: Bank of Canada, IIAC

WHAT DOES THE BOND MARKET LOOK LIKE?

The bond market is largely invisible, being decentralized, over-the-counter, and with no post-trade disclosure in Canada yet. The United States has its Trade Reporting and Compliance Engine (TRACE) system and we are studying this approach now. I discuss this in more detail in the section on transparency beginning on page 51. It resembles an onion with a series of layers. At the heart of the Canadian bond market is the Bank of Canada, which is in charge of monetary policy and open-market operations in the foreign exchange, money market, and bond markets.

Next come the money market "jobbers," whose role is to ensure the orderly maintenance of the money market, including the issuance of Government of Canada treasury bills. The money market is defined as securities issued with a term to maturity of one year or less. Treasury bills are obligations issued by the various governments. They are issued at a discount from their face value and mature at their face value so all the yield is in the amortization from that discounted amount.

Then we have the primary dealers, many of whom are also jobbers. Among other things, they are required to bid for the auction of the Government of Canada's primary bond issues. They do the bulk of the underwriting of new provincial and corporate debt, make markets in the complete array of fixed-income products, and service the fixed-income needs of the various institutional and retail investors by maintaining extensive inventories and bidding and offering on all sizes of blocks of bonds. Individual trades can be in the hundreds of millions or as little as $5,000. The lion's share of the daily $38.42 billion trading volume takes place among the Big Six investment dealers (at the time of writing, they were RBC Dominion Securities, TD Securities, CIBC World Markets, BMO Nesbitt Burns, Scotia Capital, and National Bank Financial) and their institutional and global customers. The market for individual investors is approximately 2 to 3 percent of this total. The other 97 to 98 percent is in the institutional area, where the bank-owned dealers (plus a few non-bank-owned dealers, such as Merrill Lynch Canada, Desjardins Securities, Casgrain and Co., Laurentian Securities, Penson, and HSBC) make wholesale markets in all the various fixed-income products to serve the investment needs of their institutional customers. These customers include life insurance companies, chartered banks, pension funds, mutual funds, investment counsellors, governments, and foreign investors.

PRIMARY DEALERS FOR BONDS

BMO Nesbitt Burns, Inc.

Casgrain and Co., Ltd.

CIBC World Markets Inc.
Desjardins Securities
Deutsche Bank Securities Ltd.
HSBC Securities (Canada)
Merrill Lynch Canada Inc.
Laurentian Bank Securities Inc.
National Bank Financial Inc.
RBC Dominion Securities Inc.
Scotia Capital Inc.
The Toronto Dominion Bank

It is worth pausing to note that the money that these institutions have for investment represents the aggregate savings of individuals like you! Your money is mixed in with everyone else's, thus giving the institutions very large sums of money to invest and trade. A large percentage of this money is invested in fixed-income securities to satisfy actuarial requirements, match liabilities, and guarantee fixed returns. With large blocks of money to invest, these institutions command and receive the best prices. The investment dealers vie for this business: competitive tendering for bids and offerings is the norm, and individual trades exceeding $100 million are commonplace.

Naturally, all of the bank-owned dealers serve individual investors, since they all have national sales forces of IAs. There are another 210 members of the self-regulatory body which goes by the unwieldy title of Investment Industry Regulatory Organization of Canada (IIROC), who transact fixed-income securities. There are large, independent firms such as Blackmont Capital (now MacQuarie Private Wealth), Canaccord, and GMP Capital, as well as a host of small- and medium-sized investment dealers such as Odlum Brown, Haywood Securities, and Dundee Securities.

Each of these firms has to find fixed-income products somewhere in order to satisfy their customers' needs. The bank-owned dealers help to meet these needs. They offer, via electronic delivery, retail quantities and prices of the various fixed-income products. TD Securities, Merrill Lynch, and RBC Dominion Securities are prominent in this area. In addition, Penson, Laurentian Securities, and HSBC also contribute to market making in this space. As well, a company called Perimeter CBID aggregates prices and offerings from a number of contributors and makes them available to all these same small dealers and entities. Several of the larger independents, such as MacQuarie, Dundee, Canaccord, and Odlum Brown, have their own specific fixed-income trading departments staffed by experienced personnel. They have sufficient capital and technology resources to assemble, maintain, and offer a wide range of fixed-income securities to meet the needs of their IAs' customers.

My former firm, Blackmont Capital, for example, has a department of four professionals who have enough capital to maintain inventories of sufficient size to adequately serve the needs of their entire sales force. They manage these aggregates on a fully hedged basis to eliminate market risk for the firm and to offer competitive prices at all times. With an online, real-time trading system at their disposal, they can offer their own inventory plus fixed-income securities that they do not own. This is possible owing to the presence of actively traded, large bond issues for which there exists a known market.

Knowing what spread they trade at in relation to one of the benchmark issues makes it easy to offer a security without owning it. In fact, the benchmark prices are fed electronically into this system as they change, ensuring that the IAs' customers are always seeing live prices. Also, in a typical sales force, some clients are selling securities that others will be buying. Knowing this, the trading department will keep and hedge the sold securities for later resale to its own sales force rather than to "the street," the large market-making investment dealers mentioned earlier. This is an efficient way to do business, and customers benefit through better prices. Running to and from the wholesale market for every small transaction is very expensive. Yet, that is what the smaller dealers must do, as they do not have the personnel, capital, or the inclination to keep an inventory themselves.

It is also worthwhile pointing out the different philosophies of the various investment dealers with respect to how they treat individual fixed-income investors. Most of the bank-owned dealers treat their retail customer base as a captive audience and therefore charge more for individual bonds than the smaller, more focused firms. What you need to know is whether the FI you are dealing with treats the retail fixed-income market as a profit centre or not. The best ones work at growing the business through value-added service and competitive prices. Make a point of ascertaining what approach your FI uses.

Also, there are interdealer brokers (IDBs) whose role is to act as middlemen, facilitating anonymous trades among the jobbers, primary dealers, and investment dealers. The most prominent ones in Canada are Shorcan (owned by the TMX) and Freedom (owned by Cantor Fitzgerald and the Canadian banks). The trades are done anonymously so that the dealer in question does not give up any trade secrets to his counterparties (read *competitors).* Also, it means that each dealer does not have to make multiple phone calls to attempt a transaction. The IDB displays everyone's bids and offerings electronically and pockets a brokerage fee on each transaction. These parties trade among themselves to offset transactions done with clients.

Last, we come to the individual investor whose needs are served by the different FIs. Individuals have their own specific reasons for purchasing fixed-income products directly: to generate income, to plan for retirement, and to provide safety of principal. They may need income in a foreign currency, they may wish to speculate on the price movement of bonds, or they might want to invest some money for future educational needs. Direct investment by individuals in the bond market, including GICs and ETFs, totals several hundred billion dollars.

THE CASE FOR BONDS

Why go through the bother of purchasing individual fixed-income securities? Why not take the easy route and invest in a nice bond mutual fund or ETF? The answer to the second question is that it is not in your best interest to do so! Mutual bond funds and ETFs simply do not offer the certainty required in retirement planning; their performance is erratic, and the management fees are too high. I speak from experience. For five years I managed what is now the largest mutual bond fund in Canada.

Sadly, there are too few IAs with sound enough working knowledge of fixed-income markets. The line of least resistance for them is to recommend bond mutual funds because they are an easier sell and the fees are attractive. However, they are not the ideal choice for the individual investor. Here are five reasons to choose individual fixed-income products.

Planning. Fixed-income products have specific maturity dates. That is, you know the exact date at which your principal will be returned to you and what your yield will be for the term that you hold this security. Contrast this with bond mutual funds: They do not have a specific maturity date, nor do they have a specified income level. Investors do not know what their investment will be worth at any moment or what it will be worth when they actually need their money back. Bond fund managers are constantly tinkering with their portfolios, shortening term, extending term, and trading for capital gains. This is not conducive to effective planning.

Fees. Bond funds charge management fees averaging approximately 1.66 percent per annum! ETFs offer lower management expense ratios (MERs). This takes a serious bite out of an investor's income and return. Contrast that with individual products, where there is a one-time fee at the time of purchase (averaging 1/2 to 1 percent) with no further fees until they mature and the money is reinvested or if they are sold before maturity.

Performance. The long-term results of "professional" bond fund managers are not impressive, for a couple of reasons. First, it is a well-documented fact that no one is 100 percent sure of where interest rates are going. All forecasters, traders, and market commentators are right some of the time, but nobody is right all of the time. However, this does not stop portfolio managers from guessing using a technique with the more elegant name of "rate anticipation trading." It only takes a couple of bad guesses for performance to suffer. Second, there is indexing in the bond fund management business, too, as brave portfolio managers huddle around the different bond indices in order to look good in the performance game and earn those bonuses for their professional management. They strive to beat the index as well as more than half of their peers so they will be able to market above-average performance. Also, consider that bond funds are required to calculate an annual return since they do not have a fixed maturity date. Investors owning individual bonds do not have to worry about annual returns since their yield and maturity date are known at the time of purchase. A good analogy is a baseball game. Individual investors in specific fixed-income securities know the outcome of the game before it starts even though the score (the annual return) may vary by inning. Bond fund holders have to worry every inning since they may have to leave the stadium before the end of the game without knowing the outcome.

It is difficult to have negative performance in the bond market.

Here are the annual performance results from 2002 for the broad Canadian Government Index and the Canadian Corporate Index as provided by Merrill Lynch Canada.

	2002	2003	2004	2005	2006	2007
Government Index	8.81%	6.69%	6.60%	6.56%	3.57%	4.90%
Corporate Index	8.66%	8.52%	7.32%	6.04%	4.35%	1.35%

	2008	2009	2010	2011 (to June 30)
Government Index	11.31%	-1.31%	5.76%	1.69%
Corporate Index	0.04%	15.34%	7.30%	2.56%

Corporate bonds just barely turned in a positive return in 2008 while the only negative performance came from government bonds in 2009. The principal reason for bonds to return positive returns on a consistent basis is the interest paid on bonds and the reinvestment of that interest. Granted that bond yields fell on a net basis since 2002, nevertheless there were lots of negative months. The bond market is one market where investors are advised not to sell into weakness.

Following is a table showing a group of Canada and corporate bonds with three-, five-, seven-, and ten-year maturities. Using current market yields, I increased the yield by 100 basis points or one full percent for a one- and two-year period. For good measure, I increased the yield by 200 basis points for the two-year period.

TOTAL RETURN				
	Yield (7/26/11)	Plus 1% 1 year later	Plus 1% 2 years later	Plus 2% 2 years later
Canada 2.25% Aug.1, 2014	1.70%	-0.20%	1.23%	0.76%
Canada 2.75% Sept. 1, 2016	2.14%	-1.56%	0.75%	-0.62%
Canada 4.25% June 1, 2018	2.45%	-2.51%	0.45%	-1.53%
Canada 3.25% June 1 2021	2.88%	-4.41%	-0.33%	-3.45%
BNS 3.35% Nov. 18, 2014	2.32%	0.17%	1.70%	1.12%
Bell 4.64% Feb. 22, 2016	3.10%	0.01%	2.01%	0.92%
H&R 5.00% Dec. 1, 2018	4.57%	-0.56%	2.45%	0.38%
Enbridge 4.26% Feb. 1, 2021	4.00%	-2.78%	1.05%	-1.80%

A few things stand out. For one, the lower the starting yield, the more negative the return for a given increase in yield. This makes sense as the income to be reinvested is less than that of higher yielding bonds. Thus, the corporate bonds would outperform all the government bonds for these scenarios.

The two-year total returns exceed the one-year returns for the same yield movement because there is one more year of compounding and because the bonds are now shorter in maturity by two years and thus less volatile.

Maturity Selection. Bonds come in a wide range of maturities, from thirty days to more than thirty years, allowing for appropriate retirement planning and ladder building (more on this in Chapter 8). Bond funds and ETFs do not have maturity dates so investors do not know how much money they will have when they need to redeem their units.

Liquidity. Bonds can be sold at any time, should raising money become important or should other opportunities present themselves. Daily trading volume averages over $38 billion, with the major investment dealers maintaining bids and asks on the complete array of fixed-income products that have been issued. Mutual funds can only be redeemed daily.

BOND INDICES

There are several bond indices in the Canadian bond market. One of the most widely used for bonds in Canada is the DEX Universe Bond Index™ produced by PC Bond (www.canadianbondindices.com). This index encompasses some 1,103 different bond issues totalling some one trillion dollars and is constantly being rebalanced so that it fairly represents the overall bond market. As of December 31, 2010, it consisted of 46 percent in federal bonds and federal guaranteed bonds, 27 percent in provincials and municipals; and 27 percent in corporates. The corporates are further weighted by credit rating. The average duration was 6.27 years. *Duration* is a term that refers to the average term of the bond, taking into account the weight of the interest payments. Thus, duration is shorter than the term to maturity and is a measurement of the volatility of a bond. (More on this later.) This index is further divided into maturities with 45 percent being one to five years, 24.2 percent from five to ten years, and the balance of ten years and longer at 30.8 percent. There are many other sub-indices as well.

For the twelve months ending August 31, 2011, this index returned 5.35 percent while Canadian-managed bond funds returned a median of 3.50 percent. This gap is partly explained by the fees charged to the fund by the manager. This is called the management expense ratio (MER), which averaged approximately 1.7 percent in this period (source: globefund.com).

What to do then? I referred in the introduction to a strategy called laddering, which is fully explained later. Suffice it to say here that laddering takes the guesswork out of interest rates, reduces fees, and, over time, outperforms the majority of bond fund managers. This is done with individual fixed-income securities of staggered maturities. Basically, it is the most effective way of dealing with reinvestment risk, as your investments are spread out over regular intervals. This approach eliminates the need to guess which way interest rates are going, as investing in bonds of different maturities avoids the risk incurred if all your funds were invested in one maturity and interest rates were very low when that investment matured. There will be more on this important method in Chapter 8.

It is in your best interest to take control of your financial future by arming yourself with the knowledge of how to invest in individual fixed-income products. Doing this will offer you greater certainty as to the future value of your money and cost you less in fees.

CHAPTER 2

How Do I Get Started?

It is likely that you already have a relationship with an FI and/or an IA. It may be a bank, a bank-owned investment dealer, an independent brokerage firm, a mutual fund company, a financial planning company, a life insurance company, or a trust company. All of these entities, through their IAs or agents, first attempt to sell you their products, even if they are not suitable for you. Very few IAs (my guess is 10 percent) actually have your best interests in mind. Therefore, you will have to arm yourself with all the knowledge you can and find an experienced IA to act for you.

Your IA's firm will have lots of educational material available and there are a plethora of websites to help you along. I have included this list in Appendix A. These websites offer all kinds of analytical tools. The daily newspapers offer some commentary, and television shows such as CNBC and the Business News Network (BNN) have expert commentators on a regular basis, including me. There are books available, and your IA's firm will likely offer daily, weekly, and monthly bond market commentary. Over time, all of this information will stand you in good stead as you will have a good knowledge base.

So, armed with all this knowledge, you should be able to get your broker/advisor to do what you want, shouldn't you? Not necessarily! Each pillar of the financial services industry (banks, trust companies, mutual fund companies, life insurers, investment dealers, and advisors/planners) has a vested interest in selling you what is in its best interest, not yours. Rare is the organization (or individual) that actually listens well enough to ascertain the needs of the client and takes care to make sure those needs are met, even at the expense of a sale that might produce greater near-term reward.

How and where do you find such people? The number one method is referral, from an IA's satisfied clients or from lawyers, accountants, and friends. Ask, ask, ask, and eventually you will find someone who will help you. At some point, you will likely receive what are called cold calls. These come from IAs just starting out who are trying to build their books. It is in your best interest to find IAs with experience and well-established books of business so that you are well served. It is a further bonus if they offer fee-based services and thus are not driven by the need to generate commissions on every trade. It is possible that you may not find such IAs or your account may not be large enough for them. The major investment dealers offer superb training for new IAs, which includes the fixed-income markets. Therefore, you may find a newer IA who might be suitable for you, but remember to ask, ask, ask.

This market remains a decentralized or over-the-counter market. With myriad issues to choose from and with mammoth trading volume and institutional dominance, it becomes extremely important to select the right firm and then the right adviser. The choice of a firm must be made before you pick an adviser. Extra time spent on this decision can mean significantly enhanced returns and thus a higher standard of living and more comfortable retirement!

The first step is to determine whether an investment dealer or organization takes the retail fixed-income business and its participants seriously. Look for FIs who advertise a special focus on fixed-income needs. Develop basic questions to ask would-be financial advisors. Here are some common questions, as well as the answers you should be looking for.

Q: Is the retail fixed-income desk a captive of the wholesale desk or is it master of its own destiny?

A: To properly serve individual investors, the retail fixed-income desk should be focused on providing IAs and their clients with good advice and competitive pricing.

IAs' books of business refer to how many clients they have and what the assets of those clients total.

Q: Is it a stand-alone profit centre or is the desk's compensation linked to the overall growth of the firm's fixed-income business?

A: A desk that is motivated to grow the business of the IAs will offer the best overall service.

Q: What percentage of your business is fixed-income?

A: It should be in the 20 percent to 50 percent range.

Q: How is the Bank Rate set?

A: You should be told that it's set at regularly scheduled meetings of the Bank of Canada (bankofca nada.ca).

Q: Assuming I have $100,000 in my RRSP, what kind of fixed-income portfolio would you recommend in individual securities?

A: IAs should mention stripped bonds (zero coupons), corporate bonds, real return bonds, and the concept of laddering, perhaps Exchange Traded Bond Funds (ETFs), and should not suggest bond mutual funds.

Q: What is the difference between semi-annual and annual yield?

A: It depends on the level of nominal rates. It is an important question, since GICs, for example, are quoted in annual yield terms while most bonds are offered in semi-annual terms. Most firms will convert one to the other for fair comparison. It is in your best interest to ensure that you are being offered an apples-to-apples comparison, since annual yields may appear to be higher than semi-annual yields when, in fact, they may be the same or even lower.

Q: How much commission do you charge on bond trades?

A: If they answer at all, it should be between 0.5 percent and 1 percent. They may be fee based, which is expensive for fixed-income portfolios.

Q: Do you know what duration is?

A: This is important as it represents the risk and volatility of a bond. It is the average term of a bond, including the interest payments.

Q: What is the size of your book and how many clients do you have?

A: A minimum size of $100 million and perhaps 250 clients would indicate a successful IA and one who, therefore, would not need to do frequent transactions to make a living. Ask if they are willing to do a price comparison test with other FIs. It may not be easy to get these answers, but persist. Ask friends, read the financial papers, listen, observe.

Q: If I find the right advisor, how easy or difficult is it to move my account from my existing financial institution?

A: Naturally, FIs are not keen to see customers leave and so they do not make it easy to do so. In days gone by, it was a genuine hassle to move your account. Now the rules have changed and your account must be moved, in cash or kind, within days or the FI faces fines. It also helps that almost all securities are book-based, so this transfer becomes a simple matter of a computer transfer—plus the inevitable paperwork, of course. The FI that you are moving to will expedite the transfer.

To move your account, first open a new account with the new FI. Once that is done, complete, with the help of your new IA, a Request for Transfer Form, which serves notice to your former firm that you would like to transfer your account. The former firm must reply within two days and deliver all the securities and cash, within ten days. For a complete description of this process, visit www.IIROC.ca and look in the Investor Education section.

The absolute worst part of this process is the treatment that you may receive from the FI that you are leaving. There are horror stories of the departing IA being attacked verbally and his clients being given the full court press to stay. Typically, the departing IA's accounts are divided among some more junior IAs and they really go after these clients. Sometimes, incentives are offered in the way of fee reductions and the like. If you really like your IA, go with him/her to the new FI. IAs do not move often, largely as a result of this treatment.

***

The advisors you are seeking are not likely to be rookies. They are most likely to have more than ten years of experience with a large, balanced book of clients. They will be working for an FI that has a comprehensive inventory of individual fixed-income products and a variety of tools to make your investing easier. Most major FIs have websites replete with prices, calculators, portfolio-building strategies, and, of course, offerings of all the various products.

There are also an increasing number of institutional bond salespeople who, late in their careers, become retail advisors. They can be of immense assistance to the individual investor given their knowledge of the entire fixed-income spectrum, as well as their ability to take advantage of how the bond market functions. If you are talking to a branch manager of an FI, ask if there is an IA there who specializes in fixed-income products or has a strong knowledge of and a client base in these products. Typically, IAs with only a passing knowledge of bonds are timid and unsure in approaching the trading desk personnel, who, to such IAs, appear to be a bunch of fast-talking, untrustworthy types. Unsure of themselves and of how to interact with the market, they may shy away. However, skillful handling of the information, services, and expert personnel of the typical well-staffed fixed-income department by a person steeped in the knowledge of how this market functions can produce measurable rewards for fortunate clients. Knowledgeable IAs will have access to bargain lists, and will know of important economic releases and the upcoming borrowing calendar. These IAs are well placed to add income and yield to your portfolios. The experienced advisor also gains the respect of the traders, lets them know what his or her specific areas of interest are, and thus gets calls when specific offerings appear.

Following are some representative questions and comments that IAs will use with their bond-trading department.

Q: My client can buy those bonds cheaper somewhere else.

A: This is a loaded one; most of these apparent discrepancies can be explained because this is not an apples-to-apples comparison. In other words, the client (or IA) may be comparing the identical security, but one yield may be quoted in annual terms and the other one in semi-annual terms. At 5 percent this difference is 6.25 basis points even though the price is the same (see the chapter on basic math). As well, the comparison may be hours or days old, and bond prices do change minute by minute. The securities being compared may not be exactly alike; there may be slight differences in maturity, credit, or features that may affect the relative yield between different fixed-income products. Another explanation could be that another investment dealer is offering a special sale. Worse yet, advisors may be trying to get a lower transfer price (the price at which the trading department transfers bonds to IAs). This is the IAs' cost and they add a markup to earn a commission. If they do obtain a lower price from the trader, that improvement is not necessarily passed on to clients. Needless to say, traders become wise to ploys such as these and handle the offending parties appropriately.

The relevance of this is that it is an over-the-counter market and there are inefficiencies. Clients may receive, or say that they receive, better prices from another FI. It may be because one IA is charging more commission than the other or that one firm's bond desk is running a special on a certain bond. It does underscore the point that the more experienced your IA is, the better the treatment you will receive.

Q: Why can I not buy this bond at the same price as quoted in the weekend newspaper?

A: This is a very common question. The newspaper quotations are snapshots of market prices at a particular instant, typically 4:00p.m. the previous business day. They are quotations representing only the market for transactions larger than $1 million and before any brokerage or commissions are added. The large lists of bond quotations in, for example, the weekend *Toronto Star* or the *Globe and Mail* are matrix-priced, meaning that each bond is not priced individually but in relationship to the benchmark issues. In such cases, there is no allowance for any idiosyncrasies or features of a bond that could affect its price. What happens is that a keen client, eager to learn the ways of the bond market and therefore studiously following everything, discovers a few really high-yielding bonds in the weekend paper and phones an IA on Monday morning to scoop up these bargains before those slow-moving bond traders catch on.

The advisor, of course, smelling a sale, rushes to the bond desk asking for offerings without a shred of thought. In almost every case, these bonds have certain features—usually call features—that mean that the issuer may redeem those bonds before maturity and the advertised yield in the newspaper may not be realized. (The papers may not have the inclination or the space to show the yield to call.) In addition, the issue may also be small, or a private placement, in the hands of foreigners, or the whole issue could have been stripped with no public float at all. There is a public site (www.canadianfixedincome.ca) where you can obtain live wholesale markets. These are also not prices at which individuals will be able to transact, but they do offer valuable market information.

Q: My client just inherited $350,000. What do I do?

A: A good retail fixed-income desk will ask the IA more questions as to quality and maturity preferences and then construct a customized portfolio. If an IA just recommends a bond fund, then this IA is not doing his or her job.

HOW TO GET ALONG WITH A BOND DESK

I have seen all aspects of human behaviour in managing retail fixed-income trading desks. I have built and managed three retail-oriented fixed-income trading desks since 1988. The first was for Dean Witter Canada, which was eventually sold to Midland Walwyn, which got taken over by Merrill Lynch, whose retail arm was sold off to CIBC Wood Gundy, where many of the Dean Witter IAs had come from when Wood Gundy got out of retail. What a business! The second one was built for First Marathon Securities, which needed a retail-oriented bond-trading desk to service the fixed-income needs of its rapidly growing Correspondent Network, which today clears and trades for a very large number of financial organizations: some small investment dealers, some large ones, some investment counselling firms, and some investment subsidiaries of very large FIs. First Marathon was purchased by the National Bank in 1999 and merged with Lévesque, Beaubien. NBCN became the abbreviation for the National Bank Correspondent Network. And finally, the third was another retail-focused fixed-income trading desk, this time for Blackmont Capital Inc., an independent investment dealer focused on the individual investor. MacQuarie, a prominent Australian bank, bought Blackmont from CI Financial and renamed it MacQuarie Private Wealth. To all of MacQuarie's IAs, my former department offers a complete array of fixed-income securities via an online, real-time order entry system. It also offers customized portfolio design, market commentary, and research. As well, it offers fixed-income securities to some of the more than two hundred IIROC members that do not have their own inventories.

Each of these trading desks has had the same philosophy—to be in charge of its own destiny and to be driven and compensated primarily by the growth in the retail fixed-income business. In this way, IAs know that their bond-trading desk is served by helping their business to grow.

On the one hand, I have observed thoughtless, short-term-oriented IAs adversely affecting clients' returns while alienating the trading desk at the same time. On the other, I have had the pleasure of working with enlightened, informed, intelligent, long-term-oriented IAs who reap huge benefits for their clients by adroit use of the market and the desk. No more than 10 percent of any sales force falls into this latter category—hence my focus on selecting the right advisor.

I have seen and heard it all: IAs looking for an ask when they really wanted a bid; strange trades initiated at month end with the sole motive of generating commission; outright lies (e.g., saying XYZ broker is offering something cheaper), pleading for a lower price only to keep the difference and not pass the savings on to the client; apples and oranges comparisons, days or hours apart; confusing annual and semi-annual yield, yelling and screaming when the price cannot be matched or has changed. To a person, these IAs say they cannot trust the desk and are getting ripped off, when really it is they who are hurting themselves and their clients through this time-wasting, counterproductive behaviour.

Trading desks make or take a thousand calls a day and execute more than a thousand trades per day. They know what they are doing, what the prices are right now. Some IAs attempt to outsmart them; what they should be doing is being straight with them, and they will receive the same treatment in return. IAs should also be spending more time with their clients. I am always amazed when an acquaintance tells me that not only does he not understand what his money is invested in, but that he does not see his advisor routinely, perhaps once a year at best! At stake here is the return to the client, as consistently bad behaviour makes us leery of certain IAs, and therefore their clients will suffer.

Contrast this with informed IAs who realize that the desk is on their side—at least a tool for them to use, at best an active partner in helping improve their business. They trust the traders and realize that there are bargains to be had at different times as well as (with the market knowledge of the desk) assistance in timing purchases to again help clients achieve superior yield. These astute IAs are more aware of pending release times for important, market-moving news and new-issue timing. With proper desk contact, IAs learn of temporary sell-offs or rallies to take advantage of. Trusting the desk or at least being straight with it yields huge advantages. Contrast this with the mistrustful IAs who play petty games with the traders, getting their backs up. In fact, through frequent communication with the desk, IAs may pick up gratuitous tips or advice to further their clients' (and their own) after-tax standard of living.

You want to seek out an IA who has a sound working knowledge of the fixed-income markets and who does a high percentage of business in fixed-income. Listen to the IA describe how he or she gets along with the desk; if it's not mentioned, ask. The answer will reveal a lot. Human nature is important; traders are human and will respond favourably to professional treatment. Of course, trading desks are not perfect. One mistake or misunderstanding in an over-the-counter market may colour one's opinion for a long time. However, a quick glance at the commission statistics will reveal in almost every case that the IAs who give the desk a hard time are in the lowest quartile of production. They waste too much time playing games with the desk and not enough time taking care of their clients. The top quartile of producers do not waste their time or the traders' time through childish antics. Every retail organization where I have worked has these IAs. It is the same as with a lot of other businesses, where 10 percent of the IAs handle 90 percent of the business. You want to find one of those IAs. The other

90 percent complain and play games and just waste too much time on unimportant issues.

TRANSPARENCY, TRANSFER PRICES, MARKUPS, AND COMMISSIONS

> *Transparency: that which is transparent; a transparent object or medium*

Despite efforts to make the bond market more transparent, there is still a dearth of websites where bond prices may be obtained. With the explosion in internet usage, investors are now used to finding and using useful sites. The following three organizations offer free quotes and also offer a subscription service for greater access and visibility.

CI Financial owns Perimeter CBID, which is a marketplace where several liquidity providers make available bids and offerings on a wide selection of fixed-income securities. Perimeter CBID operates a public website: www.canadianfixedincome.ca. Besides offering live markets on approximately 2,500 bonds, it also contains the previous day's closing prices, actively traded corporates, and featured quotations. For $19.95 per month, investors may subscribe to Bondview, which offers a more in-depth view of CBID's marketplace. CBID is not perfect, as it does not have all the liquidity providers, but it does present an accurate view of the retail bond market.

The TMX owns PC Bond, purchased from Scotia Capital. It has the most complete data base for bond prices and performance in Canada. The programs and analytics are aimed squarely at institutional customers, being far too expensive for individual investors. However, their wonderful site, www.canadianbondindi ces.com has a wealth of information suitable for individual investors. It offers the performance of the different sectors of the bond market on a daily and historical basis. It offers live prices on a variety of government and corporate bonds along with information as to volume traded. They do not offer a subscription service.

CanPX is a joint venture of the primary dealers in Canada plus certain inter-dealer brokers. It provides a composite display of real-time bids and offerings on a variety of bonds. It is geared to the wholesale market, also, but their website offers hourly updates on the benchmark Government of Canada treasury bills and bonds. On a subscription basis, and only available through Gmarkets (www.gmarkets.ca) are two subscriptions: All governments for $125 per month and their corporate bonds for the same amount. I recommend the corporate bond subscription, as this is the most current list of corporate bonds available. In addition, GMarkets has their own product called Pilot, which is a comprehensive view of all aspects of the financial markets. It costs $485 per month but is well worth it.

Another excellent source for individual investors is the Bank of Canada's site: www.bankofcanada.ca.

One of the main reasons—if not the main one—why investors either do not know enough about fixed-income markets or are too timid to venture into them is the lack of transparency of this giant market. As we have discussed, there is no central location for the bond market. Instead, it operates on an over-the-counter, decentralized basis. There is no ticker tape showing trades as they take place, nor is it easy to obtain a quotation. In other words, most of the bond market is opaque, not transparent. Whether *transparency* is the proper word or not is debatable. Prices of the most liquid bonds, Government of Canadas, are highly visible and widely quoted on a number of websites (www.candeal.ca and canadianfix edincome.ca are two). I feature Perimeter CBID's live quotes on my website, www.inyourbestinterest.ca and there are many provincial and corporate prices in addition to the benchmark Canadas. Of course, they represent a tiny percentage of all the bonds outstanding (some 60,000 issues) but at least it is a start. Regulators are pushing for more transparency and I am on a committee of IIROC that is exploring improvements in this area. By now, most clients can see the yields of the bonds that they have traded on their transaction statements. There is a strong push to reveal the commissions charged on each fixed-income transaction. Although most fellow committee members oppose this, I am in favour of it. Investors know how much they are charged for equity trades, so why would they not get to see how much they are paying for a bond trade? There really is not much to hide, as the fees charged on bond transactions are generally fair and do not vary significantly from equity commissions.

Policy 5 is a code of conduct for IDA member firms trading in wholesale domestic debt markets. It was developed at the behest of the Department of Finance and the Bank of Canada. Its purpose is to "ensure the integrity of Canadian debt markets and thereby to encourage liquidity, efficiency and the maintenance of active trading and lending and promote public confidence in such debt markets." You can read the entire policy at www.iiroc.ca.

In recent years, Policy 5B was added. This was aimed directly at the retail fixed-income markets. It requires all investment dealers to have written policies and procedures in place for dealings with individual investors in the Canadian retail debt market. In particular, each investment dealer must have in place a recommended commission or markup for each fixed-income product that they trade. Such a grid would look like this.

FIXED-INCOME COMMISSION GRID (per $100)		
Term	**Suggested Commission**	**Maximum Commission**
Government Bonds		
< 1 year	.1	.2
1-2 years	.25	.5
2-5 years	.5	1.0
5-10 years	.75	1.5
10+ years	1.0	2.0
Corporate Bonds		
<1 year	.1	.2
1–2 years	.5	1.0
2–5 years	.75	1.5
5–10 years	1.0	2.0
10+ years	1.0	2.0
Strips		
< 1 year	.1	.2
1–2 years	.5	.75
2–5 years	.75	1.25
5–10 years	.75	1.25
10+ years	1.0	1.75
High-yield Bonds	2.0	3.00

While not generally available, you can ask for and expect to receive a copy of your FI's grid. At the very least, your IA should be able to tell you what the grid is. As you can see, these are fair commissions (generally, the longer the term, the higher the commissions). This is for two reasons. First, the longer the maturity the less the yield is affected for a given commission, and second, it rewards the IA, as most bonds, especially strips, are buy and hold securities.

Other proposals are being pushed forward that would require retail bond-trading desks to maintain records demonstrating that their dealing prices are fair. This is a long way from implementation, but it is clear that the push is on to ensure that the retail fixed-income investor will be assured of getting a fair shake.

A huge hurdle facing bond market transparency has to do with the fact that IAs and their clients are captive to their firm's bond-trading desk. The Big Six—RBCDS, TD Securities, Scotia Capital, BMO Nesbitt, CIBCWM, and National Bank Financial—are loath to give up their monopoly and trade flow. I am positive that they will not do so unless legislation is enacted requiring them to participate in a commingled marketplace for bonds. It seems to me that if every dealer who wanted to could provide their bids and offerings to a centralized system, and also allow their clients access to the same system, that would solve the transparency debate once and for all. I am also positive that this is going to be snail-like in its progress, as the Big Six have nothing to gain from it; the whole retail fixed-income business is not a very high priority for them. Regulators do run the risk of imposing so many costs and rules on the investment dealers that the dealers will move their clients away from this already expensive business.

The retail fixed-income business has shrunk dramatically as a percentage of investment dealers' revenues as a result of plummeting nominal yields and the surge in (alas) structured products. Sadly, these products (chronicled in the product chapter) are not created in your best interest, but rather are designed to put big fees into the hands of the investment banking groups and big commissions in the hands of the IAs. As I stress, to be a do-it-yourselfer in the world of bonds, you will need to find a knowledgeable IA with a large book of business such that he/she does not need to do a lot of transactions with you to make a living. Otherwise, and I have heard from many of you, you can open an online account with a discount broker. To assist you, I have conducted my own hands-on survey of the various online fixed-income suppliers, which you will find on page 58.

The investment dealers make their markets in bonds using their own capital, unlike the stock market, where most trades occur on an agency basis (buyer and seller meet and a transaction takes place without the investment dealer needing to use capital).

Why does this difference exist, and what is being done about it? First of all, the majority of the outstanding fixed-income issues do not trade every day, with the noticeable exception of the very liquid Government of Canada benchmark issues. The reason they do not trade more frequently is that a provincial government or a corporation issue bonds of various types, maturities, and amounts. Some issues end up being owned by a few large investing institutions, leaving no "float" (refer back to the TRP example on page 29) Others may be stripped and sold as zero coupon securities. Also, some issues are too small. Foreign investors may acquire a large percentage of an issue.

Thus, quotations on almost all other bonds besides benchmarks are calculated on a matrix basis, where a certain bond is priced in relation to benchmark issue of a similar maturity. Otherwise, how would investors know what to pay for an illiquid bond? At the same time, the daily retail fixed-income transactions are estimated to number between 8,000 and 10,000, with an estimated face value of $700 million, perhaps 2 percent of the total market. This implies an average individual transaction size of approximately $70,000. With bond yields having fallen significantly in the past three years, retail transactions have fallen as indicated. They were approximately 5 percent of the market in 2008. These trades all happen privately, as each investment dealer has its own private electronic delivery system for providing bids and offerings on a complete spectrum of fixed-income instruments to its IAs and then to their customers. Discount brokers display offerings in a similar fashion, providing online tools to assist investors in selecting issues, building ladders, and calculating yields. Each system is different, and there is no public display of the trades.

In the meantime, a company called Perimeter CBID, mentioned earlier, has developed and introduced a fixed-income system that features several contributors showing retail bids and offerings to a growing list of smaller investment dealers. While it offers good software and reasonable offerings, it has one weakness: it does not have all the major liquidity providers. These dealers see no reason to provide liquidity to CBID, and remain content to distribute their fixed-income products internally to their captive sales forces.

There are more than 200 IIROC members and only 12 or so retail-oriented trading desks to service them all. What are the Big Six doing? For one, they created a company called CanDeal, which exists to make markets electronically in the most active Government of Canada issues, but only for institutional customers. There are 12 liquidity providers, the primary dealers for the Bank of Canada and the best market-makers for bonds in Canada. CanDeal was modelled after a company called TradeWeb in the United States that is now trading approximately $300 billion of fixed-income securities and related products daily online. Recently, the Toronto Stock Exchange made a $20 million investment in CanDeal, signifying its interest in this business and perhaps staking out a possible future role as central consolidator for the fixed-income business.

Where is this going? In the huge American market, only a handful of electronic bond-trading platforms remain after there were once more than a hundred. Only two are profitable.

In Canada, it is hard to imagine more than one system surviving in each of the institutional and retail spaces. It is equally difficult to imagine why the Big

Six would want to give up their private monopoly over their own sales forces and clients. Gradually, inexorably, some veils will be lifted, but there will be stout resistance from institutional bond traders, loath to share any trade information with rivals. There is a system in the United States called TRACE (the Trade Reporting and Compliance Engine for corporate bond transactions). It broadcasts, with a delay, the last sale price and other relevant trade data for U.S.-dollar-denominated, investment-grade, and high-yield corporate bonds. The delay was at the behest of the major investment dealers, who argued that immediate dissemination of corporate bond trades would put them at a competitive disadvantage. The bank-owned dealers are advancing the same argument in Canada. Nevertheless, there is enough pressure emanating from the regulators to make this happen eventually.

Transparency is a long way off, but retail investors will have more choices and more tools.

Where do I stand on this? I am in favour of greater transparency for individual investors in fixed-income securities for the simple reason that the more investors can see a market, the more they will trade in it. As a trader, that means more trading volume and that is a good thing! I also think some sort of post-trading reporting system showing at what prices bonds actually traded would help lift at least one veil from this over-the-counter market. In other words, the more information that is made available on prices and quantities of bonds, the better able the investors will be to make a decision. An open market reflects the divergent valuations of the participants, and the larger the number of competitors with market knowledge, the greater the chance that both buyers and sellers will get the best price possible.

Much of the pressure to reveal more has to do with markups and commissions. Let us first re-examine the process. The major investment dealers maintain extensive inventories, using their own capital to do so. They incur hedging costs to minimize risk, make large investments in market-making systems, communications, and back-office infrastructure. There are spread risks, yield curve risks, and credit risks. This helps explain why there is a spread between the bid and the ask sides of a market, with that spread representing the risks associated with bidding for that particular bond. For example, when bidding for an obscure corporate bond, traders must take into account its credit rating and the likelihood of finding a buyer for it. They may own it for months, and the bid will reflect that. Conversely, bidding on an actively traded Canada issue is simple because they know they can sell it right away.

When it comes to the retail offering of bonds, each trader takes all of these risks into account and offers the inventory to the sales force at what is called the transfer price, which is the price at which the trader will transfer the bond to the IAs. There is no commission built in; this is merely the traders' ask price. As this is a principal market, the IAs need to add a markup to this price to earn a commission. It is this markup that is the hot button for the regulators. Investors see how much commission they pay when trading equities, but not so when buying fixed-income securities (including GICs). Investors pay a 1 to 1.25 percent commission when buying a five-year GIC.

ONLINE TRADING SURVEY

Since publishing the second edition, I have continued to receive emails from individuals with respect to online bond trading. The biggest concern is the availability of products. Frequently, when on the Business News Network (BNN), I will recommend certain bonds, usually corporate bonds. These are bonds that are normally available to my firm, Odlum Brown, and which I regard as relatively easy to obtain. It turns out that most of the online investment dealers do not, in fact, offer as extensive a supply of bonds as Odlum Brown is accustomed to seeing on a daily basis. This is being rectified and much broader offerings of bonds should be available in the not too distant future.

There has been a significant change in the online bond trading space. The Bank of Nova Scotia (BNS) bought e*Trade Canada in the fall of 2008 and, with much ballyhoo, launched Scotia iTrade Canada in early 2009. They claimed to have made a huge breakthrough in the bond space with their "buck a bond" policy. With a minimum commission of $20 (a purchase of $20,000 face value) and a maximum of $250, iTrade claimed to have made a breakthrough in transparency by actually revealing the commission on the contract. They also said that they were using multiple providers of bond offerings with more than 2,300 issues available. It was clear that BNS had to do something, as the Scotia Online product came last in my previous survey.

Besides **iTrade, Trade, I was able to survey the online offerings of TD Water-** house (TDW), BMO Investorline, and RBC Direct Investing. CIBC was unwilling to participate and so was National Bank Financial. I tried without success to see what Questrade had to offer.

For the four firms which I surveyed, I was able to pose as an individual investor, using a dummy account but in a live trading environment.

The results follow in a table, but I will say at the outset that the clear leader here is TDW, which combined very good pricing with ease of use and decent availability of inventory. In addition, they offer the tools for an individual to build his own ladder easily.

	TDW	RBC	BMO	iTRADE
Ease of Use (1–10)	8	8	6	6
Inventory Breadth	7	9	8	9
Pricing	9	7	6	8
Tools	7	8	6	9

Notes: TDW is the only one to show a bid side for bond prices; for all the others, you must phone a representative for a bid or have the bond in your account to get a bid online. This seems reasonable except that when buying a bond, it is useful for investors to see what the bid is. ITrade has the best combination of educational materials and research. TDW is the only one which offers investors the ability to build their own ladders.

Specific Pricing Comparisons: As you review these, remember that I was able to compare each dealer's prices at exactly the same time as I could see the prices in the wholesale market, so the results are accurate in measuring their spreads from the base price.

PRICE SPREADS

	TDW	BMO	iTRADE	RBC
Canadas (3 years)	0.39	0.48	0.20	0.53
Provincials (10 years)	0.81	1.13	0.20	1.00
Corporates (7 years)	0.55	3.50	0.83	0.66
Strips (6 years)	0.53	1.73	0.42	0.65

It is important to note that iTrades prices do not include the "buck a bond" commission. Thus for a trade of $50,000, an additional $50 would be added to the total purchase cost. This would have the effect of raising the price and lowering the yield.

I did not include money market pricing as not all the dealers offered Bills and BAs, and the ones that did charged ridiculous spreads.

OTHER COMMENTS

iTrade has excellent breadth of product but has some idiosyncrasies in its corporate bond prices. It is my understanding that they blend the offerings from Scotiabond's fixed-income trading desk with those of Perimeter CBID. This does result in a broad suite of offerings. iTrade's search function was very awkward to use.

As noted, TDW is relatively weak in the product breadth category, displaying a total of 436 different issues. TDW is planning to rectify this with a new fixed-income platform that will not only include a broader suite of bonds but which will offer several new features, including an enhanced search facility, the ability to save searches for future reference, and the addition of U.S.-denominated securities. As well as having the ability to create laddered portfolios, TDW's new platform will allow investors to add bonds from their saved searches to other portfolios.

The other specific advice I have is, if you do not see the bond which you are looking for, phone the investment dealer and ask. Each of these firms told me that they were prepared to search for the specific bonds in questions on demand.

My opinion on this, after managing retail fixed-income trading desks for 22 years, is that most fixed-income trades are done with fair markups. There have been—and no doubt still are—some rogue IAs who take excessive markups, but they are the exception. Every investment dealer has internal guidelines for markups and offenders are penalized. The marketplace enforces discipline, as it is possible to check prices with other dealers. Each investment dealer generates an up-to-date list of transfer prices on a complete spectrum of fixed-income instruments. These prices are not much different in practice from one fixed-income trading desk to the next. The different prices that clients pay for the securities arise mostly from the different markups charged by IAs.

Let us go through an example. Assume an investor wishes to buy $100,000 of the Province of British Columbia 3.70 percent bond of December 18, 2020. The transfer price is $101.31 for a yield to maturity of 3.54 percent (as of July 13, 2011):

Transfer Price: $101.31
Yield: 3.54 percent
Markup: $1.00
Total price to client: $102.31

Yield: 3.41 percent
Amount client pays: $100,000 * 1.0231 = $102,310.00
(expressed another way, the client is buying one hundred $1,000 bonds priced at $1,021.31 each)
Transfer cost to IA: 100,000 * 1.0131 = $101,310
IA's commission: $1,000, or almost 1 percent

This is a typical commission for such a bond. (Please note that these calculations do not apply for fee-based accounts.) At shorter maturities, the yield is affected more for a given markup, so markups are typically lower for, say, one-to five-year maturities than they are for the longer maturities. Also, markups typically become smaller as the size of the transaction increases. My recommendation for an investor with a large sum of money to invest is to ask two or more investment dealers for competitive offerings. Knowing this, the IAs at these firms will reduce the markup in order to win the transaction. On a trade of $250,000, a markup of 0.25 percent would be typical, for a gross commission of $625.

Let us now consider stripped or zero coupon bonds. They are a rarity in the investment business, as they are excellent products for retirement planning while they offer higher percentage markups for IAs. Let us assume that the same $100,000 was going to be invested in an Ontario stripped bond of a similar maturity. The transfer price on the Ontario 0 percent December 2, 2020, at a yield of 3.81 percent, is $70.19.

Transfer price: $70.19
Yield: 3.81 percent
Markup: $1.00
Price to client: $71.19
Yield: 3.66 percent
Amount client buys: $100,000/.7119 = $140,469
Transfer cost to IA: $140,469 *.7019 = $98,266
Amount client pays: $140,469 *.7119 = $100,000
IA's commission: $1,734.00 or 1.7 percent

Again, this is a typical markup and is common throughout the business. It is not an outrageous amount, especially when you consider this is a one-time fee for what most likely will be a buy and hold situation. In any event, these fees are in line with what IAs charge for equity transactions, in the region of 1 to 2 percent.

Remember, GIC investors also pay a markup, as the issuing agents pay the investment dealers $1 to $1.25 at the five-year maturity.

The hue and cry over fixed-income market markups is somewhat misguided. This is a self-policing business and a competitive one. I think it is reasonable for IAs to make a living. Investors may ensure that they are obtaining fair prices by opening accounts at more than one investment dealer or at a discount broker. Investors are advised to obtain competitive quotations, especially for large transactions, say over $100,000. IAs who repeatedly attempt to overcharge will find their business declining. It is very useful to have an online trading account with a discount broker as it is easy to transact your own bonds.

On balance, individual investors do not pay unfair markups, as the self-policing nature of the business ensures fair pricing. Having at least two accounts at separate FIs will ensure favourable pricing, especially when you have one with an IA at a full-service firm. When contemplating a fixed-income transaction, let your IAs know that you are requesting at least one other quotation. This keeps them on their toes and they may consider lowering their markups. Should you not do this, it is standard behaviour for an IA and an FI to take advantage of a monopolistic situation. Individual investors can now keep track of a selection of real-time bond prices at, www.canadianfixedincom e.cawww.canadianbondindices.com, or at canpxonline. ca.

CHAPTER 3

Basic Math

What you'll want to remember: present value = future value/$(1 + r)^t$

It is no wonder that the investing public has a difficult time comprehending the bond market when they are told that bonds are issued in denominations of $1,000 but are priced out of $100. This $1,000 is the principal amount, or face value. Adding further confusion is that bonds are priced as a percentage of this amount, as we saw earlier.

While the minimum unit of a bond is $1,000 face value, the pricing out of $100 actually makes it easier to understand when you realize that a price of, let's say, $98 represents 98 percent of the face value of the bond, which by extension, makes one bond in this example worth $980. It is an uphill struggle, but one must remember that bond traders are simple folk and pricing out of $100 is easier. We are going to use the terms par, par value, and face value to mean the same thing—the principal amount you originally loaned.

WHAT IS A BASIS POINT?

This is a phrase commonly used in the fixed-income business and one that I use frequently in this book. Consider what 1 percent in yield represents. Most bonds do not trade at round yields such as 3 percent, 4 percent, or 5 percent. Even though they may have been issued with those yields, once they start to trade, their yield moves up and down and so they will be presented in fractional form. For example, if interest rates move upwards by one-half of 1 percent, a bond issued at 3 percent, will be quoted as yielding 3 1/2 percent. Seems simple enough; however, most of the time, the yield will not fluctuate so evenly and so you might find this same bond quoted to yield 3 37/100 percent. This is a little unwieldy, so what the simple bond folk have done is to divide 1 percent into one hundred even pieces, each one of which is called a basis point. In bond lingo, basis points are known as "beeps." Thus, 25 basis points constitute 25/100, or 1/4 of 1 percent. The bond people then replace fractions with decimal points. So, if a bond moves up in yield by one basis point, they do not quote it as yielding 3 1/100 percent but rather 3.01 percent. The previous example of the bond moving up by 37 basis points would therefore be quoted at 3.37 percent. Got it? It is important to remember the definition of basis points, as that is what we use to compare one bond with another. For example, the British Columbia 3.70 percent December 18, 2020 yield 71 basis points or "beeps" more than the Canada 3.50 percent bonds due June 1, 2020, 3.54 percent versus 2.83 percent.

This chapter is about mathematics, money, and yield. Money invested earns a return. If money is invested in bonds or other fixed-income investments, the return consists of regular interest payments plus the ultimate return of the original amount loaned. If the interest is not needed, it will be reinvested, thus earning interest on interest, a concept we label *compounding.* This is a key concept that we'll return to later.

The first concept we will discuss is *present value.* Understanding it will lead you to the full knowledge of how to correctly value a bond or, at least, to fully understand the concept of present value (and which way bond prices go when interest rates go up).

Obviously, $100 today is worth $100 today; it has no time value. Would you lend someone $100 today for, say, two years, and accept nothing but the $100 back? Unless this was a family member or an extremely close friend, you would likely ask for some interest on the loan; otherwise you would have loaned your money for nothing. Money has time value. Putting it another way, $100 due in two years is not worth $100 today—not unless it were to earn 0 percent and inflation were zero. In the real world, money earns a return and there is inflation, so in two years, $100 will grow by the amount of interest (both simple and compound) earned during that period. The present value formula calculates the present value of that future amount of money using a discount rate, or yield. This concept is vital to a solid understanding of how the bond market functions and is extremely important to retirement planning. That's why I included it at the beginning of this chapter. Here it is again: present value = future value/$(1+ r)^t$, where r is the interest rate per period and t is the number of periods.

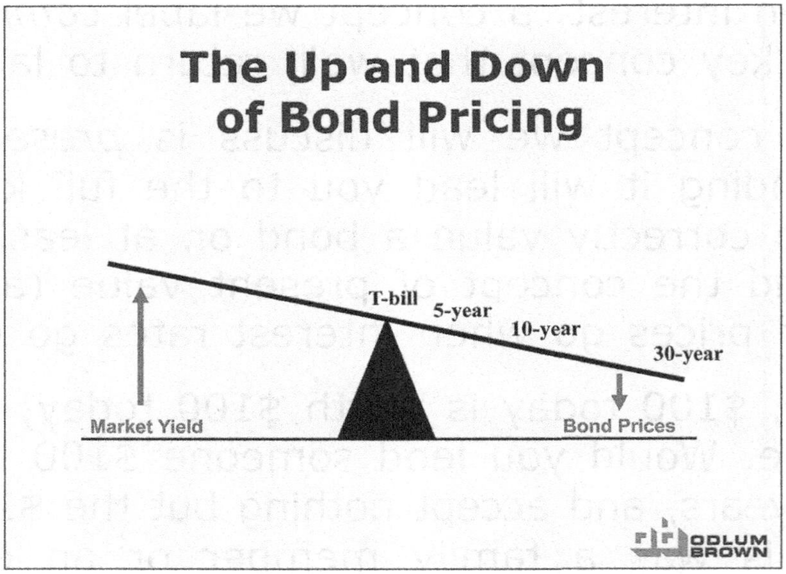

Do not despair! Present value tables have already been prepared for your ease of use and enjoyment. To determine the current value of \$100,000 due three and a half years from now at a semi-annual yield of 5 percent, you would calculate the answer thusly: $\$100,000 / (1+2.50 \text{ percent})^7 = \$100,000 / 1.0250^7 = 1/1.18868.60 = \$84,126.52$. Stated differently, \$84,126.52 today invested at 5 percent compounded semiannually will grow to $100,000 in exactly three and a half years.

Before continuing, we will spend some time discussing compound interest, since the all-important present value is merely the reciprocal of a compounded amount.

COMPOUND INTEREST

Baron de Rothschild described compound interest as "the eighth wonder of the world." Compound interest is a concept vital to the understanding of yield to maturity. Compounding means that not only does your original dollar earn interest but interest you receive also earns interest by being reinvested. In this case, we are compounding on a semi-annual basis; although this appears to complicate matters, the domestic bond market functions on a semi-annual basis. Thus, a bond paying semi-annual interest and paying 5 percent pays that 5 percent in two payments of 2.5 percent each, paid six months apart. The following example will use an original amount of $100,000. This amount will be returned at maturity, in this case three and a half years from now. There will be seven interest payments made. How much will each payment be? The original face amount times the interest rate divided by two: $100,000 *.05/2 = $2,500.

We will assume that all of these payments (except the last one, since it is paid at the same time the $100,000 is repaid) will be reinvested or compounded at the same rate (2.5 percent) for the remaining term of the investment, and so on with each successive payment. This might be a difficult concept to grasp initially, but it is how bond calculators work. It provides a common yield measuring device for us simple bond folk, since it is obviously not a real world calculation. In the real world, every interest payment will be invested at a different yield, if reinvested at all.

How $100,000 will grow at 5 percent compounded semi-annually:

Interest	Compound Interest	Total Interest	Amount	Total
$ 2,500.00	$ 0.00	$ 2,500.00	$100,000.00	$102,500.00
$ 2,500.00	$ 62.50	$ 5,062.50	$100,000.00	$105,062.50
$ 2,500.00	$ 126.56	$ 7,689.06	$100,000.00	$107,689.06
$ 2,500.00	$ 192.23	$10,381.29	$100,000.00	$110,381.29
$ 2,500.00	$ 259.53	$13,140.82	$100,000.00	$113,140.82
$ 2,500.00	$ 328.52	$15,969.34	$100,000.00	$115,969.34
$ 2,500.00	$ 399.23	$18,868.58	$100,000.00	$118,868.58
$17,500.00	$1,368.58	$18,868.58	$100,000.00	$118,868.58

Thus, $100,000 invested today at 5 percent compounded semiannually will grow to $118,868.58 in three and a half years.

Explaining this table in more detail, the first interest payment of $2,500 is received after six months. At twelve months, the next $2,500 is paid, but since the payments are being reinvested, the first $2,500 payment will have earned 2.5 percent, or $62.50, during those six months; this is the interest on the interest, or what we call compound interest. For the next payment, the $2,500 is received plus the interest earned on the first two payments plus the compound interest ($2,500 + 2,500 + 62.50) *.025 = $126.56. So, the total is now the three payments of $2,500 each plus $62.50 plus $126.56, for a total of $7,689.06, and so on, until the compounding period ends and the total future value totals the original face value plus the interest payments received (7* $2,500 = $17,500) plus the total compound interest of $1,368.58: $100,000 + $17,500 + $1,368.58 = $118,868.58.

Let us now go back to the present value formula since it will be referred to many times and is a very important concept. Since the above calculation shows the future value of a sum invested today at a certain interest rate for a specified period of time, we should be able to calculate the present value of a sum in the future discounted by an interest rate for a specified period of time. All we have to do is take the reciprocal of the future value formula. In other words, $118,868.58 discounted at an interest rate or yield of 5 percent semi-annually for three and a half years is worth $100,000 today. If you wished to express this out of a round amount like $100,000, simply divide the $100,000 by $118,868.58 to get an answer of .841265. Thus, $84,126.50 invested today at 5 percent semi-annually compounded will grow to exactly $100,000 in three and a half years. This calculation will be very important when we discuss stripped bonds in a later chapter. A present value table, calculated for a wide number of terms to maturity and interest rates, may be found in the stripped bond chapter.

Let us now return to the bond used earlier, the Canada 3.50 percent bond maturing June 1, 2020. This is a benchmark issue with some $13.1 billion outstanding. We will demonstrate how the value of this bond is really determined by calculating the present value of each of the interest payments and the principal. For this example we will assume a yield or discount rate of 2.883 percent for each of the components and that the bond was bought at a price of $104.861. In addition, we will assume that the bond was purchased on June 1, 2011, so that the first payment is in exactly six months. You can calculate all these present values yourself by using a present values table, the calculator found on my website (www. inyourbestinterest.ca), or Excel, which has bond math in its Analysis Tool Pack. (See Appendix C to see how to use Excel for bond yields)

I am assuming a cost of $104.861 for a semi-annual yield of 2.883 percent as of June 1, 2011. Price per $100 is therefore $104.861, exactly the cost of the bond.

Date	Interest Payment	Principal	Discount Rate	Present Value of $1	Value
Dec. 1, 2011	$ 1,750		2.883	0.98579	$ 1,725.13
June 1, 2012	$ 1,750		2.883	0.97178	$ 1,700.61
Dec. 1, 2012	$ 1,750		2.883	0.95797	$ 1,676.45
June 1, 2013	$ 1,750		2.883	0.94436	$ 1,652.63
Dec. 1, 2013	$ 1,750		2.883	0.93094	$ 1,629.15
June 1, 2014	$ 1,750		2.883	0.91771	$ 1,605.99
Dec. 1, 2014	$ 1,750		2.883	0.90467	$ 1,583.17
June 1, 2015	$ 1,750		2.883	0.89181	$ 1,560.67
Dec. 1, 2015	$ 1,750		2.883	0.87914	$ 1,538.50
June 1, 2016	$ 1,750		2.883	0.86665	$ 1,516.64
Dec. 1, 2016	$ 1,750		2.883	0.85433	$ 1,495.08
June 1, 2017	$ 1,750		2.883	0.84219	$ 1,473.83
Dec. 1, 2017	$ 1,750		2.883	0.83023	$ 1,452.90
June 1, 2018	$ 1,750		2.883	0.81843	$ 1,432.25
Dec.1, 2018	$ 1,750		2.883	0.80680	$ 1,411.90
June 1, 2019	$ 1,750		2.883	0.79533	$ 1,391.83
Dec. 1, 2019	$ 1,750		2.883	0.78403	$ 1,372.05
June 1, 2020	$ 1,750		2.883	0.77289	$ 1,352.56
June 1, 2020		$100,000	2.883	0.77289	$77,289.00
Total	$31,500				
Grand Total		$131,500			$ 104,861.00

You will notice that by calculating the present value of each component of the bond at the purchase yield, we arrive at the exact cost of the bond as seen above: $104,861. Thus, a bond is demonstrated to be the sum of its parts.

As you can see, a bond is merely a sum of its parts; put another way, yield to maturity is the discount rate that equates the future cash flows to today's price.

Now you see how artificial the yield to maturity calculation is, since yields at different maturities will not be identical. Put another way, the odds of each coupon payment being reinvested at the purchase yield are very, very low. For that to be the case, yields would have to be the absolute same at all the interest payment dates as at the time of purchase. We will see when we discuss yield curves that this is a very rare event. Another calculation produces the realized yield, which takes into account the effect of different reinvestment rates on the yield to maturity. This calculation is best left to calculators. What you need to remember is the longer the term of the bond, the more important the interest payments and, therefore, the more important the interest on the interest.

Following is an example of a longer-term bond, the Canada 3.5 percent due December 1, 2045. Showing the effect of different reinvestment rates illustrates how important interest is when assessing the value of a bond. These numbers represent the total amounts received if this bond was held to its maturity date with the reinvestment rate varying. The importance of reinvestment rates is also striking. In all three cases the simple interest received over the life of the bond exceeds the final principal repayment, while in two of the cases the compound interest also exceeds the principal payment.

At July 12, 2011:

CANADA 3.5% DECEMBER 1, 2045			
Reinvestment Rate	**2%**	**3.35%**	**6%**
Principal	$100,000	$100,000	$100,000
Simple Interest	$120,640	$120,460	$120,460
Compound Interest	$ 51,850	$103,409	$268,624
Total	$272,490	$324,049	$489,264

"Thrift is a wonderful virtue—especially in an ancestor," said Mark Twain. Compound interest is one of the strongest forces in the investment business and one of the keys to investing success. For example, the following table indicates how long it takes for $1 to double at different semi-annual compounding yields (pre-tax, of course).

Rate	Years to Double
4%	17.5
6%	11.7
8%	8.8
10%	7.1
12%	5.9

You may have noticed that multiplying the rate times the number of years produces an answer close to seventy-two. The "Rule of 72" says that if you divide seventy-two by the interest rate, the answer is the number of years (approximately) that it takes for money to double.

So you want to make a million? The present value of $1 million due in twenty years discounted at a yield of 10 percent semi-annually is $142,000. Therefore, $142,000 invested at 10 percent will equal $1 million in 20 years (pre-tax, but this is possible in RRSPs). At 5 percent, that same $142,000 would grow to only $381,279 in the same period, while at 15 percent it would grow to $2,562,281! These dramatic differences underscore how important it is to take advantage of high-yields when they are available. At 8 percent compounded semi-annually, $1,000 would grow to more than $2,000 in nine years, $7,106 in twenty-five years, $50,504 in fifty years, and $2,550,749 in one hundred years.

You can see that compounding is a very powerful force. Consider the tale of the numerically naive king and his mathematical daughter who happened to be a whiz at checkers. He offered her monthly prizes for scholastic achievements. His daughter told him that she wanted just one dollar to be put on the first square of her checkerboard after the first month and then to have that amount doubled every succeeding month. So, on month two it would be $2 on the second square, $4 on the third month, and so on, until the sixty-four squares were full. Well, the king ran out of money. By the tenth square, he put down $512, and by the twentieth, it had become $524,288. The amount would have been in the trillions by the time he reached square sixty-four! She was earning a 100 percent return per month.

REINVESTMENT RISK—OR, WHAT YOU SEE YOU MAY NOT GET!

It is vital that after gaining the knowledge of how important compound interest is, investors understand how much their future retirement stakes are at risk. There are two types of reinvestment risk: interest rate risk and maturity risk. The first has to do with the risk of reinvesting interest payments at lower interest rates than existed at the time of investment, and the second means having too much of your portfolio invested in one maturity, exposing yourself to the possibility of having to reinvest most or all of your money at lower interest rates (or the opposite—owning too much of a long maturity bond and watching the value of your bond decline as yields rise with no money to reinvest).

Let us again review the concept of yield to maturity of a bond. On a typical semi-annual bond, the quoted yield to maturity assumes that each and every interest payment is reinvested at that yield. They would have to remain constant at the purchase yield for the entire life of that bond! This is not likely in the real world, since interest rates are dynamic; yields are rising and falling all the time. So, this yield to maturity calculation is artificial. As we have seen, the longer the term of the bond, the more important the total interest received. For example, a 5 percent bond paying semi-annually and due in 29 years will produce

1.20 times in simple interest payments and 1.03 times in compound interest the original principal amount, assuming a constant reinvestment rate of 3.35 percent. The following table, repeated from above, underscores the importance of this reinvestment rate.

CANADA 3.5 PERCENT DECEMBER 1, 2045			
Reinvestment Rate	**2%**	**3.35%**	**6%**
Principal	$100,000	$100,000	$100,000
Simple Interest	$120,640	$120,460	$120,460
Compound Interest	$ 51,850	$103,409	$268,624
Total	$272,490	$324,049	$489,264

Since a quoted yield to maturity on a bond is far removed from the real world, you might wonder why this yield calculation is done at all. It offers a consistent way to value all bonds and helps in valuing one bond in relation to another one. Investors are at greater risk than they realize unless they are invested in a product with no reinvestment risk. Yes, Virginia, there is such a product, and it gets its own chapter later on: the zero coupon or stripped bond. To combat this reinvestment risk, I advocate a laddered portfolio of stripped bonds in an RRSP account, as stripped bonds have no interest to reinvest. I advocate the laddered approach for taxable portfolios, since the staggered maturities of a ladder allow investors to avoid the reinvestment risk mentioned above. More on this later.

The other form of reinvestment risk involves maturity selection. In day-to-day terms, planning your retirement with short-term investments is like timing a marathon runner after 100 yards and extrapolating the result over the ensuing 26 miles, 285 yards. The following high-tech chart outlines the direction of interest rates since the Second World War.

While somewhat simplified, it underscores the reinvestment risk of maturity selection. No one knows where interest rates are going, so why take a chance? Since the peak in yields in 1982, anyone who has invested retirement funds in treasury bills and GICs has discovered the unpleasant experience of having a high-yielding investment mature with much lower yields available. Another way of addressing maturity reinvestment risk is to use the analogy of real estate. Suppose you owned a property with five units for rent. The property is your capital. Would you rent all your units for the same term? This would be imprudent as when all the leases came due at the same time, there could be a recession underway and your rents could fall and/or you might lose some tenants entirely. Thus, you would be wise to rent your units out for different terms. Also, you might want some diversity in your tenants; renting to several people in the same business runs the risk of an economic setback. Applying this approach to bond portfolios means that you should diversify by maturity so that your money does not mature at an inopportune time and you should also diversify by credit to spread your risk out.

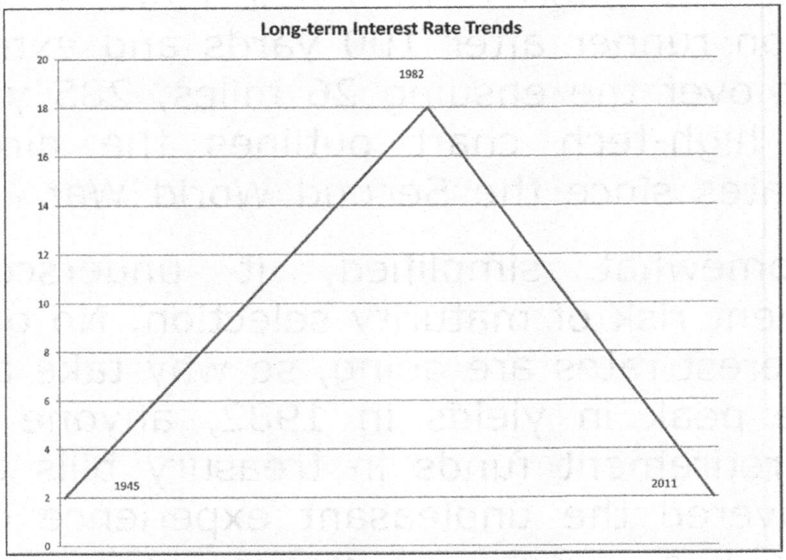

HISTORICAL YIELDS		
Year	**Five-year GICs**	**Long-term Canadas**
1982	16.14%	16.33%
1987	8.79%	8.51%
1992	7.92%	8.92%
1997	4.91%	7.38%
2002	3.93%	5.51%
2007	3.73%	4.57%
Today	3.00%	3.35%

If only I had bought those twenty-year bonds yielding 16.3 percent! As you can see, five-year GIC rates have moved progressively lower. In 1982, you could have invested in a twenty-year Government of Canada bond at 16.33 percent. But, buying the five-year GICs and renewing for five years when they matured produced progressively lower returns.

For a typical RRSP plan, the previous table underscores the long-term effects of investing in short-term investments at a time of declining yields. I am writing this book in such a period. Obviously, in a period of generally rising rates, staying short is a winning process since yields will be higher as each bond matures. The purpose of this chapter is to stress the fact that, since even the great Templeton could not find anyone who can consistently forecast the trend in interest rates, it is important to find an approach that removes or significantly reduces reinvestment risk. It is the laddered approach, and it is fully discussed in Chapter 8.

Since the domestic bond market is built around semi-annual yield and the issuers (banks and trust companies) of deposit instruments (GICs, mainly) typically quote their yields in annual terms, it is important to know the "apples to apples" comparison, since the difference can be meaningful.

Consider a one-year investment of $100,000 offered at a yield of 5.0625 percent annually and compare this with another one-year investment paying 5 percent semi-annually. Which one would you buy? On the surface you would buy the one yielding 5.0625 percent, but assuming we invest $100,000 in each of them, let us see what they return:

	Annual 5.0625 Percent	Semi-Annual 5 Percent
Interest (6 months)	$ 0	$2,500
Interest (12 months)	$5,062.50	$5,000
Compound Interest	$ 0	$ 62.50(5,000*.025)
Total Interest	$5,062.50	$5,062.50

Thus, we can say that 5 percent compounded semi-annually is equivalent to 5.0625 percent annually. Obviously, the higher the yield, the greater the difference:

Semi-annual	Annual Equivalent
4 percent	4.04 percent
5 percent	5.06 percent
6 percent	6.09 percent
7 percent	7.12 percent
8 percent	8.16 percent
9 percent	9.20 percent
10 percent	10.25 percent

Investment advisors worth their salt will provide both yields so there can be no misunderstanding. Most investment dealers now include these yields on the contracts that their clients receive. Since this is not typically the case, and since investment products are seldom offered at a nice round yield, how can you work this out yourself? You could use a simple formula. To convert from semi-annual to annual, take the semiannual yield and square it, then divide by four to calculate the number of basis points to add to arrive at the annual yield equivalent. Taking 10 percent semi-annually and squaring it produces 100, and dividing by 4 produces 25 basis points, which when added to 10 percent produces a 10.25 percent annual yield equivalent.

For a semi-annual yield such as 7.56 percent, follow the same process: 7.56 squared equals 57, then divide by 4 to equal 14.3 basis points, which added to 7.56 percent produces an annual yield equivalent of 7.703 percent.

YIELD

Yield is what an investment returns to an investor, whether expressed as dividends, capital gains, interest, or compound interest. As the compound section indicates, the rate at which money or capital grows is crucial to investment results. This brings us to the yield on bonds.

Investing in a bond paying 5 percent produces 5 percent a year in interest payments, whether payable semi-annually or not. If that interest is used or spent, a simple yield of 5 percent (pre-tax) is realized. When the interest is reinvested (say in an estate, an RRSP, etc.), then this yield becomes a different matter. When you buy a fixed-income security that offers a 5 percent yield to maturity, it implies that every interest payment will be reinvested or compounded at 5 percent to produce that yield. This is not a real-world calculation. It is merely a benchmark number to measure different bond yields: you may calculate it by buying appropriate software or downloading it from your FI. Or you could get it free from my website. The formula for converting the price of a bond to its yield to maturity is a long, iterative formula best left to calculators. Calculating the price of a bond given its yield is far easier, as it involves adding up all the present values as we have seen.

DURATION, OR WHAT YOU SEE IS NOT WHAT YOU HAVE

A ten-year bond is a ten-year bond, right? Sorry! The term or maturity of the bond may be ten years but it would only have a duration of ten years if that were the only payment you received. Returning to the Canada 3.5 percent due June 1, 2020, we observe that there are eighteen interest payments spaced six months apart plus the return of the principal. These payments are a part of your bond, and since they range in term from six months to nine and a half years, they have an impact on the average life or average term of your investment. Yields and bond prices move inversely. Perhaps I should take a minute and explain that last sentence.

Not a week goes by without someone asking me if bond prices go up when yields or interest rates go up. After working through the present value calculations, you can see that if interest rates rise, then the present value of the pieces of the bond will be worth less and therefore the total value of the bond will fall. The converse is equally true. If yields fall, the present value of all the parts of a bond rise and the total value of the bond rises.

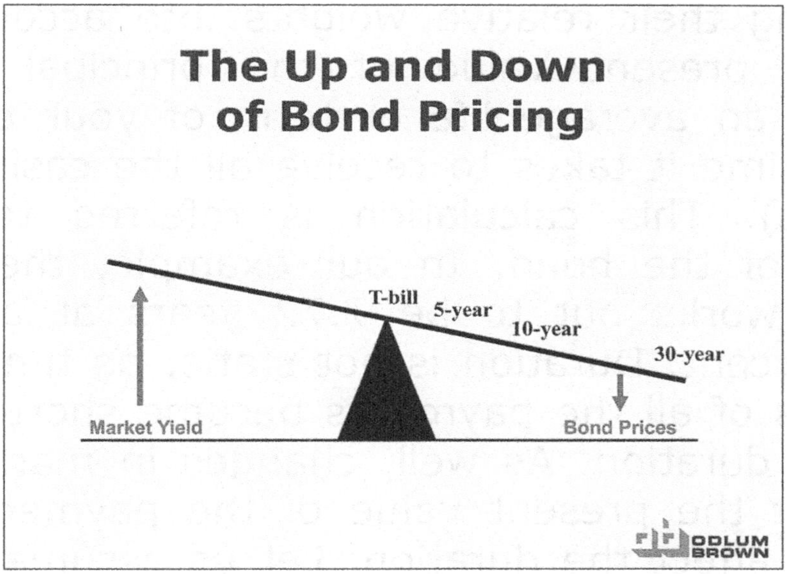

The same applies for present values of future payments: the higher the discount rate or yield, the lower the present value (and vice versa). Let us take the December 1, 2015, interest payment for example. At 2.883 percent, as we have seen, this payment has a present value of $1,538.50. Suppose we raise the discount rate to 8 percent. The present value now works out to be $1,229.38. Lowering the discount rate to 2 percent produces a higher present value of $1,600.03. Thinking about it logically, and reversing the formula, at a higher yield, you need less capital today to arrive at a specified future value (and of course the converse is true for a lower yield). Thus, to produce $1,750 in four and a half years at 2 percent you need $1,600.03 today, but if you could invest at 8 percent you would only need $1,229.38.

Each of the payments of a bond has a present value, and taking their relative weights into account along with the present value of the principal payment produces an average life or term of your bond (the average time it takes to receive all the cash flows or payments). This calculation is referred to as the duration of the bond. In our example, the average duration works out to be 7.72 years at a yield of 2.883 percent. Duration is not static: as time passes, the terms of all the payments become shorter and so does the duration. As well, changes in market yields will affect the present value of the payment stream and thus affect the duration. Let us assume we have a 6 percent bond and a 3 percent bond, both with a term to maturity or principal repayment of ten years. Which one has the shorter duration? The present value of the interest payments from the 6 percent bond will have greater value than those from a 3 percent bond at the same yield. Using a face value of $100,000, a starting yield or discount rate of 2.883 percent, and the interest payment at four and a half years produces the following:

Interest Payment	Present Value
6 percent bond:	$100,000 * 0.06/2 = $3,000 at 2.883 percent = $2,637.42
3 percent bond:	$100,000 * 0.03/2 = $1,500 at 2.883 percent = $1,318.70

The interest payments from the 6 percent bond have greater present value than those from the 3 percent bond, and so the 6 percent bond will have a shorter duration. In this case the 6 percent bond has a duration of 7.85 years, versus 8.88 years for the 3 percent bond. Another way of looking at this is to look at the present value of the two payments above. Each of the interest payments for the 6 percent bond will have a greater present value than will the same maturity interest payment for the 3 percent bond. Adding all the present values up will show that the weight of the interest payments is greater compared with the principal payment for the higher coupon bond, and this will produce a shorter average term or duration.

The reason for stressing this calculation becomes evident when selecting bonds. Duration is used as a measurement of risk. The longer the duration of a bond, the larger the price change for a given yield change. Thus if you believe that interest rates are trending lower, you would invest in bonds of long duration. IAs worth their salt will know what duration is and which bonds are appropriate for you. A shorter duration bond is less sensitive to yield changes.

The following illustrates how duration affects the price change of bonds of different maturities and durations. What I have done is take bonds of different coupon rates at two different maturity dates (five and twenty years) and measured the impact of a 1 percent (100 basis points) shift in the yield from 6 percent to 5 percent. Within the two maturities, the durations change depending on the coupon rate.

	Coupon	Duration (Years)	% Increase in Price
Five-year Bonds			
	12%	3.9	4.00
	8%	4.2	4.20
	6%	4.4	4.40
	0%	5.0	5.00
Twenty-year Bonds			
	12%	10.4	11.80
	8%	11.2	11.80
	6%	12.7	12.60
	0%	20.0	21.50

You can see the bigger price changes for lower coupon bonds of the same maturities. I included a zero coupon bond at each maturity to show that without any cash flows, these bonds have a duration equal to their maturity and have the greatest price change.

BOND PRICE DYNAMICS AND VOLATILITY

Why do bond prices change? After all, there is a fixed level of interest payments and a final repayment of principal. So, what is the point of reporting price changes for bonds daily? The daily trading volume for bonds is enormous, averaging $38.4 billion, or some five times that of the stock market. Various participants in the bond market have reasons to trade their fixed-income investments. The price of money changes frequently, as anyone who borrows or lends money knows. The reasons for this are numerous, including the changing supply and demand for money as the economic cycle changes, changes in the rate of inflation, government deficits, political turmoil, foreign exchange crises, or changes in interest rates in other countries. As well, someone investing in a bond may have circumstances change and need to sell it before maturity. Investors' expectations to inflation or other factors may also change. As well, a large pool of speculative capital trades the bond market aggressively, seeking capital gains. Time is also a factor. Consider someone who buys a ten-year bond. Five years later, that investor has a five-year bond, and new ten-year bonds may be offering a much higher yield, prompting the investor to consider exchanging the five-year bond for the ten-year.

There are a whole slew of institutional portfolio managers who are constantly analyzing the market for inefficiencies and arbitrage opportunities. They will examine relationships among thousands of bonds. For example, they may decide that the spread between ten-year Canadas and Ontarios has become too wide based on historical analysis and their own projections and thus they would sell the Canadas and buy the Ontarios, with the aim of reversing the trade if and when the yield spread narrows. Constant analysis by portfolio managers everywhere leads to an efficient market most of the time, but as with all markets, surprises occur. Astute analysts stand to benefit from knowing when there is an anomaly between two different bonds or sectors.

HOW DO BOND PRICES CHANGE AND HOW VOLATILE ARE THEY?

The following are the basic rules of bond price volatility. Bond price volatility increases as:

The maturity lengthens. Typically, as maturity lengthens, duration does too, and we already know that the longer the duration of a bond, the more its price will change for a given yield movement.

The coupon rate declines. Again referring back to duration and assuming two bonds of identical maturities, one with a 10 percent coupon and the other with one of 5 percent, the latter one has a longer duration and therefore more volatility since the present value of its interest payment stream is not as great as that of the 10 percent bond.

The starting yield increases. Let us ensure that we are all familiar with the basic tenet of bond prices and yields: Bond prices and yields move in an inverse pattern; that is, as interest rates or yields rise, the price of bonds falls (and vice versa). The longer the maturity, the greater the price movement for a particular bond.

Imagine yourself on a schoolyard teeter-totter. One end of the teeter-totter represents bond prices, the other end, yields. If someone larger than you jumps on the yield end, it will go down and you will go up to the highest level (price) that the teeter-totter will go. That is what happens to long-term bonds. If you are a little chicken and sit closer to the centre of the board and the same large bully jumps on, what happens? You do not go as far.

The following table illustrates this teeter-totter effect.

Yield Decrease	Price Increase*			
	3-year	5-year	10-year	30-year
-0.50	1.40%	2.30%	4.20%	7.10%
-1.00	2.80%	4.60%	8.60%	15.0%
-1.50	4.30%	7.00%	13.20%	23.50%
-2.00	5.80%	9.50%	18.00%	32.80%

* Assuming a coupon of 4% and a starting yield of 4%

THE YIELD CURVE: THE SHAPE OF THINGS TO COME

The yield curve compares time and yield by connecting a series of dots indicating the yield at different maturities. Practical-minded investors would expect that the longer the term they are willing to lend or invest their money, the higher the return or yield they should receive. The higher yield compensates the investor for the extra risk in lending for a longer period of time. Translating that into a graph would produce the following:

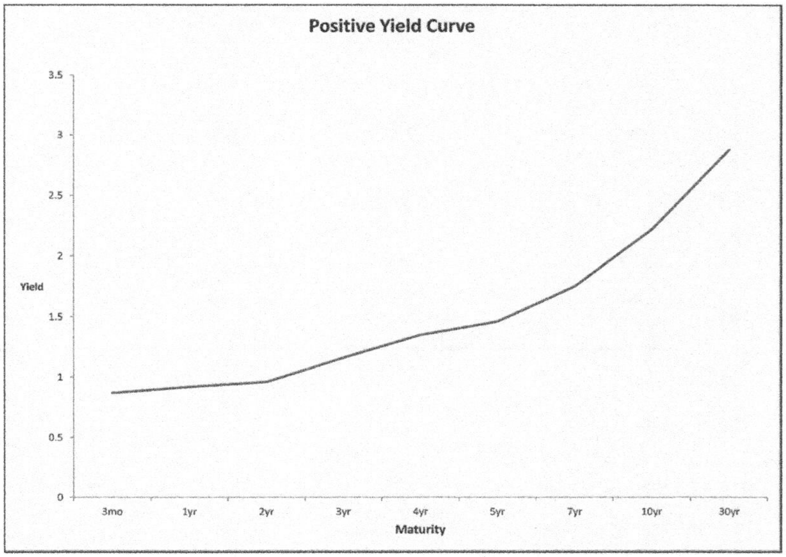

Of course, this curve is not constant; it may be steeper, that is, the upward slope may be more vertical, with long-term yields sharply higher than short-term yields. It could also be flatter, with only gradual increases in yield along the curve. (Note: All the curves in this chapter represent yields available in benchmark Government of Canada obligations, the reference points for all other securities.) The yield curve assumes different shapes at different times in the economic cycle. It can be flat, with yields identical at all maturities:

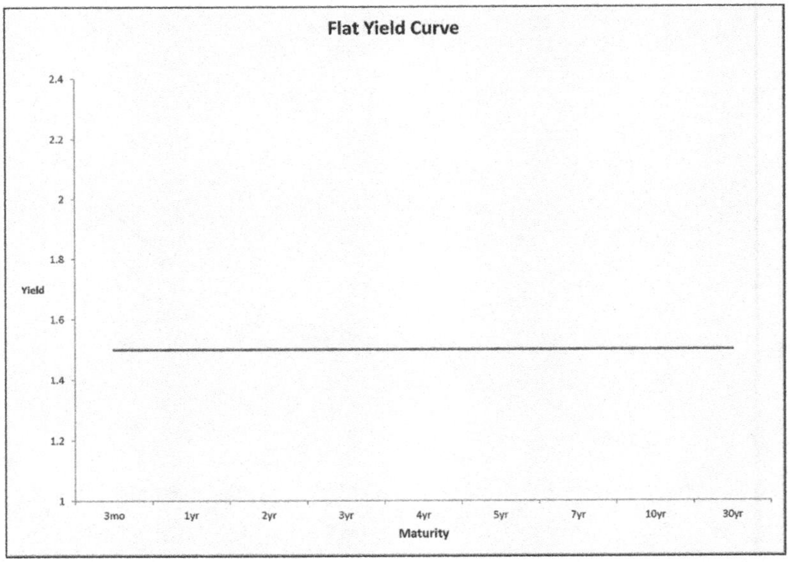

Or it can be inverted, with the shortest maturities offering the highest yields and the longest maturities the least:

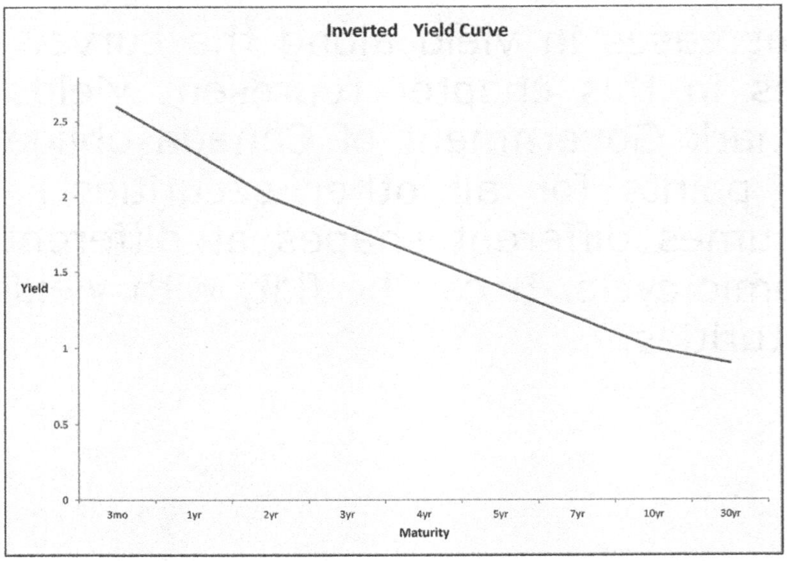

You can draw your own. On a piece of paper, draw a vertical line and a horizontal line. Using the daily newspaper or your favourite website, find the yields at the shortest maturity for Government of Canada instruments (say, three months) and, using the horizontal axis for time and the vertical for yield, place a dot where each yield belongs. You could use maturities such as six months, one year, two years, etc., all the way to thirty years. Then connect all the dots to view your curve.

Why dwell on this? What do these shapes mean? How do you get from one shape to another? What's in it for me? Dwelling on this increases your awareness of where Canada (in this case) is in its economic cycle. The shapes and the changes in the shapes assist in this analysis. When the yield curve moves from very steep to less steep, it is a sign that the Bank of Canada (or the market participants) believes that it is an appropriate time to be tightening monetary policy, which is a fancy way of saying that the economy needs to be cooled down before inflation gets out of hand. Some observers liken this approach by central banks to taking away the punch bowl when the party gets going. What is in it for you, then, is that you will have an important gauge at your disposal to be used when contemplating decisions such as whether to stay floating with your mortgage or fix it and whether to buy long-term or short-term bonds. To acquire a good working knowledge of the importance of yield curves is to understand interest cycles, to get along without an economist, and to enhance long-term returns. I really mean what I say about not needing an economist. Economists have a dismal track record in predicting economic turning points; they are about equal to your guesses and mine! Many prominent fixed-income fund managers have also admitted that they basically are guessing which way interest rates are going!

The yield curve is dynamic, with the yield relationship between one maturity and another in a constant state of flux. Why is this? For one thing, changes in the shape of the yield curve represent changing inflationary and economic expectations of market participants. At one end of the curve (the very short maturity end) is our central bank, the Bank of Canada, whose duties involve the maintenance of a stable currency, the conduct of monetary policy compatible with economic growth, and a vigilant, anti-inflationary stance. The Bank of Canada may deem it necessary to tighten monetary policy, restricting the growth of money supply and raising short-term interest rates. It can thus be responsible for pushing up treasury bill yields and the prime rate, but can it directly affect long-term bond yields and mortgage yields? The short answer is no. Beyond the shortest of maturity dates, the Bank of Canada cannot dictate where interest rates go. This is because market participants of all types, borrowers and lenders alike, combine to set market rates. For example, when the Bank of Canada begins to raise short-term interest rates, market participants may view this as anti-inflationary and thus they may feel more comfortable investing in longer term securities, whose yields then fall. This is one way that the yield curve flattens (short-term yields rise even as long-term yields fall). This happened in the first half of 2007.

At the outset there are a few theorems to advance. Almost always invest in the longest-term investments (for your particular circumstances) when it costs you the most in current income to do so. For example, ten-year bonds may be yielding 6 percent while ninety-day treasury bills yield 8 percent. This inversion of yields normally occurs at a time of maximum monetary tightness, close to interest rate peaks. When rates begin to fall, superior total returns are obtained from investing in long-term securities even though treasury bills appear to yield more. The converse of this is equally true. An investor should invest in the shortest maturities when it again costs the most in current income to do so, that is, when the yield curve is in an extremely steep configuration. In this case, ninety-day treasury bills may be 2 percent and long-term yields 6 percent. This typically occurs at a time of maximum monetary ease by central banks, when the economy is expanding rapidly and is beginning to generate inflationary pressures and when credit demand is strong. At times like this, the next major event is monetary tightening when the central bank begins to ratchet interest rates higher. Interest rates begin to rise at all maturities, so even though current income is higher in long-term investments, total returns will be worse. Your capital is at risk. In other words, capital preservation should become more important at cyclical extremes than extra current income.

One of the principal driving forces of all markets is greed. By always being greedy and reaching for higher apparent yields, investors in fixed-income products may find only short-term benefits. For instance, in the first case above, once the monetary tightening ends and inflation subsides, short-term and long-term rates will both fall. When the ninety-day treasury bill matures, ninety-day bills might then be only 4 percent while ten-year bonds may have fallen to 5 percent. Now the investor must decide whether to take the lower yield on the bills or invest in the ten-year bond at 5 percent that they could have bought at 6 percent. An opportunity lost. The converse is typically true in the other example. After a long period of monetary ease, the Bank of Canada decides to tighten monetary policy and yields rise, so that investors reaching for higher yield at the longer maturities see their principal value decline while short-term yields begin to rise.

In a coming chapter, I discuss the laddered approach to fixed-income investing, as it takes the guesswork out of the equation. Suffice it to say for now that it spreads your fixed-income investments over a variety of maturity dates. Until everyone is converted to ladders, it is important to pay attention to both the shape of the yield curve and how it is shifting. It is educational, and it demonstrates that greed (seeking higher yield) may be a false economy if in reaching for that apparent higher yield, investors are putting their principal at risk. In other words, buying a three-month treasury bill because it offers a higher yield than does a ten-year bond can be a very short-sighted decision. A similar analogy is the GIC investor who never considers anything else beyond five years when, in fact, there are times when significant gains in total returns are possible through purchasing bonds of ten- and twenty-year maturities.

In the practical advice section, I mention that a large percentage of investments become concentrated in the one-year and five-year terms. This has a lot to do with the whole GIC business, where one- and five-year terms are most common and so that is where the bulk of term matching takes place, as institutions constantly attempt to keep their assets (loans, mortgages) and liabilities (deposits, GICs) matched as to maturity. At these specific maturities, yield spreads between different issuers (Canadas, treasury bills, GICs, strips, and corporates) tend to become compressed. What occurs—and what therefore becomes an opportunity to astute advisors and investors—are yield anomalies. For example, eighteen-month investments typically offer an above average yield pickup over one-year investments. As a result, those investors willing to stick their necks out for an extra six months will be rewarded when their investment becomes a one-year investment and the yield spreads compress for the reasons advanced above. They may then sell and buy another eighteen-month investment or hold to maturity. Either way, there is a relative yield pickup. A similar anomaly often exists at five years, when a one-year extension to six years may offer a higher yield than the slope of the yield curve would suggest. In other words, the investor is rewarded with a higher yield than expected for that extra year. One year hence, the investor will have a five-year investment trading at a far narrower spread than at the time of the purchase. As with the one-year/eighteen-month anomaly, the investor may sell and reinvest in another six-year maturity or hold the investment and enjoy the extra yield.

Within the money market itself, the money market yield curve (twelve months and less) offers clues all the time about the near-term direction of short-term interest rates, a subject everyone cares about. The Bank of Canada directly influences short-term interest rates through its actions in the overnight market and the three-month treasury bill market. A little more on the overnight rate: if the Bank of Canada "tightens the system," making it more expensive for jobbers and other market participants to finance their inventories, perhaps to the point where the cost of financing exceeds the yield of the securities, interest rates tend to rise as dealers attempt to shed their inventories since they would lose money by holding them. Everyone attempting this at once is like everyone trying to get out the door at the same time. The Bank of Canada can push rates lower or keep rates low by making it possible to carry inventories at a profit, of course. Past the three-month maturity range, its influence wanes as market forces of supply and demand take over.

The money market yield curve changes frequently. Remembering the general yield curve rules, when short-term money market yields (less than three months) are a lot lower than six- and twelve-month rates (a steep curve), avoid buying the long maturities, since the curve is telling you that short-term rates are too low and/or the cycle for rates is over and rates are headed higher. Frequently, the money market yield curve is flat or inverted. This is a signal to extend term: the cycle is about to turn to lower rates, and the central bank has had to push short-term rates up sharply, typically for currency defence, not for economic reasons. Since the economic fundamentals in such cases argue for lower rates, market participants look past the near term and buy six- or twelve-month bills, knowing that once the currency stabilizes, rates will move lower again, and greater returns are to be had in the longer maturities. The accompanying chart illustrates the importance of ignoring the higher yields available when a yield curve is inverted.

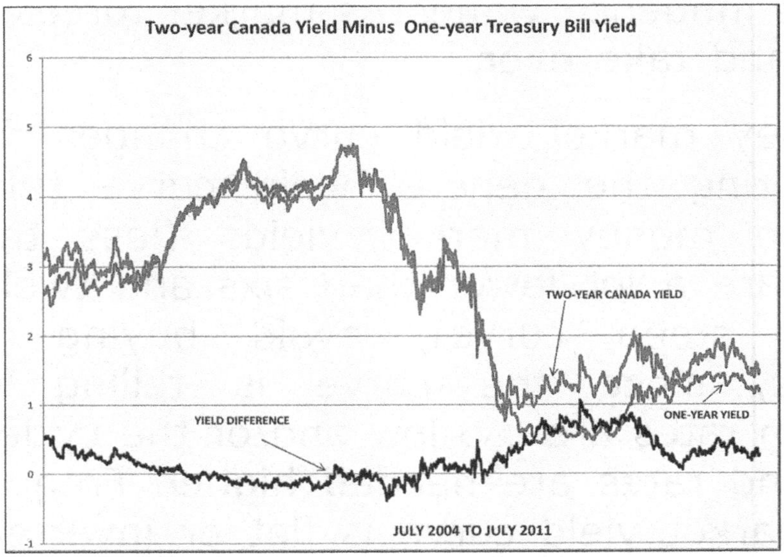

On November 19, 2007, this spread was minus 40 basis points with the two-year yield at 3.64 percent and the one-year rate at 4.04 percent. One year later, the two-year yield had fallen to 1.92 percent while the one-year was at 1.87 percent for a spread of plus five basis points. For this period, the one-year earned the 4.04 percent while the two-year returned 5.44 percent. When the crunch occurred and Lehman Brothers failed, the Bank of Canada slashed the Bank Rate to 0.25 percent and the spread between the two-year and one-year soared to 107 basis points by October 2009. On November 19, 2009, the two-year yield was 1.27 percent with the one-year yield at 0.50 percent. For this one year period, the one-year treasury bill returned 1.87 percent while the two-year bond returned 2.59 percent.

Thus, buying the higher yielding one-year bill resulted in a lost opportunity.

Investors who are well-informed can take advantage of certain anomalies that can lead to enhanced returns. These anomalies may occur if there is a very large seller of a bond of a particular maturity or if there is huge demand for another maturity. The net effect is to make a bond of one maturity less or more expensive than normally would be the case. Other factors that can produce such anomalies are a sudden surge in new-issue financings or large purchases by foreign investors. These kinds of opportunities occur at various points on the yield curve. They may alert investors that their original selected maturity date turns out to be the "expensive" part of the curve with greater yield available in a neighbouring maturity. Again, investors may return to the original maturity once the anomaly vanishes.

SUMMARY

The yield curve is a better forecaster of yields than any economist. For example, consider that one-year treasury bills yield 2 percent and two-year Canadas yield 3 percent. If you buy the two-year at 3 percent and then consider selling it after one year, what must the one-year rate be so that you would earn 3 percent? If the yield curve was unchanged, you would have earned 3 percent for the first year plus the 1 percent gain from the fact that the one-year rate was 2 percent. With the yield curve unchanged, you could buy the two-year again and earn another 4 percent. This shifting maturity strategy is a proven strategy.

The only potential drags on performance are transaction costs (so make sure you are getting competitive offerings) and the price risk of longer term securities. In addition, another rule of thumb used by some portfolio managers is to extend term when you are able to pick up an extra 20 basis points per annum.

It seems to me that this approach can enhance returns and it makes the maintenance of a yield curve very important. I encourage you to keep your own yield curve up-to-date and watch for opportunities.

MONETARY POLICY

It is very important to be aware of monetary policy, as the actions of the Bank of Canada have a bearing on the economy, profits, currency, and the bond market. I will introduce here a simple and practical way to follow monetary policy. Market professionals chart the spread between the two-year Government of Canada benchmark yield and the Bank Rate as well as the spread between the same two-year bond and the ten-year Canada benchmark. At this stage, I would like to define the Bank Rate: it is the lender of last resort rate. In other words, the Bank of Canada stands ready to supply credit at the Bank Rate to money market jobbers who would have to supply acceptable collateral. In practice, the Bank Rate is used to indicate what the overnight lending rate should be among market participants. Typically, the overnight rate is 25 basis points above the Bank Rate and it is the single rate used by the Bank of Canada to indicate to the market where it wants short-term interest rates to be. This rate is announced after each of the eight predetermined dates during the year. The target for the overnight rate is set by the Bank of Canada to "achieve a rate of monetary expansion consistent with the inflation-control target. The transmission mechanism is complex and involves long and variable lags—the impact on inflation from changes in policy rates is usually spread over six to eight quarters." (Bank of Canada Monetary Policy Report, April 2008.)

Similar to most other central banks in the developed world, the Bank of Canada has agreed on targeting a rate for Canada's consumer price inflation (Consumer Price Index or CPI). In November 2006, in agreement with the federal government, the Bank of Canada extended the acceptable annual range of 1 to 3 percent to the year 2011.

Since the Bank of Canada adopted its regular policy and Bank Rate setting meetings, the two-year Canada benchmark has become a good proxy for what market participants believe to be the trend in monetary policy. Should the market believe that the Bank of Canada is planning to lower the Bank Rate and ease monetary policy, the market will move the yield on the two-year bond below the Bank Rate with the converse being true should the market anticipate a higher Bank Rate.

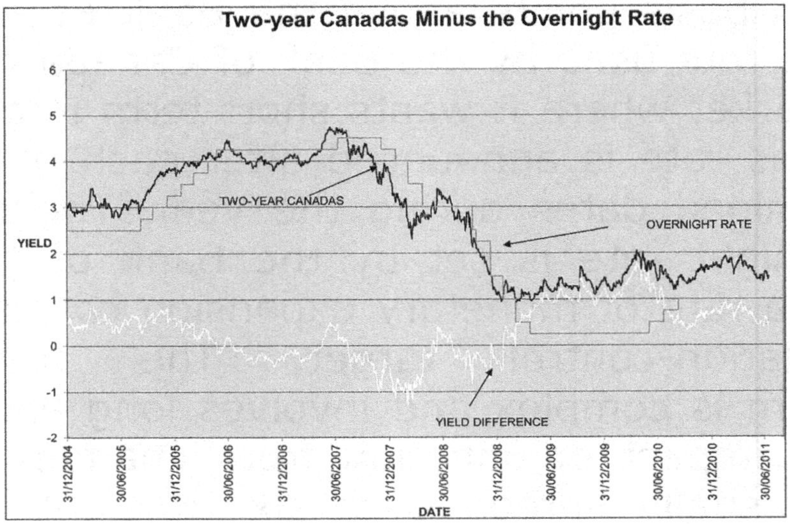

The ten-year benchmark trades independently of the Bank Rate and its yield reflects the collective will of all bond market participants. At a time of extreme monetary ease and an expanding economy, the yield spread from the two-year benchmark to the ten-year benchmark will be very wide (or steep). When monetary policy becomes less stimulating, this spread will narrow, leading to a flattening of the spread. This graph shows the recent trend in this spread:

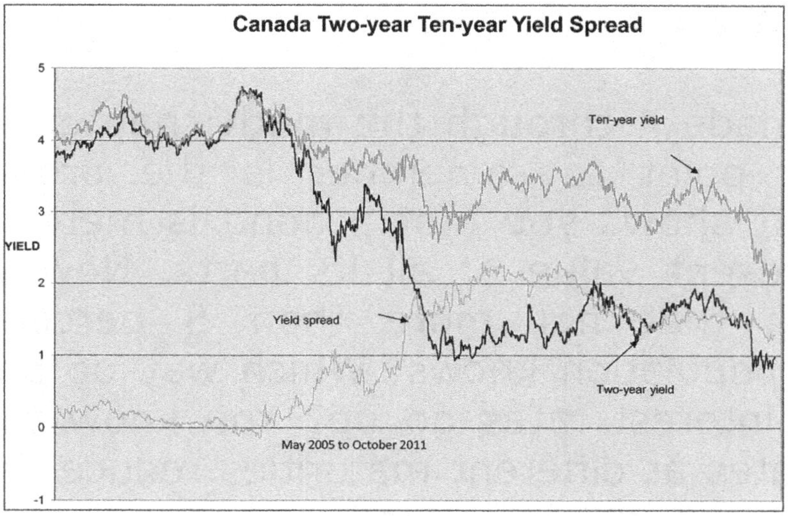

Believe it or not, this spread was negative up July 2007 after a period when the yield curve was flat. We know what happened next; the credit crisis hit with full force and the Bank of Canada began to ease monetary conditions significantly, pushing the Bank Rate down to a mere 0.25 percent in the process. The spread from two to ten years moved up sharply, reaching an extreme level of 223 basis points in June 2010. The Bank of Canada began to back away from its monetary ease but the current positive spread of 145 basis points indicates that monetary conditions are still very stimulative.

Above all else, make it a point to maintain your own yield curve and keep it current so that you maintain a good perspective on what is happening in the money market and with monetary policy.

SUMMARY

So, you made it through the math chapter! The most important point to remember is the present value concept. It shows you that a bond is merely the sum of the present value of all its parts. Now you know something that not more than 5 percent of the investing population knows: Which way do bond prices go when interest rates go up? You know that higher interest rates at different maturities reduce the present value of the parts of a bond and thus the total price or value of the bond moves lower. You also know about duration, which is a vital term as it allows you to judge the relevant volatility or risk of different bonds. (Perhaps go back to the teeter-totter. Someone who is chicken will not sit at the end of the board and thus will have less risk.) You know what basis points are, along with the yield curve, compound interest, and the important topic of reinvestment risk and bond price dynamics.

CHAPTER 4

Subprime, Credit Crunch, and ABCP

The principal reason that I entitled my book *In Your Best Interest* has everything to do with the fact that the investment industry manufactures products and sells them to you, regardless of whether they are suitable for you or not. Consequently, the recent past carried some big lessons with it. I am not going to chronicle in detail what happened, but I will stress the need for you to act in your best interest and not to accept something that is sold to you just because someone says, "Don't worry, it's AAA." My overarching view of the whole approach to fixed-income investing is to keep it simple and of high quality. The rules of the fixed-income business are simple: keep what you start with, and earn a return on it.

In the money market (maturities less than a year), you should confine yourself to government treasury bills and bankers' acceptances.

In the period leading up to the Asset-backed Commercial Paper (ABCP) credit crunch mess, Blackmont Capital was approached by a major investment dealer who wanted us to offer this ABCP paper to our sales force. It took the better part of 15 minutes before my chief trader, a very bright young man, told them that he was having a hard time understanding this and how was he going to explain it to our IAs, who in turn would have explain it to their customers. There is little doubt in my mind that this paper was sold merely on the R1 (H) rating assigned to it. There were lots of warning signals here: Of the three major rating agencies, Moody's and Standard & Poor's declined to rate the Canadian ABCP as they felt the liquidity covenants were too weak. This should have set off alarms, but who in the investing public knew that? The Dominion Bond Rating Service (DBRS) not only assigned it its highest rating, but worked with the issuing conduits to obtain this rating. One thing has come out of this, for sure: when issuers are paying rating agencies for ratings, there is an obvious bias in favour of the issuer. I know from my years as a portfolio manager and from contemporary discussion that most prominent investment institutions do their own credit analysis and do not rely on the public rating agencies. Very few such institutions had any of this paper, with the notable exception of the giant Caisse de Depot, the Quebec Pension Plan arm, which owned every one of the ABCP conduits totalling $13 billion. All of this for an extra 10 to 15 basis points over chartered bank bankers' acceptances. Before continuing, I would like to offer my take on how this developed.

The tech bubble produced a cornucopia of fees for investment bankers from the initial public offerings (IPOs) of the dotcoms. When that ended in 2000, they looked around for another cow to milk and latched on to the income trust industry, and this led to an onslaught of IPOs, to the point where even BCE and the banks were eyeing conversion. Halloween 2006 changed all that. You know where I stood on the trusts as my first edition came out in the spring of 2006: "Returns on trusts have been impressive to be sure, but at unsustainable levels. Something will change: yields in the bond market may rise, Canada could go into recession, oil prices could fall, governments could change the tax rules, or pension funds could drive prices up and yields down."

I had no idea what would happen, of course. My main assumption was that the market would sort it out.

Bay Street had to find another goose and it latched on to the asset-backed craze: ABCP, Collateralized Debt Obligations (CDOs), and Structured Investment Vehicles (SIVs), for example.

Ironically, the shrinking stock of Canada treasury bills contributed somewhat, as both nature and underwriters abhor a vacuum!

COMMERCIAL PAPER

To refresh your memory, commercial paper, in its classic, basic version, is a short-term (less than one year) obligation. Typically, it is an unsecured IOU issued by a corporation backed only by the company's promise to repay you at maturity. While there have been a few notable failures (Olympia and York), this market has operated trouble-free. Enter the asset-backed market. Asset-backed securities (ABS) have been around for a long time. They differ from ABCP in two very important ways:

1. The assets behind them are real and include first mortgages (not subprime), credit card receivables, and car and bank loans. Typically, the collateral exceeds the face value issued by 25 percent.

2. The term of the securities issued matches the term of the underlying assets, so there is no problem with maturities or reissuance. ABCP paper was mismatched with terms of 30 to 90 days with long-term assets and derivatives as security (a significant percentage being of dubious quality). There is some greed involved here, as the yield paid on the short-term ABCP is lower than the return on the assets in a positive yield curve environment. This adds to the profits. This is what made that liquidity covenant so important. When the liquidity providers declined to step in, this market came to a screeching halt and is still frozen at the time of writing. I provide an update on the ABCP fiasco on page 176.

SUBPRIME

Enter the subprime mortgage business. A very good friend opined that if these had been called what they really were/are, junk mortgages, then this problem would never have become as disastrous as it did. The implication of the word *prime* in subprime surely gave these dubious securities a greater reception than they deserved. Before this is done, as much as one trillion dollars may have to be written off by the globe's largest financial institutions. Spawned by a rosy real estate/housing market and easy money, lenders (primarily in the United States) discarded any semblance of lending standards, giving rise to such expressions attached to new borrowers such as NINJA (No Income, No Job, No Assets!). Many such individuals became homeowners, counting on inexorably rising house prices to skate them onside. This did not happen and, currently, foreclosure rates are in the atmosphere, housing prices are retreating rapidly, and consumer confidence is plummeting.

Clever banks and underwriters, anxious to get this stuff off their balance sheets, packaged them up in numerous guises and shipped them out to investors all over the world. They ended up in many of the ABCP conduits; these conduits owned upwards of 50 percent of their assets in subprime related securities or some other synthetic derivatives.

CRUNCH TIME

We have now seen the fallout from the subprime fiasco. Credit spreads on *everything* blew out to extremely wide levels. Banks and other counterparties did not trust one another, prompting central banks to step in with unprecedented actions to assist the market in returning to some degree of normality.

The TED spread is a very good gauge of credit market conditions. The *T* stands for the yield on three-month U.S. government treasury bills while the *ED* stands for the yield on three-month commercial Euro Deposits. Subtracting the former from the latter offers a good look at the conditions in the credit markets as the Eurodollar rate represents credit risk while the T-Bill rate is the risk-free rate. As you can see by the chart below, in normal times this spread is at 15 to 20 but it blew out to 264 basis points in August of 2008 before returning to normal levels. Over the summer of 2011, it has crept up over 30 as the troubles in Europe have flared up.

Even high-quality investment-grade bonds were affected significantly. There is a federal agency, Canada Housing Trust (CHT), which buys mortgages from financial institutions and packages them as bonds. They carry the unconditional guarantee of the Government of Canada while offering the collateral value of the first mortgages themselves (no subprime here!). Before the crunch, they traded at 15 basis points over an equivalent Government of Canada bond. Come crunch time, they blew out to 65 basis points over, representing a wonderful risk-free investment. They have narrowed to 20 beeps over now, but this is still too wide. A man in the moon would ask why the Government of Canada does not issue bonds in its own name and then advance the funds to CHT. This is a very good question. There is no simple answer, as this would save taxpayers a lot of money on the approximately $75 billion of these issued annually. In any case, the government needs to issue more bonds, given the previous debt paydown resulting from our surpluses. They have already begun to issue bonds on behalf of other federal agencies such as Farm Credit Corporation, so perhaps they will eventually get to CHT.

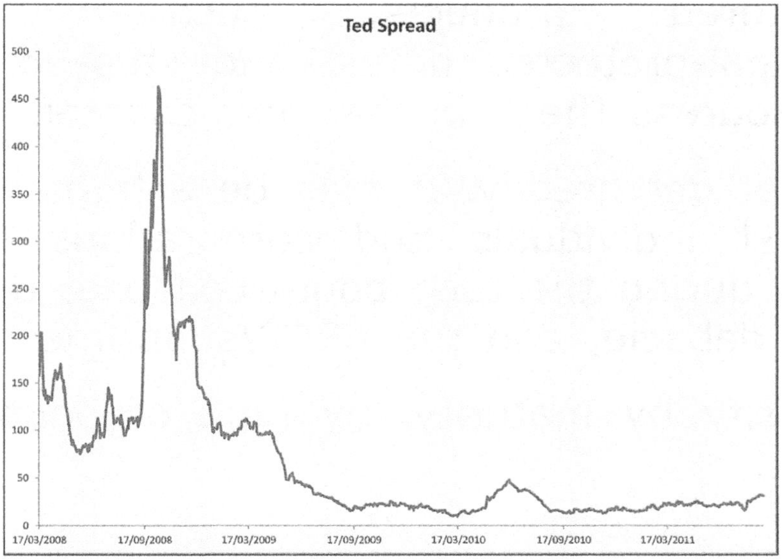

This is only one example of what transpired when the crunch came. Liquidity dried up, bids were hard to find, and good credits had to pay through the roof for credit. This crunch also lay to rest the invincibility of our chartered banks, which have had to shore up their balance sheets and no doubt will continue to do so.

As I write this, global financial institutions are raising equity capital at every chance as they need to deleverage in a meaningful way to ride out this storm. Central banks, particularly the Federal Reserve Board in the United States, have taken extraordinary measures to ensure that credit markets continue to function. The lessons from this are simple:

1. Stick with high-quality investments.
2. Do not invest in something you do not understand. This applies to all manner of structured products, such as ABCP, principal-protected notes, and step-up bonds. I will address these in the next chapter.
3. Do not get greedy. It may be a human trait but it cost individuals and corporations significant sums during the tech boom collapse, the income trust debacle, and the ABCP/subprime mess.
4. Diversify by maturity, by type of bond, and by credit.

CHAPTER 5

The Products

It is time to discuss the choices facing investors as they seek to assemble their fixed-income portfolios. This is a long chapter, so hang in there. Rule number one: keep it simple. This is sound advice for all investments, not just bonds. If you do not understand a product that is being offered to you, say no!

In this chapter, I have separated the various fixed-income products into two general categories. The first describes the standard or conventional bonds that are easy to understand and are straightforward. Included in this first section are treasury bills, Government of Canada bonds, provincial and municipal bonds, uncomplicated corporate bonds, and American and international bonds.

The second section deals with structured products of various types, including step-up notes, asset-backed securities (ABS), and the most recent scourge of Bay Street, principal-protected notes (PPNs). None of these types of securities are ever designed with your financial well-being in mind. Rather, they are created to generate large underwriting and commissions. In other words, they were designed to be sold!

My first piece of advice is to hang up or say no when your IA or financial institution attempts to sell you something that you do not understand. In addition, unlike conventional new issues where the issuing entity pays the fees and the investor receives a net yield without fees, structured notes normally have their fees buried in the offering price. If commissions totalled 3 points, for example, the opening bid on such securities would be no better than 97 and perhaps lower. In my experience, very few IAs actually understand what they are selling, but they do know that the commissions are significantly higher than on conventional bonds. The question that you must ask your advisor is: "If this product is so great, why are they being offered to me instead of being snapped up by all those savvy institutions?"

There are two basic types of issuers of bonds: governments and corporations. The government sector includes the federal government and Crown corporations, the provinces, and municipalities. Corporations that issue bonds include industrial, utility, financial, and single-purpose entities. Single-purpose entities are one-off companies like GTAA (Greater Toronto Airport Authority). Both of these groups issue different types of products.

First, let us discuss the only money market securities that you should invest in: treasury bills and bankers' acceptances (BAs). The money market (securities of less than one year to maturity) is where you park surplus funds, be they savings earmarked for a real estate purchase or for other similar outlays. This is not where you take risk.

CONVENTIONAL BONDS

TREASURY BILLS (T-BILLS)

These securities are short-term, with a maturity of one year or less (most being issued with terms of three or six months). The federal government also offers one-year bills. At the time of writing, there was $111 billion in Government of Canada T-Bills outstanding. Every second week, the Bank of Canada conducts an auction, inviting the money market jobbers to bid for the amounts being auctioned of three-, six-, and twelve-month maturities. They, in turn, bid for them according to what they consider to be the appropriate yields for the different maturities.

Treasury bills are priced at discounts from their face value. Their yield is the difference between the purchase price and the maturing face or principal amount. The following formula is used when computing the yield of a treasury bill:

$$Y = \frac{F - P}{P} \times \frac{365}{T}$$

Y = Yield
F = Face Value
P = Price

T = Number of Days to Maturity

(In this formula, *Y* is the quoted yield, *100* is the face value, *P* is the price, and *term* is the number of days remaining to maturity.) Here's an example. A 91-day treasury bill is offered at 99.013. What is the yield? (100–99.013) * 365/91 = 4 percent.

You might ask how to compute the price, if you know the yield:

$$P = 100 / 100 + (Y * \text{term} / 365)$$

Let us then work backward from the 4 percent yield from the first example:

$$\begin{aligned} P &= 100/100 + (4 * 91/365) \\ &= 100/100.99726 \\ &= \$99.013 \end{aligned}$$

You will note that this is not the same as the formula in the present value section. This is because these are short-term, money market securities and the money market functions on an annual yield basis. It is important to grasp the concept of investing in a discounted instrument and receiving your yield when the security matures at a known value in the future. We will return to this concept when we discuss zero coupon bonds, cornerstones of retirement planning.

Government of Canada T-Bills are the safest—and the lowest-yielding—money market securities. They are very liquid, with daily trading volumes of $3.8 billion.

Investors buy them for safety, to park money for a short term, for market reasons, to keep idle chequing account deposits earning something, or to put funds aside until they are needed for a specific future event (buying a house, paying taxes, etc.). Provinces also issue treasury bills and their yields are modestly higher than the federal government T-Bills.

MONEY MARKET INSTRUMENTS

Banks issue bankers' acceptances (BAs), which are corporate promissory notes stamped by the banks as guaranteed. They typically yield more than treasury bills but less than commercial paper and are also very liquid. Like T-Bills, they trade at a discount from face value. BAs are also very liquid, being acceptable collateral at the Bank of Canada's discount window. Trading volume is $5.74 billion per day.

Corporations issue commercial paper, which is merely an unsecured promissory note to repay; commercial paper is riskier and yields more than treasury bills.

Money market securities thus offer safety and income for those investors with short-term needs.

GOVERNMENT BONDS

Bonds issued by governments are issued in terms from two to thirty years and in different currencies. The bulk of these issues are straightforward, paying interest twice a year with no special features, so investors are attracted to them for their safety, yield, lack of complication, variety of maturities, and liquidity. All governments have taxing power; in fact, we taxpayers collectively provide the security for these bonds. For almost a decade, the federal government ran large surpluses, allowing for a significant reduction in our national debt. This created a virtuous circle where some of the surplus was applied to reducing debt, resulting in lower debt payments, which led to a bigger surplus to pay down more debt. This virtuous circle came to an end when the recession struck in 2007–08, and once again the federal government began to rack up large deficits.

The debt paydown period changed the way that the bond market functioned. For example, even though the federal government was paying down debt, it still recognized the importance of having liquid benchmark issues so that market participants could hedge their inventories and also provide reference points for new issue pricing. The Bank of Canada conducted a program of buying in older, smaller, less liquid Government of Canada issues and replacing them with additions to the benchmark issues at the important maturity dates: two, three, five, seven, ten, and thirty years. This program is no longer necessary, owing to the large federal deficits that Canada is facing. These become very large issues and are the most liquid in the marketplace. These issues also allow investment dealers to hedge their inventories by shorting the benchmarks against all their long positions or to hedge a new issue that is selling slowly. Swap desks, which are involved in the business of swapping fixed-rate liabilities for floating-rate ones, among other things, are frequently large buyers or sellers of these high-quality, fixed-rate benchmarks. In addition, when IAs or the media need to know what is happening in the bond market, they will refer to one or more of these issues, sometimes using the term *bellwether,* as in "The bellwether 5s of 2037 are up 50 cents in active trading."

Of course, they also provide the foundation for the yield curve, which, as we have seen, can be an important analytical tool. Also, as you will see in the zero coupon section, they are the base for the bond stripping business. They provide easy entry and exit from the bond market for those money managers who attempt to guess which way bond prices are going, for foreign investors, and for individual speculators.

PROVINCIAL BONDS

Provincial bonds are similar to the federal ones but offer slightly higher yields as their governments' taxing power is confined to their individual provinces. Here is where the various provinces trade on a yield spread basis from the Canada benchmarks:

PROVINCIAL YIELD SPREADS (in basis points) (July 2011)			
	5 Years	10 Years	30 Years
British Columbia	34	68	77
Alberta	28	56	65
Saskatchewan	29	67	70
Manitoba	34	71	79
Ontario	36	74	81
Quebec	39	79	89
New Brunswick	37	80	89
Nova Scotia	36	76	86
Prince Edward Island	38	81	92
Newfoundland/Labrador	37	75	80

These yield spreads are relatively modest and closely bunched. What a difference a few years make. In 2008, Alberta was close to paying off its debt completely and nine of the ten provinces were in surplus. Thus, borrowing requirements were modest. Now, seven of the provinces have deficits and total borrowing needs for 2011 are $80 billion.

Since the credit crunch has pushed provincial yields significantly wider, they are genuine bargains. In this day of sovereign debt problems, their credit ratings are all stable. This has not always been the case, as the ebb and flow of the political events in Quebec produced some startling swings. Also, these days, provincial issuers are adding to existing issues regularly, augmenting their liquidity and popularity. Thus, investors can pick up some extra yield in safe, liquid provincial bonds.

MUNICIPAL BONDS

Municipalities also borrow money for capital purposes. There was a time when each town or city would issue its own bonds. Those days are mostly gone. Most provinces have created municipal borrowing authorities (Alberta Municipal Finance Corp. and New Brunswick Municipal Finance Corp. are examples) that they use their lower interest costs to borrow money on behalf of the various municipalities. The bonds that they issue are guarantees of the provinces and therefore trade at the same yield as straight provincial debt. There are a few exceptions, naturally. Ontario has created regional governments, such as the Regional Municipality of Ottawa-Carleton, which assume borrowing power for all the towns and villages in their areas. Also, Canada's largest cities, such as Montreal, Toronto, and Vancouver, still issue bonds in their own names. Unlike in the United States, there are no tax advantages to owning municipal bonds in Canada.

ZERO COUPON BONDS

Imagine an investment that is high-quality, liquid, and fully compounding, with a future value that is known to the exact penny. This is the zero coupon bond. More commonly known as a strip, the zero coupon bond has become the cornerstone of the fixed-income portion of RRSPs. As the baby boomers work their way toward retirement, they are looking for more certainty, and zero coupons offer them just that. A detailed description of these bonds follows in the next chapter. Given a certain amount to invest today, you can buy a zero coupon of a specific maturity and you will know exactly what you will receive at that maturity date. As well, these are almost all government bonds and are very safe.

They are created by traders for investment dealers who purchase a block of bonds and then separate or "strip" the individual interest and principal payments from each other, applying a discount yield to these payments to compute a present value (remember the present value calculation from Chapter 3). This present value becomes the cost, and this strip will then compound at the purchase yield to the future payment amount. There are no payments received during that time, which is where the term *zero coupon* comes from.

This is a terrific retirement product. The market for strips is huge, with $187 billion of face value outstanding and trading volume of $6.3 billion per month.

RETIREMENT SAVINGS BONDS (RSBs)

Suppose you have ten years to retirement, at which time you will need regular income. Is there a product that can accomplish this feat? Yes! The RSB is a partially stripped bond. The coupon payments for the years for which you do not need income are stripped from the bond, with the rest of the bond being left intact. When the ten-year period, in this example, is up, interest payments begin, producing a regular stream of income. These RSBs are sold at a discount, reflecting the present value of the deferred income stream. In fact, they are deferred annuities that offer attractive yields and liquidity, as well. They already exist in many forms, trade in the secondary market, and can be created easily to custom specifications by your friendly stripper.

REAL RETURN BONDS

Inflation is the enemy of bonds. At an inflation rate of approximately 5 percent, a dollar's purchasing power shrinks to just 61 cents in only ten years! Since most fixed-income instruments pay a fixed rate of interest, inflation will erode the purchasing power of those payments over time. Investors, cognizant of this fact, expect to earn a real return (yield minus inflation) of 2 percent before taxes on government bonds. The question then becomes which inflation rate to use to compute a real return: the past twelve months, the average for the past five years, or the inflation expectations for the next one or several years? It appears that the expected future rate of inflation is the key variable.

The fact that inflation is so unpredictable helps to explain why I am a strong advocate of laddered portfolios. With a steady progression of maturing bonds, an investor will have money available at different times to reinvest at prevailing interest rates, which, of course, will reflect the inflation expectations at that moment. Should interest rates spike higher, then maturing funds would be available to reinvest at higher yields. The converse is true, of course, should interest rates move lower, but over the course of a couple of economic cycles, investors would find the laddered approach to be in their best interest as they spread their investments over the cycles. Furthermore, it eliminates the risk of having all of their fixed-income investments maturing at the low point of the interest rate cycle, which would almost guarantee poor real returns, as inflation and interest rates would then move higher through the economic cycle.

While the laddered approach is my preferred method of ensuring positive real returns, there is another fixed-income instrument available that guarantees real returns and which also serves as a useful proxy for inflation expectations. This is the real return bond (RRB). In Canada, RRBs are issued primarily by the Government of Canada, and they protect the future purchasing power not only of the principal but also of the interest payments. For a comprehensive analysis of these complex securities, I recommend visiting the Bank of Canada's website (www.bankofcanada.ca.)

RRBs are similar to conventional Government of Canada bonds: they are issued with a fixed coupon rate; interest is paid twice a year; and they have a specific maturity date. For example, the RRB that we will use as an example is the Government of Canada 3 percent bond due December 1, 2036.

They are unconditionally guaranteed by the Government of Canada and thus have a AAA rating. While that makes them relatively safe securities, they do have significant price swings as can be seen in the chart below. These are long-duration, low-coupon bonds and thus fluctuate widely for given changes in real yields. If you buy a real return bond (RRB) at 1 percent, say, you will receive that yield after CPI if you hold it to maturity.

Given the upward trend in RRB prices over the past few years, naturally, mutual fund and ETF funds are trumpeting the double-digit returns of their RRB funds. Beware! This is not the time to be buying RRBs at what are the lowest yields since 2003.

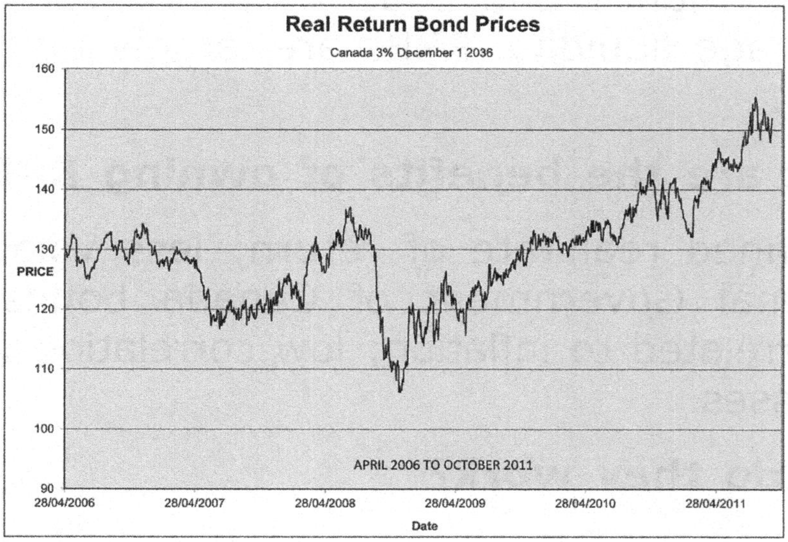

Here are some frequently asked questions about real return bonds.

Q: How do they differ from conventional bonds?

A: Both the coupon payments and the principal are indexed to the change in the Consumer Price Index (CPI); thus, they offer constant purchasing power regardless of the trend in CPI.

Q: How big is the market for RRBs?

A: There are $31.5 billion of outstanding Government of Canada RRBs with maturities ranging from 2021 to 2044. This is approximately 8 percent of the total Government of Canada bonds.

Q: How liquid are they?

A: The trading volume of RRBs is approximately $1.2 billion per month and thus they are considered to have average liquidity. RRBs are largely buy and hold securities.

Q: What are the benefits of owning RRBs?

A: Predefined real rate of return; less volatility than conventional Government of Canada bonds; returns highly correlated to inflation; low correlation with other asset classes.

Q: How do they work?

A: The coupon payments on these bonds remain fixed. What changes is the principal base. Let us use the Canada 3 percent December 1, 2036, as an example and assume that it has just been issued. Bonds are issued in denominations of $1,000. If the CPI was to rise 2 percent in the first six months, the principal would be adjusted by multiplying $1000 by 2 percent and adding this amount to the principal. Therefore:

$1,000 x 2% = $20 adjustment + $1,000 principal = $1,020 is the new principal amount

Taking half of the annual payment rate of 3 percent, the coupon payment becomes:

1.5% x $1,020 = $15.30

If six months later the CPI goes up by another 2 percent, the principal now becomes:

$1,020 x 2% = $40.40 + $1,000 = $1,040.40

The interest payment is 1.5 percent of this amount:

$1,040.40 x 1.5% = $15.60

This process is repeated every six months, thus offering investors the constant purchasing power of his/her interest income.

The principal is also indexed to the CPI; however, the inflation adjusted principal amount accrues and is only paid out at maturity. This adjustment to the principal is called the "index ratio."

Q: How do RRBs trade?

A: RRBs trade on a real yield basis.

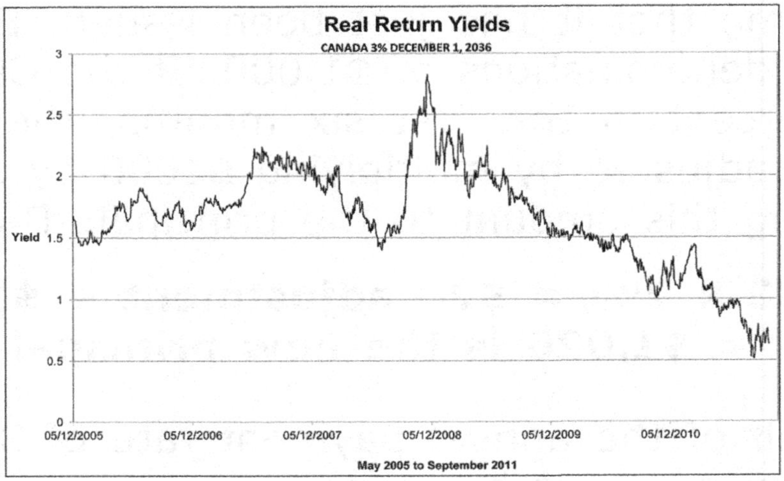

For example:

Bond: Canada 3% of December 1, 2036
Price: $137
Real Yield: 1.33%
Index Ratio: 1.12844

If investors buy this bond at $137.00 and hold it to maturity, they will earn a rate of return *after* inflation of 1.33 percent. Given a transaction of $10,000 face value for this bond at $137.00, the cost to investor is: 10 bonds x $1,370 (price of a $1,000 bond) = $13,700.

Total Cost: $13,700 x 1.12844 = $15,459.63 plus accrued interest.

Q: What are the risks of RRBs?

A: As with conventional bonds, the market price for RRBs fluctuates daily. If an investor decides to sell an RRB before maturity, he/she would face the possibility of a capital loss should the real yield rise. Real yields do fluctuate over time.

There is also the possibility that, in the event that CPI is negative, the index ratio will fall, producing less interest income. Apart from that, RRBs are unconditionally guaranteed by the Government of Canada; therefore, they are AAA securities with purchasing power protection.

Q: When is a good time to buy RRBs?

A: It is best to buy RRBs when inflation and its expectations are rising. Investors should avoid them when inflation and its expectations are falling and real yields are low. Since 2005, real yields have fluctuated between 0.87 percent and 2.69 percent, averaging 1.73 percent.

Q: How do investors buy them?

A: Should there be an appropriate time to invest in RRBs, individual investors may purchase individual RRBs based on their investment objectives and comfort level. They can be purchased through Exchange Traded Funds (ETFs) as well, with relatively modest management expense ratios.

Q: Do RRBs help in forecasting inflation?

A: Yes. By subtracting the yield on an RRB from a conventional Government of Canada bond of the same maturity, we arrive at the break-even inflation rate.

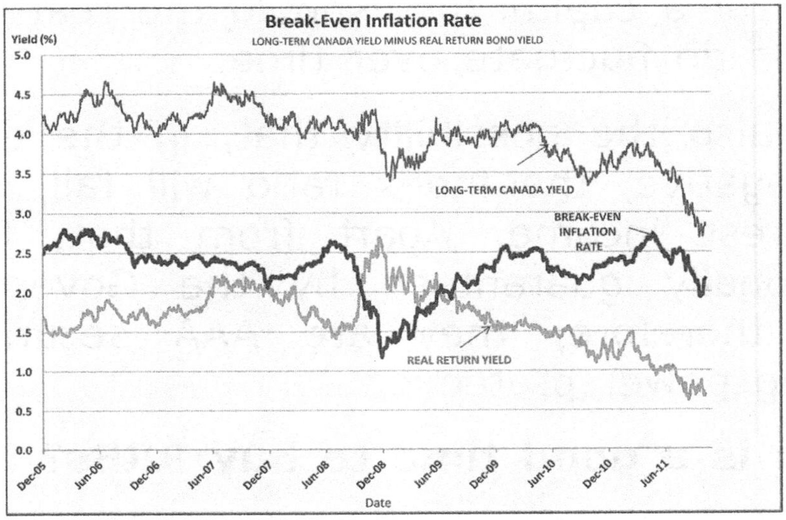

Using our example, the Canada 3 percent December 1, 2036, yields 0.91 percent at present while the Canada 5 percent June 1, 2037, yields 3.39 percent. The difference of 2.48 percent is what the market expects inflation to be over the long term.

By tracking this spread, investors can observe shifting inflation expectations. For example, at the end of 2009, this spread was 2.60 percent.

Taxation: The coupon payments on RRBs are taxed as interest income. However, the inflation adjustments to the principal are also taxed as they accrue. Thus, these bonds are best held inside a tax-sheltered account.

Summary: Real return bonds can make a sensible addition to a fixed-income portfolio, as their returns are not closely correlated to other asset classes. In conjunction with a bond ladder, they would contribute in reducing downside risk while offering stability to returns.

U.S. BONDS

The American bond market is the biggest and most liquid bond market in the world. Canadian investors sometimes need to buy U.S.-dollar securities. This could be because they intend to retire in the United States and would therefore need U.S.-dollar income, because they have a negative view of the Canadian currency, or due to the fact that interest rates are higher there.

The American market, of course, offers a broad and diverse product list. The market is divided into three separate categories: the domestic market (for U.S. government, agency bonds, stripped bonds, and domestic corporate bonds); the Yankee market (which refers to U.S. dollar bonds issued by Canadian borrowers); and the municipal tax-exempt market (which has no appeal for Canadian investors as they trade on an after-tax basis).

With respect to American government and corporate issues, there may be tax considerations that may make them unattractive to a Canadian investor. Nevertheless, the U.S. Treasury bond market offers immense liquidity and very narrow bid-ask spreads. In Canada, the bid-ask spread is typically five to ten cents on benchmark Canadas, whereas in the United States, it is 1/64 (.015625) of a cent on a U.S.

government bond! Active traders and speculators are assured of liquidity and tight pricing, even for small quantities.

The American market also offers U.S. government strips and real return bonds (called TIPs). U.S. government bonds and domestic corporates are now fully eligible for Canadians after the recent removal of foreign content restrictions. As the most liquid Government of Canada benchmarks are considered the bellwethers in the Canadian bond market, U.S. benchmark bonds are the bellwethers for the entire global bond market. The U.S. ten-year benchmark issue (currently the 2.125 percent due August 15, 2021) is the most closely watched individual bond in the world. Therefore, it would be in your best interest to start following it from the daily newspapers, online from sites such as Bloomberg.com, or from your IA's firm. If your IA's FI has it on its website, make a point of tracking it. While you may not be considering investing in U.S. government bonds, this particular bond and its yield affect a lot of other bond and equity markets, so a big change in the price of it could affect your investment decision in any number of investment categories. Perhaps a surprise uptick in the rate of inflation might cause a sudden sharp decline in the price of the U.S. ten-year benchmark (and a corresponding rise in its yield). A lot of these sharp swings prove to be temporary or are overdone, thus presenting you with an investment opportunity or window to take advantage of.

The Canadian bond market is tightly correlated with the American bond market, so it pays to be aware of what is happening there. There is a steady parade of economic statistics in both the United States and Canada that can move markets. Learn about these from your IA and ask for the calendar of upcoming releases or look for them in publications such as *Barron's* or the *Financial Post,* or online at www.bloomberg.com. They come out at specific times of the day and some are more important than others. It will pay off for you to be attentive to these releases.

Thus, the American bond market is important to you even if you are not contemplating an investment in it. Later, in the technical section, we cover how to chart bonds. The U.S. ten-year benchmark would be the first to chart.

Should you have needs for U.S.-dollar fixed-income investments, you might also consider Yankee bonds. A Yankee bond is one issued by a Canadian borrower in U.S. dollars.

The Yankee market is an attractive alternative for Canadian investors. For example, the Province of Ontario may choose to issue bonds denominated in U.S. dollars. Even though the principal and interest are payable in U.S. dollars, these bonds are *not* considered foreign content, since they were issued by a Canadian entity, nor do they have any adverse tax implications. (Of course, following the 2005 budget, foreign content is no longer an issue for Canadian investors.)

The major Canadian investment dealers have American subsidiaries that make markets in all of the U.S. pay bonds, making it relatively easy to obtain bids and offerings. American yields are almost always lower than Canadian yields, although that was not the case during the period of time when our currency strengthened and we experienced triple surpluses (budgetary, trade, and current account). Our yields have now moved above U.S. yields again. The spread among the various maturities expands and contracts, offering some excellent opportunities for traders and investors alike. For example, from the perspective of a Canadian investor looking to buy U.S. government bonds, the spread at the ten-year maturity for government bonds since 2004 has ranged from a positive spread of 55 basis points to a negative spread of 77 basis points.

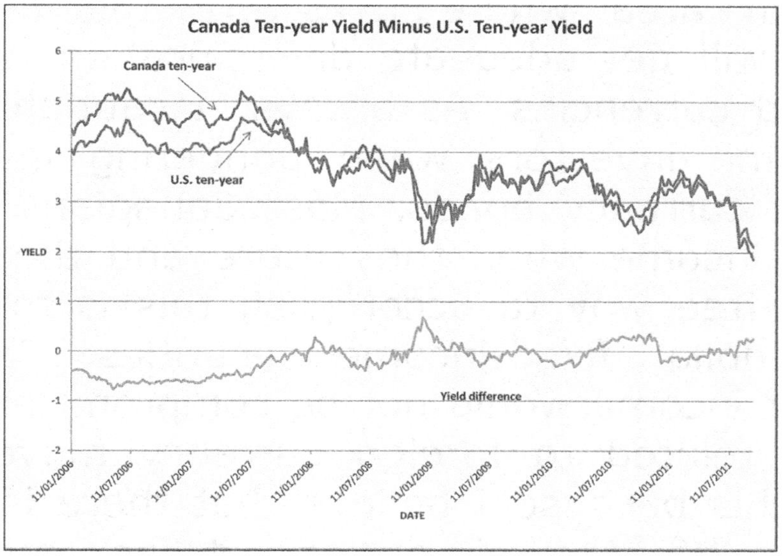

The American corporate bond market is so broad and diverse that it is a daunting task for any individual to sort through the myriad of choices. I recommend that you consider bonds having nothing less than an AA rating. Failing that, I direct you to the ETF section (see section entitled "Chapter 9: Exchange Traded Funds (ETFs)") where you will find an excellent choice of U.S. corporate bond ETFs.

INTERNATIONAL BONDS

With the recent strength of the Canadian currency, domestic fixed-income investors are becoming more interested in foreign currency bonds. It is natural for snowbirds to consider American pay bonds as they may need U.S.-dollar income in retirement. Perhaps some Canadians will need Euro income. In the recent past, emerging market bonds have performed well;

this is an area where ETFs are the answer, as investors will get adequate diversification both as to bonds and currencies. As always, I caution domestic fixed-income investors when pondering investments in foreign currency bonds. Most Canadians will need Canadian income when they retire and the simplest, most risk-free way to accomplish this is to invest in Canadian-dollar fixed-income securities. Thus, your retirement income would not be compromised because of losses related to foreign currency movements. I mention this because I believe that there is a strong possibility of the Canadian dollar appreciating significantly in the long run as a result of our superior fiscal condition and our abundance of natural resources such as wheat, corn, oil, natural gas, uranium, and potash.

The turmoil in the Eurobond markets has produced some startling increases in the yields of various countries. As tempting as these yields are on the bonds of Greece, Ireland, Spain, Portugal, and Italy, it is prudent to avoid them as this mess is nowhere close to resolution and there is the potential for "haircuts." This refers to the risk of bondholders suffering a reduction in income and principal should issuers restructure their debt. The best sovereign credits are found in the emerging markets and in certain specific countries, including Canada and Norway. BMO offers an ETF (ZEF) which invests in emerging market bonds. The bonds in question are all denominated in U.S. dollars and BMO hedges the currency exposure back to the Canadian dollar. Visit their website (www.etfs.bmo.com) for a complete description.

CORPORATE BONDS

It is in your best interest to learn as much about corporate bonds as possible for two essential reasons: they offer more yield than do government bonds; and, unlike governments, some corporations go out of business, so investors must pay close attention to credit ratings.

First, let us review what a bond is. When we discuss the bond market, we are referring, in a broad sense, to all the fixed-income instruments that trade. In the narrow definition, a bond refers to an obligation that is backed by specific assets. These could include factories, rail cars, airplanes, or credit card receivables. Investors would have first claim on these assets in case of default. Let's use the first mortgage on a house as an example. A financial institution lends you money to help buy a property, but in return, it has a first mortgage or claim on it if, for some reason, you default on your payments.

So, what are bonds called that are not backed by specific assets? They are called debentures. Technically, what the Government of Canada and the provinces issue are debentures, but in practice, we call their issues bonds.

Practically all the corporate bonds issued these days are also debentures, so debenture holders have an unsecured claim on corporate assets. Governments issue bonds to cover a deficit or to refinance a maturing issue. Corporations have more specific reasons for issuing debentures, such as building factories or pipelines. Sometimes they are paying off bank debt incurred when building those assets. A bond issue can be tailored to the life expectancy of an asset.

There is a wide array of corporations, but we will try to break them down into a few categories: utilities, industrials, financials, and single-purpose entities. To facilitate assessing the creditworthiness of corporations, there are several agencies that produce credit ratings on all the debt, both short-term and long-term, issued by companies (for example, Moody's, Standard & Poor's, and Dominion Bond Rating Service). They assign a credit rating for each debt layer of a company and are constantly reviewing them, issuing upgrades and downgrades when necessary. The debt layer refers to the fact that different corporate bonds rank differently on a company's balance sheet. A first mortgage bond would have first claim on specific assets, while debentures would have a general claim on a company's assets and subordinated debentures would rank behind all others. Note that they all rank ahead of equity holders.

One critical level for corporate credit ratings is the investment-grade level. BBB is the lowest level at which many institutions may invest in corporate bonds. Below that level—BB (High) or less—bonds enter what is called the high-yield bond or junk-bond levels, where fewer lenders venture and where financing becomes more difficult. Credit ratings begin at AAA (or "triple A") for the best borrowers and descend from there. Each level has three tiers, for example AAA (High), AAA (Mid), and AAA (Low). Then there are AA, then A, and then BBB, with each level having the same three tiers. These ratings are not foolproof, but they provide a very useful reference point for investors.

In addition, the major investment dealers all offer comprehensive research on companies. While a great percentage of it is aimed at the equity value of a company, there is specific research available regarding the debt quality of corporations, investment grade and not. Corporate bond offerings are normally accompanied by the credit rating. If not, ask for it. You should also check to see if the rating has changed recently or whether it is under review.

Following the ABCP mess in Canada and similar developments in the United States, rating agencies have received some flak and have attracted a lot of attention, leading to increased efforts to regulate them. For sure, their reputations have been tarnished. At the end of the day, simply buying something because it is rated AAA is not good enough if you do not understand what is being offered to you. There is little doubt that ABCP was sold only on its credit rating.

Most financial institutions conduct their own credit analysis, since they view the various rating agencies as biased in favour of the issuers (who, not surprisingly, pay the rating fees!).

Corporate bonds frequently have elements not typically found on other bonds. Government bonds typically pay interest semi-annually and pay the principal at maturity. While there are some similar corporates, they normally have additional features.

The most common one is a callable feature, meaning that the corporation, under certain conditions, may call the debentures back from the investors. Why would a company call its bonds back? It could be because it has enough cash and wishes to reduce its indebtedness, or a corporate event such as a merger or takeover might have occurred. What would such a feature look like? Here is a specific example: in 2011, Bell Canada issued $500 million 3.65 percent bonds due May 19, 2016, at $99.928, to yield 3.67 percent, 116 basis points above the Canada yield curve. The call feature states that this company may call, or redeem, this issue, but only at the greater price of $100 or 29 basis points above the Canada yield curve, whichever price is higher. In this case, even though investors may have their principal returned to them prematurely, it is on relatively attractive terms—87 basis points better than when it was issued. If this bond had been called the day after it was issued, BCE would have had to pay bondholders $103.94 to yield 2.80 percent.

Overall, call features are not in your best interest, as your investment may be called from you when you did not want your money back. The option to call is in the issuers' hands.

Following the unsuccessful legal challenge by Bell Canada bond and debenture holders, who argued that their bonds should have been redeemed instead of diluted to junk ratings, lenders have fought back and have had some success in obtaining better protection. One such issue is the Telus Corp 5.95 percent due April 15, 2015. Its indenture contains provisions that, in the event of a change of control and/or that its credit rating were to fall below investment grade, the bondholders have the right to have the issuer redeem these bonds at a price of $101. I expect that we will see a lot more such provisions as lenders fight to defend their principal.

HIGH-YIELD OR JUNK BONDS

With nominal interest rates so low these days (even though real yields are about where they normally are), many investors are tempted to reach for the very high yields offered by corporate bonds issued by companies whose credit ratings have fallen below the investment-grade levels. When that happens, many investing institutions can no longer buy them and, in fact, some may have to sell them. What typically happens is that the price of the bonds falls precipitously, offering what appear to be very high yields. The bid/ask on these types of bonds becomes very wide ($3 to $5), with poor liquidity and sudden, large price swings. Your IAs may offer certain of these bonds to you. Many of these situations have worked out (Telus, Nortel, Hudson's Bay, and others), but there have been some spectacular flameouts (Air Canada). I recommend the following approach to these "fallen angels":

Diversify your risk. If you wish to invest in them yourself, buy several different issues.

Shop around. Prices may vary widely from one FI to another, and IAs like to charge higher-than-average markups on these bonds.

Do your homework. With the high-yield bonds, it is important to understand the value of the company and what the equity is worth. Obtain equity research on the individual companies and ask your IAs for debt research, too. The major FIs all have fixed-income research on corporate bonds.

Consider high-yield mutual funds and ETFs. These are the only mutual funds I would ever suggest. ETFs (Exchange Traded Funds) are an excellent choice because the fees are significantly lower than those of mutual funds and you will receive broad diversification. One such ETF is XHY-T. It is invested in the U.S. high-yield bond market but is hedged back to the Canadian dollar.

***

So, how do you go about investing in corporate bonds? Very carefully. But with due diligence and a knowledgeable IA with a good firm, you can start to earn some incremental yield. Most new corporate issues are sold only to institutional investors because it is economical for the underwriters to do so. It is all about money. Most IAs get a 50 percent payout on commissions whereas institutional groups are paid a lot less, so it behooves a major dealer to sell as little as possible to the retail investor.

There are some issuers who insist that some of their issues be distributed to retail customers and a few who do specific retail-targeted deals, but they are the exception. Therefore, most of your retail corporate bond investing will be done in the secondary market and with certain mid-term note (MTN) issuers. MTN issuers file what is called a shelf prospectus, which permits them, on short notice, to bring a bond issue to market without the need for a full prospectus. This process allows them to take advantage of a sudden drop in yields or perhaps to fill a void in the market when there is not much supply and lots of demand. Regular borrowers such as car companies and utilities are the largest issuers of MTNs.

So how do you proceed? Let us examine the laddered approach. In the corporate bond world, you not only want different maturity dates but different issuers as well, to spread out your credit risk. Needing income but not much risk, investors may put together a ladder of the higher-rated corporates (household names such as the big banks, TransCanada PipeLines etc.), which will produce higher yields than would a ladder of government bonds. There will be moments when investors are tempted to invest in something that appears to offer an exceptional yield when compared to other corporate bonds. There is usually a good reason why something appears to be cheap, so it is in your best interest to dig deep to learn more. There could be a punitive call feature, or the company in question may be facing a downgrade to less-than-investment-grade status. As I prefer one-to ten-year ladders, there will be ten different credits, so that no more than 10 percent of your funds are invested in any one credit.

FIXED/FLOATERS

Typically issued by the banks, these bonds look like this: Royal Bank 6.75 percent June 4, 2012/2007. To qualify as Tier 1 capital, these bonds were issued with a ten-year maturity but only paying a fixed rate of interest for five years, after which they "float," at three-month bankers' acceptances plus 100 basis points if the bank does not call them. In practice, these bonds are called at the end of the fixed period, as there is no reason for a bank to pay 1 percent over BAs. This is because BAs trade at small-yield spreads over treasury bills and banks can borrow money very cheaply. This is an artificial floating rate, and the bonds are valued to the end of the fixed-rate period.

However, it happened during the credit crisis that one such fixed/floater issued by a European institution was not called and this sent a shiver through the Canadian bond market. None of our banks failed to call their fixed/floaters, but the bonds still fell out of favour quickly. Now that the new capital rules are about to be implemented, the banks are issuing a new generation of these subordinated fixed/floaters. These new debentures incorporate new language in their indentures that reduces the incentive to call at the five-year term and are being marketed as ten-year securities. However, from 2013 on, under the final Basel 111 Guidelines, this new debt is still likely to be called after five years.

CONVERTIBLE DEBENTURES

Convertible debentures are hybrid securities that combine the features of a conventional debenture with the option of converting, under certain circumstances, into the underlying equity of the issuer or another company.

They are similar to conventional bonds as they offer a fixed-income stream of interest payments plus the repayment of principal at maturity. They rank ahead of the underlying equity on a company's balance sheet and are therefore relatively safer.

Due to the convertible option however, the coupon rate on the convertible debenture is lower than for an equivalent non-convertible debenture. Most convertibles issued in Canada are unsecured by the issuer. There are no specific assets pledged and they are not rated by the credit rating agencies. Another notable feature of convertible debentures is that, unlike conventional bonds, almost all of them listed on the Canadian Exchanges.

Since they offer a convertible feature, convertible debentures prices tend to fluctuate along with the underlying equity. This is certainly more typical when the stock price rises.

When the stock price falls, the convertible debenture will fall too until it reaches its value as a bond. Thus, it stabilizes even as the stock price continues to fall. This occurred frequently in 2009 and the term "busted convertible" became commonplace, referring to convertible debentures that were so far out of the money that they traded as bonds. If the stock price exceeds the conversion price, the debentures are said to be "in the money" and will trade virtually lockstep with the common share.

When the underlying equity is near the conversion price, the convertible is said to be "at the money." At this level, the convertible debenture will be influenced both by the equity price change as well as the change in interest rates.

Convertible debenture issues almost always come with a feature which allows the issuer to redeem the debentures prior to maturity at the call price. An issuer would call an issue to possibly refinance at a lower rate or to force conversion.

They are issued for a number of reasons. The coupon rate is lower than that of a non-convertible debenture issued by the same company. This reflects the value of the conversion option so the issuing company saves interest costs.

The issuing company's credit rating or size does not allow it to issue conventional bonds.

A company can avoid or delay dilution to its shareholders by issuing convertibles. For example, perhaps a company is planning to use the proceeds to make a capital investment. When such an investment comes on stream and begins to contribute to earnings, the company would force conversion on its debentures.

Here is an example of a recently issued convertible debenture:

Issuer: H&R Real Estate Subordinated Debentures

Market Price: $101.00
Coupon Rate: 5.90%
Share Price: $18.00
Annual Dividend: $0.61
Maturity Date: June 30, 2020

Each $1,000 debenture is convertible into 42.5532 shares of H&R Real Estate Investment Trust (HR-U). They are therefore convertible at $1,000/42.5532 = $23.50 per share.

H&R may call them anytime after June 30, 2016, at $100.00. Investors have the option of converting before the debentures are called.

Intrinsic Value is calculated by multiplying the number of shares per bond times the value of the shares. In this case it is 42.5532 shares x $18.00 = $765.96 (also known as $76.60 per $100 in conventional bond terminology).

The **Premium** is the difference between the market value of the debenture and its intrinsic value: $101.00 - $76.60 = 24.40 points. The premium exists to reflect the value of the conversion option in addition to the current yield advantage versus the yield on the underlying equity.

CASH FLOW ADVANTAGE	
Current yield on bond (not yield to maturity)	5.84%
Current yield on the common stock	-3.34%
Cash Flow Advantage	2.50% per annum

The next calculation displays the period of time needed to recoup the premium paid for the bond. The first calculation is the income per $100 debenture. That is simply the coupon rate times 100. In this case, it would be 5.90% x 100 = 5.90.

The next calculation provides the amount of income that would be produced using the equivalent amount of shares per $100 debenture and multiplying it by the annual dividend. This would be 4.3 (42.5532/10) x 0.61 = 2.62.

The payback period is the conversion premium divided by the difference between the annual income on the $100 debenture and the annual income on the equivalent amount of shares. In this case, $24.40 / (5.90-2.62) = 7.44 years.

Thus, the premium would be recouped before maturity from the time of purchase. Please note that these variables are dynamic. In H&R's case, the company has signalled that it will be raising its dividend payments gradually, so this calculation will change.

Nevertheless, the debenture holders will have the added security of owning the debenture along with more income. Should H&R increase its dividend significantly, that should help boost the share price and, indirectly, the debenture price.

Convertible debentures in Canada are typically less-than-investment grade and not rated. Therefore investors with a moderate to high risk tolerance might include them in a well-diversified portfolio. Thus, these debentures have credit risk, interest rate risk, and call risk.

When considering investing in convertible debentures, the first step would be to examine the underlying equity of the issuing company. Contact your investment advisor or portfolio manager for specific investment ideas and recommendations. Next, investors would examine the features of the bond; in particular, the call price is important, as is the forced conversion clause. This kicks in when the price of the equity is well above the conversion price. The company in this instance would call the bonds, thereby forcing the debenture holder to convert to the common shares.

The conversion premium is also very important. One of the first things to do is to calculate the cash flow payback period as illustrated earlier. Thus, look for a payback period in years such that the net income gain from owning the debentures versus the equivalent amount of stock pays off the premium before the bond matures. These relevant valuation metrics are available from your IA on request.

Summary: Convertible debentures will perform well in rising equity markets while adopting more bond-like behaviour during equity market downturns, thus mitigating downside risk. They offer investors the upside of equities while retaining the characteristics of a regular fixed-income security, namely a fixed stream of interest payments plus the repayment of principal at a specific date. They offer some diversification benefits and, therefore, would also contribute to lower portfolio volatility. They rank ahead of equity on a company's balance sheet and thus offer an extra layer of security.

STRUCTURED PRODUCTS

This section will describe fixed-income products that you will be avoiding for the most part. These are products that have been assembled by various investment bankers and their propeller heads. The primary reason for structuring all these products is to permit financial institutions to move assets off their balance sheets so as to free up capital and improve the return on equity. For the most part, they are not created in your best interest, but rather to separate you from your money. They have been created to be sold, not bought. If these were such great investments, retail investors would never even see them. In fact, the institutions cherry pick these products, leaving the toxic waste for the man in the street. Large fees are involved in creating these products and large commissions are paid to IAs and FIs for selling them. Unlike primary issues in conventional bonds, the fees are buried in the product so that the opening market will be well below issue price.

I have to say that Canada has avoided some of the worst of the structured product fallout in that our mortgage-backed securities are a lot better quality than those found in the United States. However, principal-protected notes should have never been foisted on the investing public.

MORTGAGE-BACKED SECURITIES

Since the early 1990s, financial institutions have been selling off large parts of their mortgage portfolios by packaging them up and selling them as securities called mortgage-backed securities (MBS). These securities offer the quality of the National Housing Act guarantee plus a first mortgage on the properties themselves. As well, they offer a blended monthly payment of principal and interest. Of course, they are the flip side of a mortgage. As anyone who has bought a house and financed via a mortgage knows, monthly payments consist of both principal and interest. With MBS, investors are receiving a blended payment, and yet when they sell them, many of them complain because their principal amount has shrunk.

In an MBS pool, the various payments are recorded, and what is called a "pool factor" is calculated, indicating what percentage of the original principal remains. There are different kinds of MBS pools, the most common being non-pre-payable (where borrowers may not pay down their principal early) and pre-payable (where they may). The pre-payable pools have greater volatility, since the borrowers can pay off their principal in lump sums. The non-pre-payables thus offer a more predictable cash flow. I am always astonished when I hear IAs complain that their clients' original face value has shrunk by a significant amount. They just don't get this principal repayment idea.

The appeal of MBS, besides their quality, is the monthly income. Given the problems that that IAs and clients have with the principal payment issue, the investment bankers have managed to get a few borrowers to issue monthly pay bonds where the monthly payment is only interest. There are several issuers, so ask your IA for a list. Should these issues not be available, it is possible for your IA to construct portfolios where the interest payment dates are staggered to produce monthly payments. Sometimes they can even be laddered! But overall, MBS are usually too complicated for individual investors. My advice, if you need monthly income, is to buy monthly pay bonds that pay just interest monthly or to construct a portfolio whose interest payments fall in such a way that you receive a cheque each month.

In addition, mortgages are sold to the Canada Housing Trust, which resells them as Canada Mortgage Bonds (CMBs), carrying the full guarantee of the federal government plus the security of the first mortgages. There is no subprime debt in these bonds. In addition, bond holders receive interest only so there is no confusion about receiving principal back on a regular basis. They trade at a yields premium to Government of Canada bonds, so they are an excellent choice for those seeking top quality with some extra yield.

STRUCTURED NOTES

Crown corporations, provinces, and banks issue structured notes aimed primarily at the individual investor. While not necessarily in your best interest, you will need to know about them. Let's first discuss step-ups. Step-up bonds are issued mostly by provinces, Crown corporations, and banks. They are not straightforward. They are called step-ups because they have several potential maturity dates. Interest is paid at a certain rate to a certain date, at which time the interest rate "steps up" to a higher rate, and so on. They offer an attractive yield spread over the corresponding maturity dates of conventional bonds. So, what's the catch? They are callable by the issuer at each date. This means that the issuer or borrower may return your money to you at any of the callable dates; subsequently, there is a lot of uncertainty about the life of your investment. Also, if the issuer does not call the bond, it is usually because rates have risen and the yield you are receiving is below where new step-ups or conventional bonds are being offered, and so the value of your investment goes down.

They can be attractive investments at certain times but should be avoided when interest rates are rising, or when the yield curve is becoming flatter.

ASSET-BACKED SECURITIES

These bonds have been around for a long time. They are created typically by a company such as Canadian Tire, which has credit card receivables. It packages them together and issues a bond using the receivables as collateral. In other words, the credit card payments flow through to the bond holders. In order to ensure that the bonds are adequately backed, issuers typically over-collateralize the bonds, perhaps to the tune of 125 percent of the size of the bond issue. This takes care of any possible shortfalls from delinquent or defaulted payments. Other collateral used included car loans, bank loans, and mortgages. Given the fact that these were real assets with over-collateralization, they behaved like conventional corporate bonds with a healthy yield spread from Government of Canadas. As well, they were issued in terms that matched the maturity of the underlying assets and thus there were no liquidity issues. The chartered banks issued short-term ABS and backed them up with their own balance sheets so that, even during the credit crunch, they were paid off easily.

Enter Asset-backed Commercial Paper (ABCP). The purpose of mentioning it again here is just to illustrate how products become unsuitable. Suffice to say that these third-party conduits issued commercial paper backed by assets of five years or so. DBRS assigned their highest credit rating to this paper, even while Moody's and Standard & Poor's declined to rate it because of the weak liquidity covenants. I doubt that many investors in ABCP knew that. They were sold R1 (High) paper. These are such complex securities that IAs really did not know what they were selling. The assets backing this paper were nowhere near the quality of typical ABS. Rather they were stuffed with toxic subprime mortgages and other synthetic assets. The maturity mismatch caused the liquidity condition to kick in but the liquidity providers determined that they did not have to intervene to roll this paper. The rest is history. see section entitled "Chapter 10: Income Trusts, Royalty Trusts, and Real Estate Investment Trusts" for an update.

PRINCIPAL-PROTECTED NOTES

Another growth industry has developed in principal-protected notes (PPNs), another product which has been designed solely with fees in mind and not the well-being of the individual investor.

They are issued typically by chartered banks as debt instruments; they guarantee your principal back at some distant maturity (five to ten years) plus the possibility of some upside in returns by being linked to some underlying basket of equities or commodities or hedge funds. They are created by taking your $100 and investing about $70 of that in a zero coupon or similar instrument that will grow to $100 by maturity date. The balance of the $100 is usually invested in some kind of futures or derivative securities. It is entirely possible that you may just receive your initial principal back after a number of years, meaning that you would have done better with a savings account. There were so many layers of fees involved in creating PPNs and so little disclosure that the federal minister of finance produced new regulations on June 11, 2008, the main intent being to improve disclosure in many aspects of PPNs, including repayment terms, fees, risks, and redemption terms.

My advice is simple: Avoid them entirely. You can create your own using a strip bond or a regular bond and then investing in an ETF in the market or commodity of your choice. These PPNs are a scourge and it is timely that they attracted the attention of the Department of Finance. The events of the credit crisis almost brought the PPN market to its knees because of the extreme gyrations in securities markets.

TRUST CAPITAL SECURITIES (TRUCS)

Yet another hybrid security that individuals would be wise to avoid is the capital trust security or Trust Capital Security (TruCS). These securities go by different names as the issuers crave the publicity, so we have BoaTs (BMO), TD Cats, and so on. They were created with the banks' interests in mind, not yours.

They are complex. A bank sets up a capital trust and distributes nonvoting units (TruCs), but retains the voting rights. It takes the proceeds of the TruCs distribution and buys a subordinated debenture from the bank. Thus, the capital trust receives interest payments from the debenture and funnels it through to the TruCs holders. These TruCs were considered to be innovative capital instruments, qualifying them as Tier 1 capital. However, the Basel 111 capital treatment allowed banks for non-compliant capital securities to amortize down at 10 percent a year to 2022. There is some debate about whether this is a "Regulatory Event," in which case most Capital Trust Securities could be called before 2022. In early 2011, the Office of the Superintendent of Financial Institutions (OSFI) urged the banks not to call these securities early.

It appears that none of the Big Five will call these securities before 2022. Nevertheless, there are certain issues which may be called and investors are advised to check with their IAs to ascertain the status of whatever issues they may own.

CHAPTER 6

Preferred Shares

The asset category of preferred shares is an important one for taxable investors. Preferred shares typically have long durations and, as such, they also help to reduce reinvestment risk. Further, the advantageous treatment of preferred-share dividends results in attractive after-tax yields compared with bonds. What percentage of preferreds an investor includes in an overall portfolio needs to be thought out carefully, but they do warrant reasonable presence in a balanced portfolio.

Preferreds are more stable than common shares, rank ahead of common shares on a balance sheet, and, yet, their dividends receive the same favourable tax treatment as do the dividends on common shares. Thus, investors receive a stable, fixed flow of dividends with favourable tax treatment.

Before getting into all the details, it's worth discussing recent developments. Preferred shares slumped badly during the credit crisis but have performed very well in the past three years. There were, and still remain, several anomalies in markets stemming from that very scary period of time. Common shares in our chartered banks were hit very hard as the credit crisis reached full bloom. None of the banks cut their common share dividends and so the yields on their common shares ballooned. For example, the yield on BMO's common shares hit 11.64 percent on February 23, 2009, with the common trading at $24.51. The yield on the BMO 5.80 percent Series 15 perpetuals (explained below) was 7.42 percent then at a price of $19.64.

One year later, the common share price had more than doubled to $54.70 to yield 5.11 percent while the preferred advanced to $25.02 to yield 5.80 percent. The spread was thus 69 basis points in favour of the preferreds and today the spread stands at 84 basis points. Given the fixed nature of their dividends and lack of ownership, preferred shares should yield more than the common shares of the same issuer.

Back then, and in the period following, I was on record as favouring the common shares of preferred-share-issuing institutions, as I felt strongly that the total return from investing in those common shares would be far greater than of the preferreds. This was proven to be the case but I took a lot of flak from dyed-in-the-wool preferred investors. Now that the yield spread has been restored in favour of preferreds, we can now assess them on their own merits.

March 2008 saw the beginning of a new wave of preferred shares: the rate reset shares. Issued primarily by the chartered banks at a time of great uncertainty, they were designed to offer investors another wrinkle. The options on all preferreds are in the hands of the issuers; the investors can only accept what is offered. In this case, and taking the TD Series AG as an example, it was issued in January 2009 with a dividend rate of 6.25 percent, 438 basis points over the Canada 2014 maturity. When the call date of April 30, 2014, rolls around, TD may renew this issue at 6.25 percent or call them and reissue them at a narrower spread versus Canadas. As yield spreads have narrowed considerably since then, TD could reissue these with a reset spread of only 100 basis points. Thus investors know that their fat 6.25 percent yield will disappear. Further, this series is trading at $27.31 (as of July 17, 2011), versus its par value of $25 because of lower market yields.

While Canada's banks emerged virtually unscathed from the credit crisis, they are still subject to the new international bank rules, designed to head off future credit crunches. It appears to be almost certain that preferred shares are not going to be allowed as Tier 1 capital and, as a result, all of these rate resets are likely to be called and NOT reissued in the 2013 to 2015 period. There are billions of these outstanding.

In addition, bank perpetual preferreds are likely to be called in 2022, a year which has been dubbed by James Hymas, president of Hymas Investment Management Inc., as a "deemed retractable" date. This is because 2022 is the regulatory deadline for the new bank rules. Uncertainty abounds with respect to the treatment of preferred shares issued by insurance companies, also. The preferred share market is going to change a lot and shrink in the process.

Nevertheless, it is still a market, so let's examine it in some detail and list the pros and cons of investing in preferred shares.

ADVANTAGES

After-tax income. This is the main reason for taxable investors to invest in preferred shares. Normally, their dividends are higher than are those on the common shares issued by the same entity. However, the tax treatment for them is the same; they are taxed at a lower rate than is interest income to offset the double taxation of earnings. Using Ontario as an example, in 2011, an investor would pay 46.41 percent on interest income and just 28.19 percent on dividend income. For every $100 of interest income, an investor would retain only $53.49, while if the same $100 was from dividends, an investor would retain $71.81. Expressed another way, an investor would need $1.34 of interest income to equal the after tax income from dividends. This ratio is important when comparing bond yields to preferred yields.

Safety of principal. Preferred shares rank ahead of common shares on a balance sheet, both from the payment of dividends and in the case of an insolvency.

"Preferred" status. Sometimes, preferred share dividends can be "cumulative," meaning that any dividends in arrears would have to be paid before a company could resume payments to common shareholders.

Publicly traded. They are listed on public stock exchanges and thus visible to market participants.

DISADVANTAGES

Credit Risk. While the majority of preferred shares issued in Canada are by the chartered banks, there are many other issuers. Similar to bonds, the rating agencies, primarily Dominion Bond Rating Service (DBRS) and Standard & Poor's (S&P), assign credit ratings to the preferred share issues. Similar to the corporate bond market, long-term preferreds such as perpetuals are more susceptible to credit spreads than are shorter-term ones. P2 (Low) is the lowest rating considered investment grade for preferreds.

Call risk. The issuer almost always has the option of calling a preferred share issue on predefined terms. They only do so when it is in their best interest, not the investors'.

Liquidity risk. As with bonds, liquidity may dry up on certain issues, as they may be small or they become concentrated in a few investors' hands.

Yield curve risk. Many preferreds, such as perpetual, have long durations, making them susceptible to swings in bond market yields.

Tax risk. The relative appeal of preferreds could be taken away by the stroke of the federal finance minister's pen.

TYPES OF PREFERRED SHARES

Let's take a look at the various types of preferreds. There are also cumulative and non-cumulative issues. And remember, there are investment-grade issues and non-investment-grade issues, as well.

RETRACTABLE PREFERRED SHARES

There are two types of retractables. The first is the hard retractable.

This type of preferred is becoming rare, since it actually gives investors options regarding their investment. Specifically, a hard retractable gives the investor the right to require the issuer to redeem the shares at par value on a specific date. Imagine that! Naturally, these are sought after and thus have lower yields than other classes of preferreds. Here is one example of a hard retractable: Brookfield Investments 4.70% BRN.PR.A P2(L).

These shares are callable anytime at $25.00. At present (July 19, 2011), they are trading at $25.25. When analyzing retractables, not only do you look at the current yield (in this case 4.65 percent), but you also need to calculate the yield to the worst. In this case, since the call price is $25, the yield to worst would be negative, i.e., minus 5.11 percent. These shares do not stray far from the call price once the retraction date is reached.

SOFT RETRACTABLES

This type of retractable allows the issuer to pay the holder in either cash or common shares. Historically, most soft retractables have been paid in cash to avoid the dilution caused by issuing more common shares. If the issuer pays in shares, it is calculated by using 95 percent of the weighted average price for the preceding 20 trading days. Also, these shares are redeemable by the issuer on a predetermined scale. This is typically at a premium initially, with the price sliding toward par value. Thus, investors must look at the yield to worst before buying.

For example, the TD Bank 4.70% Series M, TD.PR.N P1(L). These shares are redeemable by the issuer anytime under this schedule: by April 30, 2012, at $25.25; or by April 30, 2013, at $25.00.

They are retractable by the holder under the following terms: beginning January 31, 2014, at $25.00 cash or ($2.00+95 percent of the weighted average price for the preceding 20 trading days).

At the current market price of $25.50, they yield 4.58 percent currently, 3.59 percent to the 2014 retraction date, but minus 4.37 percent to the next call date.

A lot of the soft retractables are now callable with the yield to worst being negative. Thus, they are not considered to be of good value right now.

FIXED-RATE RESET PREFERREDS

As mentioned at the beginning of this chapter, this type of preferred became very popular with investors; however, once again, investors have no options. The issuers have all the cards.

These shares are issued with a fixed dividend rate for a typical term of five years. They were issued at a certain yield spread from the equivalent maturity Government of Canada bond. In the example used, TD Series AG, it was issued in January 2009 with a dividend rate of 6.25 percent, 438 basis points over the Canada 2014 maturity. When the call date of April 30, 2014, rolls around, TD may renew this issue at 6.25 percent or call them and reissue them at a narrower spread versus Canadas. As yield spreads have narrowed considerably since then, TD could reissue these with a reset spread of only 100 basis points. Thus, investors know that their fat 6.25 percent yield will disappear. Further, this series is trading at $27.24 (as of July 19, 2011), versus its par value of $25.00 because of lower market yields. This is a current yield of 5.74 percent and a yield to the first call date of 2.83 percent. With the increasing likelihood that they will be called and not reissued, they are relatively expensive and could be exchanged for a higher yielding alternative.

STRAIGHT PERPETUAL PREFERRED SHARES

These preferreds have no maturity date and pay a fixed dividend rate as long as they are outstanding. Of course, the issuer has the right to call the shares while the investor has no rights at all. As mentioned earlier, the chartered banks (and possibly the life insurance companies) may have to call these on the "deemed retractable" date in 2022. While there is no certainty that this will take place, we can put a yield to maturity on the perpetuals as a guideline as to what the yield would be if they were indeed called in 2022.

With their fixed dividend rate and no maturity, these are long-duration securities and will react more to changes in long-term bond prices than any other preferred shares. Here is an example of a straight perpetual preferred:

> **BMO** 5.3% Series 5 **BMO.PR.H P1(L)**
> **Price:** $25.95(7/19/11)
> **Call date:** February 25, 2013, and thereafter at $25
> **Current yield:** 5.10%
> **Yield to worst:** 3.38%
> **Yield to 2022:** 4.84%*

*This is hypothetical.

FIXED FLOATING-RATE PREFERREDS

This class of preferred shares pays a fixed dividend until the next reset date, which is also normally the next call date. If the shares are not called, the investor has two options: Locking in at another specific dividend until the next reset date. This rate is determined by the issuer and is typically based on a percentage of an equivalent maturity Government of Canada bond yield; and exchanging for a floating-rate preferred share. This type of preferred floats at a monthly or quarterly basis, with the bank prime rate being the reference point.

These are similar to the rate reset preferreds mentioned earlier but their floating terms are not very attractive. They are also perpetual, so they don't have maturity dates.

FLOATING-RATE PREFERRED SHARES

These shares pay dividends on either a monthly or quarterly basis and they typically float in relation to the prime rate. They may have a minimum dividend rate and some of them have a mechanism by which the dividend may be raised or lowered monthly depending on whether or not the preferred trades within a certain price band.

They are callable only by the issuer, naturally, with no retraction rights. These shares would be useful during a period of time when the Bank of Canada is raising the Bank Rate. Here's an example:

> **BCE Inc. Series Y BCE.PR.Y P2 (L)**
> **Price:** $24.10 Dividend $3.141 as of July 12, 2011
> **Next Reset Date:** August 12, 2011
> **Reset details:** 80% of Prime Rate

SPLIT AND STRUCTURED PREFERRED SHARES

It is beyond the scope of this book to do a complete analysis of split shares. There are far too many variations on this theme to include here, so I thought that it would be best to examine the underlying concept. At its simplest, a split share has two components: one share receiving only dividend income and the second nothing but capital gain or loss. Split shares offer a fixed maturity date, offering more certainty than most preferreds; in addition, they typically offer retraction features plus higher yield than soft retractables.

There is a plethora of choices in this category, so one must do one's due diligence or ensure an IA or FI provides the essential information.

Rather than delve into the many complex split shares available, I will offer one example. As there are derivatives involved frequently with these types of structures, investors must take great care to understand what they are looking at.

An example of a split based on one common share is BAM Split Corp. (BNA.PR.D). Rated P2(L), the dividend split has a dividend rate of 7.25 percent with a maturity or retraction date of July 9, 2014. The present market price is $26.80, with a current yield of 6.76 percent and a yield to maturity of 4.97 percent.

An example of a split using multiple common shares is Big 8 Split (BIG.PR.C). The underlying common shares are from BMO, RBC, TD, BNS, CIBC, Great West Life, Manulife, and Sun Life. The dividend split has a 5.75 percent dividend rate with a maturity date of December 15, 2013. At today's market price of $12.78, the current yield is 5.40 percent, while the yield to maturity is 3.19 percent. They are callable at $12.00, beginning December 15, 2011, however, and the yield to that date is-8.80 percent.

ETFs

Given the complexities of preferreds, and the shifting landscape for them, investors might want to consider ETFs as a way to invest in these products, which for a modest fee offer the diversity not easy to replicate through investing in individual shares.

Claymore S&P TSX Dividend Fund (CDZ.T) and iShares Dow Jones Select Dividend Fund (XDV.T) are two choices. They have both performed well—XDV has an MER of .50 percent while CDZ's is .60 percent—and are better choices than dividend mutual funds.

Also, there are managed funds available. One such fund is the Malachite Aggressive Preferred Fund (MAPF). While it is sold as a private placement, and thus may only be purchased by accredited investors, it is managed by James I. Hymas, President, Hymas Investment Management Inc., who is one of Canada's foremost experts on preferred shares. If your circumstances do not permit you to invest in his fund, you would be wise to sign up for his monthly newsletter, a comprehensive analysis of the preferred share market in Canada.

Investors are best served by buying individual preferred issues as there is greater certainty in this approach. Should their circumstances be such that they are unable to buy individual issues, whether it be not enough capital or knowledge, then ETFs fill a valuable role by providing diversification at a reasonable cost. Managed funds are more expensive and, similar to managed bond funds, returns are affected by the active management of the fund.

SUMMARY

Preferred shares offer tax advantages for investors, owing to their attractive after-tax yields; at the same time, they are less volatile than the common shares of the same issuers. However, they are complex, and without any options in their hands, investors are subject to the whims of the issuers.

The shifting landscape for preferreds brought about by the BASEL III bank rules may result in the shrinkage of the preferred share market as the rate resets and the perpetuals issued by our banks (and perhaps the lifeCos) seem likely to be called. Investors may then be forced to seek out alternatives. There are, and will continue to be, non-bank preferreds from other entities to consider. Investors are advised to seek as much information as possible before reaching any investment decisions about preferred shares. The ETF route looks attractive from my perspective.

CHAPTER 7

Zero Coupon Bonds

The next two chapters deal with the two most important aspects of fixed-income investing for individual investors: zero coupon bonds and the laddered approach to portfolio construction. Combining these simple but very effective products and strategies will add yield to your portfolios and enhance your retirement nest egg.

While these are my primary tools for you, I have also come to believe that there could be a spot in your fixed-income portfolios for real return bonds (RRBs), the percentage of which will vary with where their real yield is.

In addition, with my positive economic view for Canada, I think that there is also room to include high quality REIT convertibles on a selected basis to add yield and to allow for some enhanced returns.

Known commonly as "stripped bonds," "strips," or "zeros," zero coupon bonds (so called because they are bonds that pay no interest) have become cornerstones for retirement planning. I will use the term *strips* to describe them henceforth. Strips are also called coupons, residuals, TIGRs, Sentinels, and Cougars. They are created by treating each interest payment on a bond as a separate security or obligation to pay a certain finite amount at a specified future date. What follows is an example of the cash flow of an actual bond, the one that we have been using throughout the book as an example, the Canada 3.5 percent due June 1, 2020. We will assume a face value of $100,000, a market price of $104.861 and a yield to maturity of 2.882 percent (as of June 1, 2011). The total cost would equal $104,861 (100,000 * 1.04861). (There is no accrued interest since it is paid on June 1.)

Almost all domestic bonds pay interest twice a year, so each payment equals $1,750 ($100,000*.035/2).

Date	Interest	Principal
Dec. 1, 2011	$ 1,750	
June 1, 2012	$ 1,750	
Dec. 1, 2012	$ 1,750	
June 1, 2013	$ 1,750	
Dec. 1, 2013	$ 1,750	
June 1, 2014	$ 1,750	
Dec. 1, 2014	$ 1,750	
June 1, 2015	$ 1,750	
Dec. 1, 2015	$ 1,750	
June 1, 2016	$ 1,750	
Dec. 1, 2016	$ 1,750	
June 1, 2017	$ 1,750	
Dec. 1, 2017	$ 1,750	
June 1, 2018	$ 1,750	
Dec. 1, 2018	$ 1,750	
June 1, 2019	$ 1,750	
Dec. 1, 2019	$ 1,750	
June 1, 2020	$ 1,750	
June 1, 2020		$100,000
	$31,500	
	Grand Total	**$131,500**

As you can plainly see, this bond has nineteen components, eighteen interest payments, and one principal payment—the repayment of the initial loan. Since each of these payments is a separate obligation of the borrower, there is no reason they cannot be separated from each other and then treated as individual securities. In fact, evaluating the present value of each of these parts allows us to calculate the value of the bond.

Date	Interest Payment	Par Value	Discount Rate	Present Value of $1	Value
Dec. 1, 2011	$ 1,750		2.883	0.98579	$ 1,725.13
June 1, 2012	$ 1,750		2.883	0.97178	$ 1,700.61
Dec. 1, 2012	$ 1,750		2.883	0.95797	$ 1,676.45
June 1, 2013	$ 1,750		2.883	0.94436	$ 1,652.63
Dec. 1, 2013	$ 1,750		2.883	0.93094	$ 1,629.15
June 1, 2014	$ 1,750		2.883	0.91771	$ 1,605.99
Dec. 1, 2014	$ 1,750		2.883	0.90467	$ 1,583.17
June 1, 2015	$ 1,750		2.883	0.89181	$ 1560.67
Dec. 1, 2015	$ 1,750		2.883	0.87914	$ 1,538.50
June 1, 2016	$ 1,750		2.883	0.86665	$ 1,516.64
Dec. 1, 2016	$ 1,750		2.883	0.85433	$ 1,495.08
June 1, 2017	$ 1,750		2.883	0.84219	$ 1,473.83
Dec. 1, 2017	$ 1,750		2.883	0.83023	$ 1,452.90
June 1, 2018	$ 1,750		2.883	0.81843	$ 1,432.25
Dec.1, 2018	$ 1,750		2.883	0.80680	$ 1,411.90
June 1, 2019	$ 1,750		2.883	0.79533	$ 1,391.83
Dec. 1, 2019	$ 1,750		2.883	0.78403	$ 1,372.05
June 1, 2020	$ 1,750		2.883	0.77289	$ 1,352.56
June 1, 2020		$100,000	2.883	0.77289	$77,289.00
Total	$ 31,500				
Grand Total	**$131,500**			**$104,861**	

You will notice that by calculating the present value of each component of the bond at the purchase yield, we arrive at the exact cost of the bond as seen above: $104,861. Thus, a bond is again demonstrated to be the sum of its parts.

We have now made each of these payments into a separate security and can offer them as discount securities, which compound at a given yield to a precise future value. Think of them as longer-term treasury bills, where the yield is the difference between the value at time of purchase and the known future value. Following is a chart that shows how to find the present value of a stripped bond. I have included a few examples to illustrate the process of amortization as well as the price movements for different yield changes. Merely find the intersection of a yield and a maturity point and you will find the present value or price.

COST OF $100 PRINCIPAL OF ZERO COUPON BONDS

Years	3%	4%	5%	6%	7%	8%	9%	10%	11%	12%
1	$97.09	$96.15	$95.24	$94.34	$93.46	$92.59	$91.74	$90.91	$90.09	$89.29
2	94.22	92.38	90.60	88.85	87.14	85.48	83.86	82.27	80.72	79.21
3	91.45	88.80	86.23	83.75	81.35	79.03	76.79	74.62	72.52	70.50
4	88.77	85.35	82.07	78.94	75.94	73.07	70.32	67.68	65.16	62.74
5	86.17	82.03	**78.12**	74.41	70.89	67.56	64.39	61.39	58.54	55.84
6	83.64	78.85	74.36	70.14	66.18	62.46	58.97	55.68	52.60	49.70
7	81.18	75.79	70.77	66.11	61.78	57.75	54.00	50.51	47.26	44.23
8	78.80	72.84	67.36	62.32	57.67	53.39	49.45	45.81	42.46	39.36
9	76.49	70.02	64.12	58.74	53.84	49.36	45.28	41.55	38.15	35.03
10	74.25	67.30	**61.03**	55.37	50.26	45.64	41.46	37.69	34.27	31.18
11	72.07	64.68	58.09	52.19	46.92	42.20	37.97	34.18	30.79	27.75
12	69.95	62.17	55.29	49.19	43.80	39.01	34.77	31.01	27.67	24.70
13	67.90	59.76	52.62	46.37	40.88	36.07	31.84	28.12	24.86	21.98
14	65.91	57.44	50.09	43.71	38.17	33.35	29.16	25.51	22.33	19.56
15	**63.98**	**55.21**	**47.67**	41.20	**35.63**	30.83	26.70	23.14	20.06	17.41
16	62.10	53.06	45.38	38.83	33.26	28.51	24.45	20.99	18.03	15.50
17	60.28	51.00	43.19	36.60	31.05	26.36	22.39	19.04	16.20	13.79
18	58.51	49.02	41.11	34.50	28.93	24.37	20.50	17.27	14.55	12.27
19	56.79	47.12	39.13	32.52	27.06	22.53	18.78	15.66	13.07	10.92
20	55.13	45.29	**37.24**	30.66	25.26	20.83	17.19	14.20	11.75	9.72
21	53.51	43.53	35.45	28.90	23.58	19.26	15.74	12.88	10.55	8.65
22	51.94	41.84	33.74	27.24	22.01	17.80	14.42	11.69	9.48	7.70
23	50.42	40.22	32.11	25.67	20.55	16.46	13.20	10.60	8.52	6.85
24	48.94	38.65	30.57	24.20	19.18	15.22	12.09	9.61	7.65	6.10
25	47.50	37.15	29.09	22.81	17.91	14.07	11.07	8.72	6.88	5.43

Let's work through these examples:

- Move to year 20 and across to the 5 percent column; there you find a value of $37.24. This is the present value of $100 due in 20 years at a semi-annually compounding yield of 5 percent.

- Staying with the 5 percent column, move up to year 15 and now the value has amortized to $47.67; by year 10 it becomes $61.03; with 5 years left it becomes $78.12; at maturity it reaches $100. These prices represent the present value at 5 percent for those different maturities. This process is called amortization.
- Move to year 15 and the 4 percent column and you observe a price of $55.21. Now move over to the 7 percent column and you see that the value at that yield would be $35.63. Strip bonds rise and fall as interest rates change, but if held to maturity, they will reach that future value no matter where yields go in the interim.
- Go back to row 20 and the 5 percent yield column ($37.24). Now go to Row 15 and 3 percent and you find $63.98. Wow, you say, my money has almost doubled in five years! Go across to the 5 percent column again and you find $47.67. That is what the amortized value would have been at 5 percent. The difference between $63.98 and $47.67 is the actual capital gain, with the balance of $10.43 being the amortized value.

Strips are that rarest of investment products: they are actually of benefit to individual investors, especially in the facilitation of retirement planning, while at the same time they answer IAs' biggest criticism of fixed-income products: low-percentage commissions. Strips produce 1 to 1.5 percent commissions on average for IAs but still produce excellent yields for investors. At the same time they are an optimum choice for retirement planning, in that a finite future nominal value is known at the time of purchase. There are not many win-win securities!

Also remember our old friend reinvestment risk. There are no interest payments to reinvest, which we know can have a serious impact on actual or realized yield (or, if you prefer, on your ability to retire). Many of those regular payments or dividends are left idle, often being too small for investment in individual products. The appeal of strips is as investments that will grow to a precise future amount at an attractive yield and without any tiny amounts to worry about reinvesting.

Here are a couple of examples showing how investors could double or triple their money, in nominal future value, using $10,000 as a starting amount:

Province of Ontario 0 percent September 8, 2026, at $50.00 4.59 percent. Future value: $10,000 / .5000 = $20,000 Thus, with this zero coupon trading at approximately 50 percent of its future or maturing value, the $10,000 present value may be invested in over $20,000 of future nominal value.

Hydro Quebec 0 percent January 16, 2035, at $33.33 4.70 percent. The future value is $10,000 / .3333 = $30,000. This example shows how $10,000 can grow to $30,000.

As retirement looms, more certainty is welcome. Stripped bonds ease the uncertainty by allowing investors to know exactly in nominal terms what their retirement pot will be worth.

For this section, I am reverting to the example of the baby boomer couple and what their initial ladder looked like on December 1, 2005. The reason for doing so is to trace this portfolio to demonstrate how a ladder works and also to show how reinvesting results in capturing the compound interest. In this chapter, I track this coupon ladder from 2005 until 2010.

Consider the case of a baby-boomer couple in their early fifties with an RRSP of $283,349; they are empty nesters and their children have repaid them for university. They still own real estate, so they have an equity investment. Common shares and mutual funds have fluctuating market values with no certainty as to what their market value will be when the money is needed for retirement. Individual bonds have finite maturity dates but have all those bothersome semi-annual interest payments that clutter up the RRSP, often remaining uninvested.

The first example shows the future value of this couple's RRSP without any additional contributions using an actual ten-year stripped bond. Ontario Hydro 0 percent due November 26, 2015. Purchase Price: $64.18 to yield 4.49 percent. Future value = $283,349 / .6418 = $464,111.

You say there is no guarantee what the purchasing power of that future value will be? Absolutely right! To guard against the possible erosion of this amount through inflation, what we do is revert to the laddered approach (mentioned already and explained in detail in the next chapter), which allows for annual reinvestment. The following table sets out how such a portfolio looked then:

DECEMBER 1, 2005

Issuer	Coupon	Maturity	Quantity	Price	S/A Yield	Ann Equiv	Total Value
B.C.	0.000%	Dec.18/06	$ 35,000.00	97.00	2.932%	2.953%	$33.950.00
Ontario	0.000%	Dec. 2/07	$ 35,000.00	94.06	3.081%	3.105%	$32,921.00
B.C.	0.000%	Dec. 1/08	$ 35,000.00	90.65	3.248%	3.275%	$31,727.50
B.C.	0.000%	Dec. 18/09	$ 35,000.00	86.97	3.480%	3.510%	$30,439.50
Ontario	0.000%	Dec. 2/10	$ 35,000.00	83.28	3.691%	3.725%	$29,148.00
Quebec	0.000%	Dec. 1/11	$ 35,000.00	79.17	3.931%	3.970%	$27,709.50
B.C.	0.000%	Dec. 18/12	$ 35,000.00	75.08	4.109%	4.151%	$26,278.00
Ontario	0.00%	Dec. 2/13	$ 35,000.00	71.42	4.251%	4.296%	$24,997.00
Ontario	0.000%	Dec. 2/14	$ 35,000.00	67.76	4.370%	4.418%	$23,716.00
Ont. Hyd.	0.000%	Dec. 26/15	$ 35,000.00	64.18	4.491%	4.541%	$22,463.00
			$350,000.00		4.246%	4.29	$283,349.50

As you can see, the future value of this portfolio is exactly $350,000—$66,650 more than the amount this couple had to invest! This is a "sleep-at-night" portfolio. We could have chosen nothing but the 2015 year maturity as shown above, in which case the future value would have been much higher: ($283,349 / .6418 = $464,111). However, choosing that route exposes these investors to reinvestment risk. Should rates rise sharply in intervening years, they would be at a disadvantage with no money to invest at those higher yields. However, by laddering the portfolio, a constant stream of maturities is available for reinvestment. The above total of $350,000 in future value thus understates what the final amount will be since each maturing coupon will be re-invested, adding to the future value.

One year later, this portfolio looks like this. Note that the $35,000 was invested in $54,816 of future value in the Manitoba 2016 issue. I left the other coupons at their initial yields.

DECEMBER 1, 2006							
Issuer	Coupon	Maturity	Quantity	Price	YTM	Ann. Equiv.	Total Value
Ontario	0	Dec. 2/07	$ 35,000.00	$96.98	3.082%	3.105%	$ 33,943.00
B.C.	0	Dec. 18/08	$ 35,000.00	$93.62	3.246%	3.273%	$ 32,767.00
B.C.	0	Dec. 18/09	$ 35,000.00	$90.02	3.480%	3.511%	$ 31,507.00
Ontario	0	Dec. 2/10	$ 35,000.00	$86.38	3.691%	3.726%	$ 30,233.00
Quebec	0	Dec. 1/11	$ 35,000.00	$82.31	3.932%	3.970%	$ 28,808.50
B.C.	0	Dec. 18/12	$ 35,000.00	$78.20	4.108%	4.150%	$ 27,370.00
Ontario	0	Dec. 2/13	$ 35,000.00	$74.48	4.252%	4.297%	$ 26,068.00
Ontario	0	Dec. 2/14	$ 35,000.00	$70.75	4.371%	4.419%	$ 24,762.50
Ont. Hydro	0	Nov. 26/15	$ 35,000.00	$67.09	4.491%	4.542%	$ 23,481.50
Manitoba	0	Sept. 5/16	$ 54,816.00	$63.85	4.649%	4.703%	$ 35,000.02
			$369,816.00		3.930%	3.970%	$293,940.52

DECEMBER 1, 2007							
Issuer	Coupon	Maturity	Quantity	Price	YTM	Ann. Equiv.	Total Value
B.C.	0	Dec. 18/08	$ 35,000.00	$96.43	3.502%	3.532%	$ 33,750.50
B.C.	0	Dec. 18/09	$ 35,000.00	$92.34	3.931%	3.969%	$ 32,319.00
Ontario	0	Dec. 2/10	$ 35,000.00	$88.90	3.957%	3.996%	$ 31,115.00
Quebec	0	Dec. 1/11	$ 35,000.00	$84.85	4.150%	4.193%	$ 29,697.50
B.C.	0	Dec. 18/12	$ 35,000.00	$81.68	4.050%	4.091%	$ 28,588.00
Ontario	0	Dec. 2/13	$ 35,000.00	$78.22	4.134%	4.177%	$ 27,377.00
Ontario	0	Dec. 2/14	$ 35,000.00	$74.94	4.162%	4.206%	$ 26,229.00
Ont. Hydro	0	Nov. 26/15	$ 35,000.00	$72.00	4.156%	4.199%	$ 25,200.00
Manitoba	0	Sept. 5/16	$ 54,816.00	$68.87	4.303%	4.349%	$ 37,751.78
B.C.	0	Dec. 18/17	$ 54,390.05	$64.35	4.436%	4.485%	$ 35,000.00
			$389,206.05		4.080%	4.120%	$307,027.78

DECEMBER 1, 2008							
Issuer	**Coupon**	**Maturity**	**Quantity**	**Price**	**YTM**	**Ann. Equiv.**	**Total Value**
B.C.	0	Dec. 18/09	$ 35,000.00	$96.00	3.936%	3.975%	$ 33,600.00
Ontario	0	Dec. 2/10	$ 35,000.00	$92.45	3.958%	3.997%	$ 32,357.50
Quebec	0	Dec. 1/11	$ 35,000.00	$88.40	4.152%	4.196%	$ 30,940.00
B.C.	0	Dec. 18/12	$ 35,000.00	$85.00	4.056%	4.097%	$ 29,750.00
Ontario	0	Dec. 2/13	$ 35,000.00	$81.50	4.131%	4.174%	$ 28,525.00
Ontario	0	Dec. 2/14	$ 35,000.00	$78.10	4.160%	4.204%	$ 27,335.00
Ont. Hydro	0	Nov. 26/15	$ 35,000.00	$75.00	4.161%	4.204%	$ 26,250.00
Manitoba	0	Sept. 5/16	$ 54,816.00	$71.88	4.300%	4.346%	$ 39,401.74
B.C.	0	Dec. 18/17	$ 54,390.05	$67.29	4.427%	4.476%	$ 36,599.06
Ontario	0	Dec. 2/18	$ 58,333.00	$60.00	5.173%	5.239%	$ 34,999.80
			$412,539.05		4.245%	4.291%	$319,758.11

DECEMBER 1, 2009							
Issuer	**Coupon**	**Maturity**	**Quantity**	**Price**	**YTM**	**Ann. Equiv.**	**Total Value**
Ontario	0	Dec. 2/10	$ 35,000.00	$99.05	1.001%	1.004%	$ 34,667.50
Quebec	0	Dec. 1/11	$ 35,000.00	$96.85	1.646%	1.653%	$ 33,897.50
B.C.	0	Dec. 18/12	$ 35,000.00	$93.26	2.340%	2.353%	$ 32,641.00
Ontario	0	Dec. 2/13	$ 35,000.00	$89.72	2.761%	2.780%	$ 31,402.00
Ontario	0	Dec. 2/14	$ 35,000.00	$85.78	3.119%	3.144%	$ 30,023.00
Ont. Hydro	0	Nov. 26/15	$ 35,000.00	$81.72	3.428%	3.458%	$ 28,602.00
Manitoba	0	Sept. 5/16	$ 54,816.00	$77.46	3.841%	3.877%	$ 42,460.47
B.C.	0	Dec. 18/17	$ 54,390.05	$71.82	4.181%	4.224%	$ 39,062.93
Ontario	0	Dec. 2/18	$ 58,333.00	$67.45	4.446%	4.495%	$ 39,345.61
B.C.	0	Dec. 18/19	$ 54,988.00	$63.65	4.569%	4.621%	$ 34,999.86
			$432,527.05		3.133%	3.161%	$347,101.88

DECEMBER 2, 2010							
Issuer	Coupon	Maturity	Quantity	Price	YTM	Ann. Equiv.	Total Value
Quebec	0	Dec. 1/11	$ 35,000.00	$98.50	1.521%	1.527%	$ 34.475.00
B.C.	0	Dec. 18/12	$ 35,000.00	$96.07	1.971%	1.980%	$ 33,624.50
Ontario	0	Dec. 2/13	$ 35,000.00	$93.02	2.426%	2.441%	$ 32,557.00
Ontario	0	Dec. 2/14	$ 35,000.00	$89.85	2.694%	2.712%	$ 31,447.50
Ont. Hydro	0	Nov. 26/15	$ 35,000.00	$86.09	3.028%	3.051%	$ 30,131.50
Manitoba	0	Sept. 5/16	$ 54,816.00	$82.86	3.292%	3.319%	$ 45,420.54
B.C.	0	Dec. 18/17	$ 54,390.05	$77.11	3.724%	3.759%	$ 41,940.17
Ontario	0	Dec. 2/18	$ 58,333.00	$73.29	3.922%	3.961%	$ 42,752.26
B.C.	0	Dec. 18/19	$ 54,988.00	$69.00	4.145%	4.188%	$ 37,941.72
Ontario	0	Dec. 2/20	$ 53,558.00	$65.35	4.300%	4.346%	$ 35,000.15
			$451,085.05		3.102%	3.128%	$365,290.33

As is evident, reinvesting each maturing coupon in a ten-year strip results in a steady increase in the future value, from $350,000 in 2005 to $451,085 in 2010, while the total market value increased from $283,349 to $365,290!

This removes interest rate guessing from this couple's retirement planning. It contrasts sharply with a mutual bond fund or an ETF, where the future value will not be known until the funds are needed and, in addition, the investors have no control over maturity selection. Thus, we have eliminated both types of reinvestment risk. There are no interest payments to reinvest, and the maturities are staggered to eliminate the risk of putting all the eggs in the wrong basket.

Now, let us strip a bond. The market for stripped bonds is immense. As of May 31, 2011, there had been $101.15 billion in face value of bonds stripped, with a resulting face value of strips outstanding of

$187.6 billion. Trading is very active, averaging approximately $3.6 billion per month. Once again, we will use the Canada 3.5 percent bond due June 1, 2020. We are using a cost of $104.861 to yield 2.882 percent as of June 1, 2011.

To strip these bonds we need another tool or two. For one, we need to know the Canada yield curve (the yield on Government of Canada bonds). You may wish to refresh your knowledge of the yield curve from the chapter Basic Math. In any event, each interest payment when stripped will be sold at a yield relative to the yield on the Canada yield curve at a similar maturity. Thus, as the yield curve slopes upward, each interest payment would be sold or valued at progressively higher yields. The other significant variable here is the yield spread from the Canada yield curve to each future payment date. The curve and the spread in basis points that each payment would be valued at follows:

ZERO COUPON YIELD CURVE			
Term (years)	Canada Bond Yield	Spread to Zero Coupon Curve	Zero Coupon Yield
0.5	1.05	-0.070	0.980
1.0	1.23	-0.030	1.205
1.5	1.36	0.000	1.369
2.0	1.59	-0.650	1.525
2.5	1.75	-0.095	1.675
3.0	1.86	-0.050	1.810
3.5	2.00	0.077	1.923
4.0	2.03	0.000	2.030
4.5	2.14	0.000	2.138
5.0	2.30	-0056	2.244
5.5	3.36	-0.016	2.344
6.0	2.42	0.024	2.444
6.5	2.51	0.036	2.546
7.0	2.61	0.036	2.646
7.5	2.69	0.040	2.733
8.0	2.77	0.044	2.814
8.5	2.82	0.059	2.879
9.0	2.88	0.060	2.940

This spread is a function of several factors, including supply and demand, not only for the bond itself but also for the stripped bonds at different maturities. As well, the strippers need to make a profit. How do they do that? Applying the prevailing market spreads for the interest payments to each payment and adding up the pieces produces a present value either higher or lower than the cost of the bond. If the present value exceeds the cost, then the stripper sells the components separately and pockets the difference. In this example, the Canada yield curve is normal or upward-sloping but in a very steep fashion, and so the yields are progressively higher. You will note that every interest payment sold at a lower yield than the quoted yield to maturity of the bond in question (2.883 percent) produces a profit, while every payment sold at a higher yield produces a loss. In other words, every interest payment sold at a lower yield than the purchase yield produces a higher present value than at 2.883 percent, while every payment sold at higher yields produces a loss. As long as the net of the profits and losses is a profit, then the bond is stripped. The stripper does not care where the profit comes from. Following through with this thought, if the yield curve were perfectly flat (yields the same at all maturities), then most of the interest payments would have to be sold at a lower yield for the bond to be stripped profitably.

In the example below, the first column is the derived zero coupon yield from the previous page. The second column takes that yield and calculates the present market price of each $1,750 coupon payment. The third column multiplies the market price of each coupon payment times the $1,750 coupon payment to produce the total stripped value.

The fourth column calculates the value of each coupon payment, applying the constant purchase yield of 2.883 percent. The net profit is calculated from the sum of all these calculations:

Coupon Date	Zero Coupon Market Yield	Market Price	Value of $1,750 Coupon	Present Value at 2.883%	Profit/ Loss
12/01/2011	0.98	99.511	$1,741.44	$1,725.13	$16.31
06/01/2012	1.21	98.806	$1,729.11	$1,700.62	$28.49
12/01/2012	1.37	97.974	$1,714.55	$1,676.45	$38.10
06/01/2013	1.53	97.007	$1,697.63	$1,652.63	$45.00
12/01/2013	1.68	95.915	$1,678.51	$1,629.15	$49.36
06/01/2014	1.81	94.737	$1,657.90	$1,605.99	$51.91
12/01/2014	1.92	93.521	$1,636.62	$1,583.17	$53.45
06/01/2015	2.03	92.237	$1,614.15	$1,560.67	$53.48
12/01/2015	2.14	90.875	$1,590.31	$1,538.50	$51.81
06/01/2016	2.24	89.443	$1,565.25	$1,516.38	$48.87
12/01/2016	2.34	87.969	$1,539.46	$1,495.08	$44.38
06/01/2017	2.44	86.439	$1,512.68	$1,473.83	$38.85
12/01/2017	2.55	84.837	$1,484.65	$1,452.90	$31.75
06/01/2018	2.65	83.196	$1,455.93	$1,432.25	$23.68
12/01/2018	2.73	81.58	$1,427.65	$1,411.90	$15.75
06/01/2019	2.81	79.97	$1,399.48	$1,391.83	$7.65
12/01/2019	2.88	78.429	$1,372.51	$1,372.05	$0.46
6/01/2020	2.94	76.897	$1,345.70	$1,352.55	-$6.85
6/01/2020	2.94	76.897	$76,897.00	$77,289.00	$-392.00
			$105,060.50	**$104,860.10**	**$200.45**

In this case, stripping $100,000 of this bond would have produced a profit of $200.45. As you can see, there was profit in all the coupons until June 1, 2020, after which the yields were higher than 2.883 percent, resulting in losses. You can see the importance of the principal (or residual) component. The stripper would not strip this bond unless the price of it fell suddenly or if he or she could sell the residual for a higher price. In this case, the stripper may have extracted a higher price for the residual to enhance the profits. Some institutional investors will pay a premium for a residual versus a coupon for the same term since it is easier to invest larger sums in the residual. In this case, if the stripper could have sold the residual ten basis points lower at 2.84 percent, that would have added a further $295 for each $100,000 of par value stripped.

Naturally, this raises questions. Why is there any profit in this? Wouldn't dealers or others arbitrage all the profit away? Any government bond can be stripped, simply by ensuring that the sum of the parts exceeds the cost; it is a sum-of-the-parts business. When an investment dealer strips a bond, it is usually a multi-million-dollar transaction, and not all of the pieces will be sold immediately. Typically, a stripper will calculate the break-even yields for the strip (i.e., yields at which the present values for the pieces equal the cost of the bond) and then compare those yields to the street bid side (i.e., what other investment dealers would pay for all the pieces) to calculate the bailout value of the strip. If that is marginally profitable, and the stripper believes that sufficient demand exists so that a high percentage of the strip could be sold at the ask side (i.e., the transfer price to the IAs), then the profitability is enhanced.

This is so since the spread between the bid and the ask is fairly wide in strips, typically 5 to 15 basis points depending on term, credit quality, and supply and demand. Since investment dealers carry large inventories of strips of all types and maturities, there are financing costs, hedging costs, spread risks, and yield curve risks to consider. Frequently, demand for strips may be weak or institutional and/or retail investors may be net sellers, which means that inventories swell. In that case, dealers make their products cheaper to lighten inventories, and with the wider spreads, new stripping is less profitable or not profitable until the overhang is cleaned up.

What happens if the selling continues? What can the investment dealer do? Well, believe it or not, particularly with Canada strips, they can be put back together or reconstituted and sold as regular bonds. Since most Canada bonds pay interest on June 1 and December 1, the Bank of Canada has made these coupon payments fungible, meaning that they can be added to any of the bonds with June 1 and December 1 interest payment dates. This makes the reconstitution process easier and adds efficiency to the stripped bond marketplace. Owing to numerous factors, such as foreign investors and new issues, anomalies appear that create stripping opportunities. As the strip market has matured and become more efficient, profit margins have been squeezed, but with the costs and risks associated with maintaining a large inventory, there is usually some gross profit visible in the strip market.

What happens if the yield curve is flat or inverted? The strip curve changes. In the case of the flat yield curve, the strips would be sold at lower yields than the Canada curve, while in an inverted yield curve environment; the strip profit would be in the longer maturities with losses at the front end.

Who are the buyers of strips? Strips are not suitable for taxable investors, since the annual amortization of the strips counts as income and must be declared. Taxable investors would pay tax on income that they had not actually received! Thus, the sheltered plans (principally pension funds and RRSPs) dominate the market. However, there are other large investors who from time to time have a significant appetite for strips. Chartered banks and trust companies frequently invest GIC monies when mortgage demand is weak and strip yields are higher than GIC yields (a fairly frequent occurrence). Provincial sinking funds also make use of strips, as provincial governments are obliged to set aside funds for debt repayment. Strips are ideal for offsetting debt since they have a known future value. Insurance companies often balance assets and liabilities and fund structured settlement cases. The duration of long-term strips is valuable in matching long-term liabilities. Strips are also purchased by other non-profit organizations and foundations that do not need current income.

Virtually all the stripping activity involves federal and provincial bonds, although certain corporations (e.g., Bell Canada) have issued strips. In fact, since 1989, corporate strips have been sold on a private placement basis to institutional investors. Beginning in 2002, and in a rare moment of Bay Street cooperation, the CARS™ and PARS™ program was launched. CARS stands for Coupon and Residual Securities. To be eligible for investment by individuals they had to be issued under prospectus (you can find examples at) www.sedar.com. One of the principal reasons the programs were created was that many financial institutions owned bonds issued back in the era of double-digit yields, putting the market value on them so high that no one would buy them. A bond is the sum of its parts, so once it was possible to issue CARS, the institutions could realize the market value for their holdings and investors could obtain higher yields than on Canada and provincial strips. They were, and still are, much less liquid than the government strips, with much wider bid-ask spreads.

They are meant to be buy-and-hold securities. They can be exciting, as any holder of Bell coupons will attest. Before Halloween 2006, it appeared that BCE was heading for Income Trust status and that all Bell Canada bonds (and the strips) would be called on advantageous terms to the holders. Fast forward to the BCE leveraged buyout and discover that BCE is now into high-yield or junk status and there are almost no bids for longer term Bell strips. Of course, now BCE is a solid investment-grade credit and the market for Bell strips has improved somewhat. Corporate securities are always vulnerable to event risk.

Thus, in the event that you are considering investing in corporate strips, my advice is to buy the highest quality ones (used to be the banks) and stick to short-term maturities (five years maximum) You may find that they are hard to find and that is because they are gobbled up by institutions and are almost always higher yielding than GICs.

The yields on the Canada strips trade at certain spreads from the Canada yield curve; provincial strips trade at differing spreads from the Canada strips, depending on credit rating, term, and supply/demand. Clearly, if you believe the lesser-rated provinces will honour their obligations, then some yield pickup is available. Currently, at the ten-year maturity, British Columbia strips are offered 87 basis points higher in yield than Canada strips.

There have been several strips done of Canadian issuers in U.S. dollars that are fully eligible for RRSPs without being considered foreign content. This, by the way, applies to any bond issued by a Canadian issuer in any currency. In addition, bonds or strips of certain supra-national borrowers, the most prominent of which is the World Bank, are also RRSP-eligible and not considered foreign content. The liquidity in these foreign currency strips is not good, so the bid-ask spread is wide and often there is no supply.

Let us digress for some history of the stripping business.

THE EARLY DAYS OF STRIPPING BONDS

This is a trip down memory lane. You have absorbed the importance of strips for retirement planning and how you can invest to the last dollar. It was not always so easy.

Stripping bonds began in Canada in 1981–82. In those days, we used hand-held calculators to work out the mathematics of stripping. A thirty-year bond becomes 61 separate securities (60 semi-annual interest payments plus the principal) when stripped, and so we had to calculate the present value for each of them, add them all up, and see if the sum exceeded the cost of the bond, all the while hoping that the market would not move against us!

Back in those days, bonds were all in physical form; either registered in the owner's name or unregistered (a bearer bond). Thus, when stripping bonds, we actually used scissors to separate each coupon of a bearer bond from the others and from the principal portion (residue or residual). These coupons were not much bigger than a postage stamp and were "bearer," which meant essentially that they were akin to cash, as they were payable on demand to the bearer at maturity or at the discounted market price before maturity. These small bearer instruments were an administrative nightmare!

The basis unit for stripping back then was $100,000 face value. Using a bond with a 5 percent semi-annual coupon for simplicity's sake, each individual coupon would have a face value of $2,500 ($100,000*.05/2). The principal or residual portion, of course, had a face value of $100,000.

The primary investors were individual investors for their RRSPs and institutions such as pension funds and insurance companies that could match known liabilities by investing in strips to mature at the same time as the liability was due. Anyway, let us say that XYZ Pension Fund needed a $10 million strip maturing in thirty years. ABC investment dealer would ascertain the cost of buying the whole bond and then add up the present value of all the pieces, estimating where the various coupons could be sold. Happy with the sums, the dealer would proceed to strip the bonds. The "cage," or back office, then has to take the 100 separate bonds (100 * $100,000 = $10 million), take the scissors to all of those little coupons, and stuff all of the $2,500 coupons into separate envelopes! They would then be put in a vault.

Then, of course, the dealer would begin to sell all of these envelopes (or parts of them) to investors of all kinds. If a retail investor wanted to purchase $10,000 face value, they would have to be removed from the envelope and segregated. The principal portion was thus highly prized, as it was a larger piece of paper (8 1/2" by 11") and was bigger in face value ($100,000), so it was easier for an investor to deploy larger amounts of money by buying the residual. As you could guess, the residuals were keenly sought after and commanded a significant premium over coupons of the same maturity. Illustrating this point, using the above example, the investment dealer would have to strip $400 million of bonds to create enough coupons to provide the $10 million face value.

Also, in those days, many institutional investors required physical delivery to their addresses, be they in Victoria or Halifax, or to their custodian (trust company). You can conjure up the image of armoured trucks criss-crossing the country stuffed full of these envelopes. The recipients, of course, would then have to stuff them in their own vaults. You can imagine the fun trying to keep all of this straight and trying to keep track of maturing coupons. One of the most prominent zero coupon buyers practically ran out of room and was partly responsible for the change to a book-based system.

I can remember taking a flight to Halifax with $45 million of bearer residuals in my bag in order not to miss settlement by a day! I collected the cheque and took my client to lunch.

This administrative nightmare did not go unnoticed. Eventually, the investment business gave birth to a zero coupon product derived from physical bonds. These bore names such as TIGRs, Sentinels, and Cougars (to name the most prominent). A block of bonds was taken and registered in a trust company's name. There were no coupons; rather, a cheque was sent to the trust company as each coupon or residual matured. The trustee would then distribute the proceeds on a proportional basis to the registered owners. Investors received nice, fancy, big pieces of paper telling them that they owned the relevant portion of the underlying bond. Of course, there were two types: alter-ego, which meant that the investor could only buy the actual face value of the coupon in question (or a multiple thereof), and non-alter-ego, which meant that each underlying coupon could be sold in fractions as long as all the fractions added up to the appropriate face value.

This approach saved countless headaches and costs at the retail level, but many institutions could not buy them because of their investment bylaws, so they never really took a significant percentage of the stripped bond business. Once the industry moved to a book-based system, these derived instruments traded at a healthy discount from conventional strips.

Eventually, book-based stripping evolved to where the bonds are held by the trustee for CDS (Clearing and Depository Securities Inc.) and no physical stripping is done. It is all computer blips now, so the need for these alternative evidences of ownership disappeared. However, there are millions outstanding, and investment dealers make markets in them, as well.

SUMMARY

We know that the value of a bond is nothing more than the sum of its parts. Obviously, one dollar due in 20 years is not worth one dollar today. What is it worth? Discounting it at an interest rate or yield to determine its worth, applying this discount rate to that future value, and employing the present value formula produces the answer. Thus, $100,000 due in 20 years discounted at a semi-annual yield of 5 percent produces a present value of $37,243. Expressed in reverse, $37,423 invested at 5 percent semi-annually will grow or compound to $100,000 in 20 years. Where does this yield or discount rate come from? In the case of the stripped bond market, it is a function of the yields for the Canada curve at that maturity, supply and demand for strips, and the mathematics of stripping.

Zero coupon bonds are a very important retirement planning tool. As retirement moves closer, investors require more certainty, and strips offer that. Furthermore, they can be rolled into a RRIF easily and would not have to be sold. A laddered strip portfolio will serve investors well by taking away reinvestment risk while still providing precise future values, all the time being invested in high quality, primarily government, securities. Just imagine: a high quality, fully compounding investment product that is ideally suited for retirement planning!

CHAPTER 8

Building a Ladder to Success

I was a portfolio manager for two of Canada's most prominent financial organizations, managing billions of dollars of other people's money in the form of life insurance, pension funds, and mutual funds. I invested the first dollar for what is now Canada's largest public mutual bond fund (Investor's Bond Fund) in 1979. Investors Group (now IGM) has since split this fund into two funds—the Government Fund and the Corporate Fund. It is worth remembering as you read this chapter that I have a balanced perspective on both individual fixed-income securities and mutual bond funds.

LADDERING

There is a tried-and-true strategy for fixed-income investing that ensures above-average results. It is called the laddered or staggered-maturity strategy. Simply, this involves dividing a given sum of money into equal portions and investing these portions in bonds of regularly spaced maturities. For example, assuming an amount of $250,000, one could divide this into ten amounts of $25,000 and invest each amount in maturities of one year, two years, and all the way to ten years.

What is the rationale for such a strategy? First, it eliminates the risk of having all the money invested in a single maturity, thus avoiding the possibility of having to reinvest it a lower rate upon maturity. Second, it takes the guesswork out of interest rates. No one money manager has ever consistently and accurately forecast the direction of interest rates. The laddered strategy takes away the guesswork, since there is always something about to mature for reinvestment while the rest of the funds are spread out in the various maturities. The net effect is to smooth out long-term returns and avoid the yield traps, as I discussed in the yield curve section. Third, it allows for diversification by issuer, thus reducing credit risk.

Sticking with our one-to ten-year ladder example, when the one-year bond matures, that money is reinvested in a ten-year bond, since the previous ten-year bond now has a nine year term to maturity. Examples following will illustrate this. First is the laddered portfolio that I used in the last edition. Then, as I did with zero coupon ladders in the Zero Coupon chapter, I reinvested the maturing bonds since then to illustrate how ladders work. These examples are portfolios with interest-bearing securities in them. Typically, these are taxable portfolios, meaning that the investors require the income. Thus, I did not add the annual income back into the portfolios. Should these portfolios be added to an RRSP, then the interest payments would be added to the portfolio when sufficient funds would make it practical to do so. Also, since this is a buy-and-hold strategy, provincial and corporate bonds should be used, and enhanced compound yield will result. This is because Government of Canada bonds, the most liquid, are also the lowest yielding, and you do not need the liquidity in a buy-and-hold portfolio. The extra yield from investing in higher yielding provincials and corporates will compound over time to provide a greater retirement amount. Here is an example of what a laddered portfolio looks like:

AUGUST 8, 2008

Issuer	Coupon	Maturity	Quantity	Price	YTM	Ann. Equiv.	Total Value
Thomson	4.35%	Dec. 1/09	$ 25,000.00	$100.16	4.219%	4.264%	$ 25,040.00
CIBC	3.75%	Sept. 9/10	$ 25,000.00	$98.46	4.530%	4.582%	$ 24,615.00
GE Capital	4.75%	May 2/11	$ 25,000.00	$100.56	4.527%	4.579%	$ 25,140.00
Royal Bank	4.53%	May 7/12	$ 25,000.00	$100.35	4.426%	4.475%	$ 25,087.50
Manitoba	4.25%	June 3/13	$ 25,000.00	$102.25	3.734%	3.769%	$ 25,562.50
Royal Bank	4.71%	Dec. 22/14	$ 25,000.00	$98.50	4.987%	5.049%	$ 24,625.00
Telus	5.95%	Apr. 15/15	$ 25,000.00	$101.27	5.717%	5.799%	$ 25,317.50
Nfld. Hydro	4.30%	Oct. 3/16	$ 25,000.00	$100.68	4.200%	4.244%	$ 25,170.00
Ontario	4.30%	Mar. 8/17	$ 25,000.00	$100.87	4.178%	4.222%	$ 25,217.50
Suncor	5.80%	May 22/18	$ 25,000.00	$101.50	5.598%	5.767%	$ 25,375.00
			$250,000.00		4.612%	4.666%	$251,150.00

Duration 4.53 years
Annual income $11,672.50

Let us examine this portfolio. You will notice there are no Government of Canada bonds in it. Since this portfolio is not going to be actively traded, there is no point in investing in the lowest-yielding bonds in the bond market when there are good-quality provincial and corporate issues available that offer higher yield that will compound in your favour (remember the compound yield section). The average duration of this portfolio is 4.53 years. The most important feature is that the maturities span the length of approximately two business cycles. This portfolio will likely outperform the majority of professional fund managers because you are not paying annual management fees, you hold no Canadas, and you are not guessing which way interest rates are going. Following is what this portfolio looks like after the 2009 maturity and the 2010 maturity.

DECEMBER 1, 2009							
Issuer	**Coupon**	**Maturity**	**Quantity**	**Price**	**YTM**	**Ann. Equiv.**	**Total Value**
CIBC	3.75%	Sept. 9/10	$ 25,000.00	$101.50	1.783%	1.791%	$ 25,375.00
GE Capital	4.75%	May 2/11	$ 25,000.00	$104.08	1.824%	1.832%	$ 26,020.00
Royal Bank	4.53%	July 5/12	$ 25,000.00	$106.09	2.105%	2.116%	$ 26,522.50
Manitoba	4.25%	June 3/13	$ 25,000.00	$106.97	2.174%	2.186%	$ 26,742.50
Royal Bank	4.71%	Dec. 22/14	$ 25,000.00	$108.16	2.961%	2.983%	$ 27,040.00
Telus	5.95%	Apr. 15/15	$ 25,000.00	$111.00	3.674%	3.708%	$ 27,750.00
Nfld. Hydro	4.30%	Oct. 3/16	$ 25,000.00	$105.68	3.363%	3.391%	$ 26,420.00
Ontario	4.30%	Aug. 3/17	$ 25,000.00	$105.85	3.426%	3.455%	$ 26,462.50
Suncor	5.80%	May 22/18	$ 25,000.00	$107.31	4742%	4.798%	$ 26,827.50
Emera	4.83%	Dec. 2/19	$ 25,000.00	$100.64	4.749%	4.805%	$ 25,160.00
			$250,000.00		3.080%	3.107%	$264,320.00

Duration 4.32 years

Annual income $11,792.50

SEPTEMBER 9, 2010							
Issuer	**Coupon**	**Maturity**	**Quantity**	**Price**	**YTM**	**Ann. Equiv.**	**Total Value**
GE capital	4.75%	May 2/11	$ 25,000.00	$101.80	1.934%	1.944%	$ 25,450.00
Royal Bank	4.53%	May 7/12	$ 25,000.00	$104.20	1.947%	1.956%	$ 26,050.00
Manitoba	4.25%	June 3/13	$ 25,000.00	$106.30	1.874%	1.883%	$ 26,575.00
Royal Bank	4.71%	Dec. 22/14	$ 25,000.00	$107.83	2.759%	2.779%	$ 26,957.50
Telus	5.95%	Apr. 15/15	$ 25,000.00	$110.91	3.369%	3.397%	$ 27,727.50
Nfld. Hydro	4.30%	Oct. 3/16	$ 25,000.00	$107.39	2.960%	2.982%	$ 26,847.50
Ontario	4.30%	Mar. 8/17	$ 25,000.00	$107.30	3.053%	3.076%	$ 26,825.00
Suncor	5.80%	May 22/18	$ 25,000.00	$110.87	4.137%	4.179%	$ 27,717.50
Emera	4.83%	Dec. 2/19	$ 25,000.00	$103.00	4.430%	4.479%	$ 25,750.00
B.C.	3.70%	Dec. 18/20	$ 25,000.00	$99.747	3.730%	3.765%	$ 24,935.00
			$250,000.00		3.019%	3.044%	$264,835.00

Duration 4.54 years

Annual income $10,855.00

As is evident, each maturing bond was invested in a new ten-year bond as the previous ten-year became a nine-year bond with the passage of time. Also, I did not reinvest the income, as it is typically spent in a taxable account. I was able to purchase $25,000 of each of the two new bonds as they were at or close to par. As this was a period of falling interest rates and a steep yield curve, most of the prices have risen. This is one of my principal points about ladders, particularly ten-year ones. There is no guesswork and the maturity diversification pays off. Even though the funds from the maturing bonds were reinvested at lower yields, the rest of the portfolio, especially the five-to ten-year bonds, appreciated significantly. Many investors, awaiting higher yields during this period, might have deployed funds in the money market. With the ten-year ladder, your money is always fully invested and you do not run the risk of having too much of your money in the wrong maturity. The converse is true in a period of rising bond yields; while the longer maturities would fall in value, proceeds from the maturing bonds would be invested in the higher yields in the ten-year maturity, thus increasing income and yield.

Also note that the portfolio is diversified by credit. My rule is to have no more than 10 percent in any one credit. In this case, I have two positions in Royal Bank. I could exchange one of them for a different credit or I could wait for the 2012 bond to mature and deploy the funds in a different credit then.

This illustrates another feature of ladders; they do not have to be passive, hold-to-maturity portfolios. Rather, there are often opportunities in one of the maturities to exchange one bond for another to enhance income and yield. In the 2010 portfolio, for example, the Ontario 4.30 percent due 2017 could be traded (at the time of writing), after transaction costs of 1 percent, for BCE 5 percent due February 15, 2017, for a yield improvement of 81 basis points. The B.C. 3.70 percent of 2020 could be traded for Great West Lifeco 4.65 percent August 13, 2020, for a pickup in yield of 58 basis points. Why were these other bonds in the portfolio in the first place? There may have been no suitable alternatives at the time or they were relatively inexpensive.

There are variations on this theme, of course. Some investors prefer short-term ladders, others long-term, and some have maturities every second year or every six months. One also can invest a percentage in foreign pay securities for currency diversification. As well, some investors may wish to put, say, 75 percent of their portfolio into a laddered configuration and deploy the balance where they feel the maximum returns may be obtained.

Over time, this approach has outperformed the majority of professional fund managers for the essential reasons that there is no guesswork involved, no annual management fees, and the funds are invested in bonds yielding more than Canadas. It is true that fees on individual fixed-income transactions average 1 percent, but note that for the above example only 10 percent of the portfolio matures annually, so, in effect, investors pay annual fees of only one-tenth of 1 percent compared with the average MER of 1.67 percent for managed bond funds.

The ladder provides an investor with specific maturing amounts at specific dates. It permits investors to avoid the all important reinvestment risk of having all their money invested in the wrong maturity.

This strategy can be applied to both taxable accounts and retirement accounts. For RRSPs, a stripped-bond ladder may be used (see previous chapter), while interest-bearing bonds are normally employed in the taxable account. A younger investor may choose a long-term ladder. If investors are not starting with enough money for a complete ladder, they can select individual rungs, nicely spaced out, and fill in the gaps as funds become available. For instance, with $20,000, investors could begin by investing $10,000 in a one-year bond and the other $10,000 in a ten-year bond, then perhaps add a five-year maturity later, and so on. Laddering offers investors a great deal of flexibility and customization.

How do you choose the rungs on the ladder? If you have found a good IA, his or her organization should have an extensive inventory from which to choose. If you are dealing with an online or discount broker, they should provide the tools to enable you to construct such a portfolio yourself. Your aim should be to choose the highest yielding bonds for each rung that meet your credit quality threshold. The issue of credit quality is an important one and was addressed in the corporate bond section.

This approach is also important in RRSPs. Even though the plan is sheltered, the same investment principles apply, except that you would build a ladder of strips; since strips can be rolled into an RRIF, there is no compelling need to concentrate maturities at retirement age. Consider the following RRSP laddered portfolio, repeated from Chapter 5, constructed for a typical boomer couple. Assume that they are in their early fifties, empty nesters, their children have repaid them for their university costs, and they have a combined RRSP of $283,349.50.

This is the most recent update for the zero coupon ladder created for the boomer couple who had a starting amount of $283,349.50. Please refer back to the Zero Coupon chapter for the annual progression.

DECEMBER 2, 2010							
Issuer	**Coupon**	**Maturity**	**Quantity**	**Price**	**YTM**	**Ann. Equiv.**	**Total Value**
Quebec	0	Dec. 1/11	$ 35,000.00	$98.50	1.521%	1.527%	$ 34,475.00
B.C.	0	Dec. 18/12	$ 35,000.00	$96.07	1.971%	1.980%	$ 33,624.50
Ontario	0	Dec. 2/13	$ 35,000.00	$93.02	2.426%	2.441%	$ 32,557.00
Ontario	0	Dec. 2/14	$ 35,000.00	$89.85	2.694%	2.712%	$ 31,447.50
Ont. Hydro	0	Nov. 26/15	$ 35,000.00	$86.09	3.028%	3.051%	$ 30,131.50
Manitoba	0	Sept. 5/16	$ 54,816.00	$82.86	3.292%	3.319%	$ 45,420.54
B.C.	0	Dec. 18/17	$ 54,390.05	$77.11	3.724%	3.759%	$ 41,940.17
Ontario	0	Dec. 2/18	$ 58,333.00	$73.29	3.922%	3.961%	$ 42,752.26
B.C.	0	Dec. 18/19	$ 54,988.00	$69.00	4.145%	4.180%	$ 37,941.72
Ontario	0	Dec. 2/20	$ 53,558.00	$65.35	4.300%	4.346%	$ 35,000.15
			$451,085.05		3.102%	3.128%	$365,290.33

Note that the future value has grown to $451,085 from the initial value of $350,000 while the total portfolio value is $365,290 versus the initial value of $283,349.50. This illustrates the compounding nature of zero coupon bonds. Also note that I did not allow for any annual contributions from the couple; this of course would have added significantly to the total values if they had contributed the maximum allowable.

You will note how the face value keeps increasing as the maturing face value is reinvested in a new ten-year strip without new contributions. The total value will vary, of course, depending on market yields. In this case, I have used current market yields.

SUMMARY

The laddered approach is a tried-and-true approach to fixed-income investing and is in your best interest. It is simple, easy to implement, and leads to above-average results. Better yet, it is a strategy that you can implement yourself.

CHAPTER 9

Exchange Traded Funds (ETFs)

At the time of my last edition, my attention was focused on the difference between individual fixed-income securities and fixed-income mutual funds. I gave ETFs a passing mention. Now they have proliferated to the extent that they are dominating the fund space. Hardly a week goes by without a new entrant arriving with a variety of funds. Recently, companies such as Vanguard and RBC have announced their entrance. The former is a giant U.S. entity and will make its presence known immediately. The latter entrant is interesting; Canada's banks, with the exception of BMO, have left this space alone, no doubt fearing the cannibalization of their mutual fund business, which has far higher fees. TD, in fact, was in the ETF space and exited several years ago. Now it seems that the ETF space is too large to ignore, especially as more and more individual investors get used to the lower fees and extensive choices. RBC must have decided that their mutual fund business was at risk and chose to enter the ETF space in order not to lose assets. Even within the fixed-income space, there is a wide selection of funds available. This naturally leads to the need for guidance so that individual investors can make appropriate choices. This chapter will include both fixed-income mutual fund and ETF analysis.

Let us begin by re-examining the differences between individual fixed-income products and mutual bond funds.

Mutual fixed-income funds or bond funds never mature. Investors do not know what their funds will be worth in the future. Why is this? Portfolio managers are paid to manage portfolios, and they are paid handsomely. The typical management expense ratio (MER) averages 1.7 percent per year, and is charged to the fund. Therefore at the start of any year you are already behind the starting line. Put another way, if a bond fund produces 5 percent, and fees are 1.5 percent, the net returns will be 3.5 percent. The fund managers will attempt to recoup that management fee by brilliantly outperforming all the other fund managers. You may or may not receive outstanding returns after the management fee is deducted from the fund's returns. Of course, they still collect if performance is subpar or negative!

So, how does one portfolio manager outperform the peer group? Luck and guesswork, mostly. You may come across the expression "rate anticipation trading," which describes this approach. It means guessing which way bond prices are going and positioning the portfolio accordingly. Sounds easy. Interest rates are about to climb, so sell the entire portfolio, go into treasury bills, and preserve capital while at least earning money market returns. Then, just when interest rates have reached their peak, invest the entire portfolio into the longest term bonds and reap substantial capital gains plus the income minus the management fee. Does this ever happen? Rarely! Why not more frequently? The majority of fixed-income fund managers fret and tug at their locks as they attempt to have their portfolios closely track the relevant bond index with enough difference to have slightly better performance than their peer group. No one fixed-income portfolio manager has ever got it right all the time.

Also consider that bond funds are required to calculate an annual return since they do not have a fixed maturity date. Investors owning individual bonds do not have to worry about annual returns since their yield and maturity date are known at the time of purchase. Remember the analogy of a baseball game. Individual investors in specific fixed-income securities know the outcome of the game before it starts even though the score, or annual return, may vary inning by inning. Bond fund holders have to worry every inning since they may have to leave the stadium before the end of the game without knowing what the score will be!

The majority of fund managers are doomed to be average because no one gets it right every time. They care less about how well your money is doing than they do about their relative performances, on which their bonuses hinge. Few investment organizations demand a positive return before considering bonuses. Independent performance measurement companies assemble a universe of data, producing results comparing all the fund managers by results over different time periods. The data is broken down into four sections called quartiles, with the point between the second and third quartile called the median. Every manager wants to be consistently in the second quartile or higher, and better than the bond index. It does not matter if the bond market is in a tailspin with negative returns. If the bond market's total performance was-10 percent and Portfolio Manager X was at-8 percent and the bond index was at-9 percent, the manager gets to keep his/her job with a possible performance bonus!

In my experience, people I meet with funds invested in bond funds have no idea what securities are in those funds! It is possible to review carefully the quarterly (sometimes semi-annual) statements when they are released, eight or so weeks after the period ends. Unfortunately, it is only a snapshot, but hardly anyone looks anyway. There is no way to tell whether the fund manager totally changed the structure of the fund in the meantime. As well, there may have been a new fund manager appointed with a different investment philosophy who could have made significant changes to the portfolio without your knowledge.

It is safe to say that it is extremely unlikely for an individual's unique investment objectives to be met by any fund manager who has relative performance as the top criterion, rather than the individual investment objectives of thousands of unit holders. You may request the quarterly transactions of your portfolio manager—not a widely advertised fact—to better understand what is happening to your money.

There are attempts to analyze and compare fixed-income funds for the investing public. An analysis of all mutual funds is offered at www. globefund.com or at www.fundlibrary.com. They break out the composition of the funds into their various categories and provide other details, namely the average term and the percentage held in cash reserves, Canadas, provincials, corporates, strips, and foreign currency bonds. While only a snapshot and out of date, it does reveal a lot about the investment strategies and philosophies of the different investment organizations. A high percentage in cash means the fund manager expects interest rates to rise and is defending the unit value of the fund, since there is no market risk in short-term treasury bills. Conversely, fund performance would suffer if interest rates were to fall, since the portion of the fund invested in the money market would not appreciate in value. A high percentage held in Canadas may give you a warm, safe feeling, but be aware that they are the lowest-yielding securities in the Canadian bond universe. In order to compensate for this lower yield, portfolio managers trade Canadas actively and aggressively, carrying out rate anticipation trading (guessing), switches, and yield curve plays. It is a big casino, folks! While a certain percentage of Canadas may be needed for liquidity purposes, a consistently high concentration in Canadas means that high-risk trading practices are employed with a strong possibility of poor performance. If, the bulk of the fund is instead invested in higher yielding provincials and corporates, that extra yield compounds in the unit holder's favour, making it harder for the "guessers" to keep pace. Of course the guessers are not always right, and this makes the gap even wider.

Belatedly, certain investment organizations are making more special-purpose fixed-income funds available to allow investors more opportunities to tailor make their portfolios. There are now short-term government funds, corporate funds, zero-coupon funds, and high-yield (or junk) funds. In this case you may find these funds suitable, as the returns may be high enough to make it acceptable to pay the management fees.

Exchange traded funds, or ETFs as they are commonly known, are investment funds that trade on stock exchanges, similar to equities. They have become popular since their fees are much lower than those of mutual funds and since they offer broad diversification among all security classes, from bonds to commodities. They are also listed so that liquidity and visibility are not issues. An ETF holds assets such as stocks, commodities, or bonds and its price closely approximates its net asset value as it trades throughout the day. Typically, ETFs track indices and, since they are passively managed, their fees are significantly lower than those of mutual funds. By tracking the index, ETFs duplicate as closely as possible the performance of the particular index, less the fees of course. Mutual funds have much higher fees and active management of those funds often produces returns far below the index. Thus, investors who want to "buy" the market, can do so knowing that the results will not be surprising.

The first ETF was called The Toronto Index Participation Shares and was introduced in 1990. ETFs have been in existence since 1993 in the U.S. and 1999 in Europe. In 2008, the SEC authorized the creation of actively managed ETFs.

In the past few years, the number of ETFs has exploded. Globally, there were 2557 ETFs with $1.367 trillion in assets at February 28, 2011. At present in North America, the U.S. has $929.1 billion in 919 ETFs and Canada has $40.3 billion in 169 funds.

Investors have a bewildering choice of funds, ranging from short-term corporate bond funds to a triple-leveraged S&P bear fund, from a long bullion ETF to a double-leveraged U.S. Treasury bond bear fund. Investing should be as simple as possible.

It is inevitable that the mutual fund industry will continue to lose market share to ETFs. The management expense ratios of mutual funds in Canada are very expensive and something will have to give. Their monopoly is over.

ETFs IN CANADA		
	#ETFs	Assets Under Management (AUM) (in $US)
iShares	38	29.60
Claymore	29	5.90
BetaPro	62	3.00
BMO Asset Mgt.	40	1.90
Totals	169	40.30

As I have written about and commented on many times, I am totally opposed to fixed-income mutual funds for two reasons: first, the MERs take a huge bite out of performance; and investors have no idea what their money will be worth when they need it.

On the other hand, fixed-income ETFs have sharply lower fees with no active management. While they offer no guarantee of the future value of the fund, at least investors will get returns close to that of the underlying index.

There are short-term governments, the DEX* bond index, real return bonds, short-term corporate laddered funds, high-yield bond funds, and so on. Thus, investors have many choices for diversification.

[* The DEX bond indices are produced by PC Bond analytics, Canada's premier provider of fixed-income indices and performance. It is owned by the TMX Group. (www.canadianbondindices.com)]

Choice, of course, can be daunting.

Facing the plethora of fixed-income ETFs, investors are forced to "guess" which fund or combination of funds is best for them. Investors may need the help of an Investment Advisor to explain all the options.

Laddered ETFs do exist. For example, Claymore offers two laddered ETFs but they are not structured as I would structure them. They are also short-term but they do offer low fees for smaller amounts of money. They are essentially the DEX short-term Government and Corporate funds.

While I remain a staunch advocate of investing in individual fixed-income securities, I can recommend a few fixed-income ETFs. High-yield bond ETFs allow investors to receive broad diversification in high-yield bonds. Since it is very difficult for anyone to choose their own individual high-yield bonds, these ETFs fill a valuable role. iShares offers XHY, which invests in a broad selection of U.S. high-yield bonds and is hedged back to Canadian dollars. BMO also offers a high-yield fund, ZHY, of a different index in the U.S. and it is similarly hedged.

Also, ETFs in international bonds fill a need also as it is very expensive and difficult for individuals to invest abroad. BMO offers an Emerging Markets fund, ZEF, which is also hedged to our currency.

PROS AND CONS OF ETFs

Before delving into fixed-income ETFs, I thought that it would be useful to set out the advantages and disadvantages of ETFs for individual investors.

ADVANTAGES

Easy to understand. Most ETFs track their underlying index and thus are straightforward.

Diversification. They make it easy for investors to achieve broad diversification.

Buying power. The bonds in the ETFs are bought at wholesale levels. (Individual investors sometimes experience difficulty obtaining what they believe to be fair prices. This aspect partly offsets the MER fees.)

Low fees. MERs are significantly lower than those of mutual funds. (With the exception of one Horizon Beta Pro fund, ETFs aren't actively managed.)

Transparency. ETFs have transparent portfolios that are re-priced throughout the trading day.

Liquidity. They are valued throughout the day and trade visibly on stock exchanges

Flexibility. They offer the ability to invest in particular sectors.

Performance. They typically outperform mutual funds because of the lower fees.

DISADVANTAGES

Costs. Although the fees are low, ETFs trade as equities do so transactions have commissions.

Performance. The fees detract from performance such that ETFs rarely outperform the underlying index.

Uncertainty. In the case of fixed-income ETFs, there is no certainty of future value.

FIXED-INCOME ETFs

At last count, Canada had 34 fixed-income ETFs. iShares has 11, totalling $5.92 billion, Claymore has 8, totalling $2.6 billion, and BMO has 15, totalling $402 million, for a grand total of $8.92 billion. Horizon betaPro has an actively managed Corporate ETF (HAB) but it is a brand new fund. In entering the ETF space, RBC has introduced Target Maturity Date Corporate Bond ETFs with maturities from 2013 to 2020. These ETFs are unique in Canada in that they only hold corporate bonds maturing in the target maturity. Thus, investors will know that they will get their money back in the target year.

Further, these ETFs allow individuals to build their own ladders, with eight maturities to select from. Fees are just 0.3% per annum. These ETFs do hold all the corporate bonds in their respective maturities. This is good in the sense that there is broad diversification, but it also means that investors are exposed to all the corporate bonds in that maturity. Nevertheless, these ETFs are a very useful addition to the Canadian ETF landscape. Claymore's so-called "ladders" are really just the one-to five-year DEX short-term government and corporate indices, and are too short in any event. BMO's Target Maturity funds, while useful, are not as straightforward as those of RBC.

These companies have some similar funds. For example, both iShares and BMO have Bond Universe funds that use the DEX Bond Universe Index. There are other similar funds and yet the companies also have unique ETFs.

Claymore offers one-to five-year Government and Corporate Ladder ETFs. iShares offers two U.S funds hedged to the Canadian dollar. They use the iBoxx High-yield Index and the iBoxx Liquid Investment Grade Index. BMO uses the Barclay's High-yield Very Liquid Index and also offers an Emerging Markets Fund. BMO offers more maturity selections. For example, they offer short-term, mid-term, and long-term corporate ETFs. They also have a unique series of funds that aim to keep a constant maturity.

One example of this is ZXA, a 2013 constant bond maturity. They keep the maturity constant by buying a combination of BMO ETFs that together match the target term to maturity. As the maturity shortens, BMO sells enough units and invests the proceeds in the money market until, when the 2013 maturity date approaches, the ETF is all short-term instruments.

BMO also offers 2015, 2020 and 2025 maturities. This approach offers more specificity to fixed-income ETF investing. In a typical ETF, the underlying index keeps changing as bonds mature and new bonds are added. Thus, an investor would not know what the future value of his money would be. Let us examine some of the basic information of two popular ETFs

The first one is XBB-DEX Universe Bond Index Fund. It can be found at www.ca.ishares.com. The second one is XCB-DEX All Corporate Bond Fund Index.

XBB-T (as of July 8, 2011)
Management fees: 0.30%
Total holdings: 473

Sector Breakdown	
Federal Government	43%
Provincial Government	26%
Financial	13%
Other Corporate	18%

Maturity Summary	
1–5 years	47%
5–10 years	25%
10 years+	28%

Average term: 9.25 years
Average duration: 6.33 years

This fund is a relatively safe fund, having 79 percent in government bonds. It has a long duration though, 6.33 years, meaning that it is more volatile than funds with shorter durations. Also, with the heavy concentration in government bonds, it will produce lower yield and income than most corporate bond ETFs. You can get far more information, such as individual holdings and performance and credit ratings by visiting the iShares site. The full prospectus is also available there.

XCB-DEX All Corporate Bond Index Fund	
Management Fees	0.40%
Total Holdings	463
Sector Breakdown	
Financial	49%
Infrastructure	14%
Energy	12%
Communication	11%
Other	14%
Maturity Summary	
1–5 years	41%
5–10 years	31%
10 years +	18%
Average term 8.29 years	
Average duration 5.50 years	

This fund has different characteristics. First, it has a shorter duration and is thus less volatile. Second, it has almost 50 percent of its holdings in financial bonds. This flies in the face of my oft-cited rule of not investing more than 10 percent of a fixed-income portfolio in one sector or credit. The credit meltdown surely underscores the prudence of such an approach. In addition, I feel strongly that maturities should be more evenly distributed in the laddered style.

While this purports to be an all-corporate index, it is impossible for the ETF manager to buy every single issue in the index without distorting the many illiquid corporate bonds in the index. What managers employ is a process called "sampling," in which they buy a representative group of bonds. This is not well known so investors should know that they are not necessarily getting exactly what is advertised.

SUMMARY

While this chapter covered both fixed-income mutual funds and ETFs, the focus was on ETFs because they offer more advantages. Fixed-income ETFs offer these advantages over mutual funds:

- **Lower fees** than mutual funds. ETFs are passive funds and the MERs reflect that. Typically ETFs are not actively managed, so unit holders receive the return of the underlying index less the MER.
- **Diversification** for smaller amounts of money. It can be difficult when starting out to construct a portfolio of individual bonds with limited funds.
- **Buying power.** The bonds in the ETFs are bought at wholesale levels.
- **Transparency.** The units trade on public stock exchanges and the portfolios are visible.

- **Liquidity.** Investors may trade them just as they would common shares. They may also buy them on margin or sell them short.

ETFs are here to stay and offer some advantages for individual investors, particularly for those investors who own mutual funds. But the proliferation of different types of ETFs presents investors with a confusing list of choices. Although I remain a staunch advocate of investing in individual bonds, I can recommend ETFs in two areas: high-yield bonds and emerging markets. ETFs here offer the investor diversification and wholesale pricing in areas in which choosing individual bonds can be very challenging. If you must go the ETF route, follow my basic tenets by not guessing. By that I mean, do not bet the ranch on rates rising by investing in short-term funds or the converse of investing in long-term bond ETFs if you are convinced that yields are going to fall. Always maintain both maturity balance and credit balance.

CHAPTER 10

Income Trusts, Royalty Trusts, and Real Estate Investment Trusts

ABCP UPDATE

Canada's contribution to the subprime credit meltdown was the $32 billion collapse of the Asset-backed Commercial Paper (ABCP) issued by 20-odd conduits. This paper was backed by assets of dubious quality with a large percentage being synthetic derivatives. This paper was sold to retail and institutional investors alike as a short-term security, with a 30-to 90-day maturity range. Rated AAA by DBRS (Moody's and S&P refused to rate it), it offered a modestly higher yield than did treasury bills and bankers' acceptances. The assets backing this paper were much longer, so there was a serious mismatch. All was good as long as investors rolled over the paper at maturity or as other buyers were willing to take it on. As well, two liquidity providers were standing by in case buyers could not be found.

Of the 200-plus members of IIROC, the self-regulatory body of the investment industry, only 28 dealers sold this paper. I was at Blackmont (now MacQuarie) at the time, and neither Jamie Price, my chief trader, nor I could make head or tail of these securities. If we didn't understand this paper, how were we going to explain it our advisors, never mind our clients? We sold none of this paper.

When the crunch hit, investors began to wonder about the quality of the assets backing this paper; they wanted their money back when the paper matured. The so-called liquidity providers bailed out on a technicality and refused to buy the paper. Thus, this $32 billion market froze solid in August of 2007.

The principal underwriters were National Bank Financial (NBF), Scotia Capital, and Canaccord. The latter firm repaid all its retail investors in full, NBF was fined $75 million, while Scotia ponied up $25 million for their role here.

A commission was created, with Purdy Crawford heading it up. By December 2007, this committee cobbled together something called the Montreal Accord. It took 17 months of wrangling before a comprehensive restructuring was formally approved on June 21, 2009. What emerged were three new vehicles, Masters Asset Vehicles 1, 2, and 3. Believe it or not, DBRS, which had given the original paper a AAA rating, rated the new paper single A! Lately, DBRS has indicated that this paper may be in for an upgrade.

Trading has been sparse in this paper, with initial trades in the $18 per $100 for the MAV 1s and $12 for the MAV 2s. At present, these issues are trading at $78 and $74 respectively. Their coupon rate is BAs minus 50 basis points, so they are only paying 0.50 percent.

INCOME TRUSTS, ROYALTY TRUSTS, AND REITs

Of the 255 income trusts in existence when the federal government levelled the tax field on November 1, only 68 remain, and half of those are Real Estate Investment Trusts (REITs). They were grandfathered; in fact, it was their model that led to the IPO bandwagon for conversion to trusts when the underwriting community, desperate for revenue, seized upon the tax loophole for income trusts.

The remaining income trusts, which did not revert to corporation status, are a variety of business and royalty trusts. Some of the reasons for not converting are: the cost of converting; foreign income is exempt; and foreign ownership can exceed 50 percent.

Of course, most distributions have been cut, but this equity class still offers decent yield. Investors, having been burned by substituting income trusts for bonds in the period prior to November 1, 2006, now understand that income trusts are equity investments.

REITs

Real Estate Investment Trusts were grandfathered from this new tax regime. They remain as one of the most attractive vehicles for investors to invest in the real estate market. They are mostly publicly traded, which is an attractive feature given the illiquidity in owning real estate directly. They also focus on a variety of different sectors of the real estate market, such as apartment buildings, shopping centres, commercial buildings, hotels, and health care.

They also offer investors the leverage associated with the real estate market. To the extent that they can borrow money at a lower cost than the returns on their real estate investments, investors benefit from higher payouts.

Many of the REITs have convertible bonds outstanding; during the depths of the credit crisis, many of these convertibles offered higher yields compared to the underlying units. That advantage has largely disappeared as credit conditions improved. While their yields are not as attractive relative to the common as they once were, they offer decent yield and, as debentures, they rank ahead of the underlying units from the point of view of distributions and in the event of dissolution of the company.

One such example is the H&R 5.90 percent, due June 30, 2020. Rated BBB, these debentures are convertible into the common shares of H&R REIT at $23.50 per share. They are callable on June 30, 2016, and thereafter at $100.

At today's (July 25, 2011) price of $107.50, they offer a yield to maturity of 4.85 percent and a yield to the first call date of 4.20 percent.

The current yield (5.90%/$107.50) is 5.49 percent, which compares to the yield on the underlying common of 4.15 percent. Thus, there is a yield advantage in owning these convertibles. Plus, they rank ahead of the common shares on the balance sheet. They do not have value as convertibles, however, since they are likely to be called in 2016 and the conversion premium of 16 percent will not be paid off for 10.3 years.

There is an abundance of analysis on REITs available from the various financial institutions. Should you wish to own individual REITs, it should be possible to obtain the necessary research for you to make an informed decision.

There is the ETF route for those who prefer the diversification offered by ETFs. iShares offers XRE-T, which attempts to replicate the performance of the S&P/TSX Capped Reit Index:

MER: 0.55%

Inception: 2002

Current yield: 5.45%

Performance:

Six months to June 30, 2011	14.22%
2010	21.89%
2009	53.50%
2008	-38.11%
2007	-5.88%
2006	23.75%
2005	24.28%
2004	13.11%

This is very attractive performance.

BMO offers an ETF with different characteristics. It is ZRE-T. It tracks the Dow Jones Canada Select Equal Weight REIT Index and thus its holdings are an equal weight, unlike the iShares ETF, which tracks the index and thus has unequal weightings. Its MER is also 0.55 percent with a current yield of 5.98 percent. It has only been around since May of 2010, so performance data is limited. It has returned 10.96 percent year-to-date and 30.13 percent for the latest 12 months.

SUMMARY

REITs have been much sought after in the past two years, not only because of their attractive yields in a low-yield environment but also because of the limited universe of income trusts from which to choose. In addition, the fundamentals for REITs have been attractive in Canada, with a buoyant real estate market and inexpensive cost of funds. They certainly deserve a place in a balanced portfolio, but they are not a substitute for bonds unless you can invest in some decently priced convertible bonds.

Earlier in the book, I made reference to the fact that I hear from a lot of investors who yearn for the day when bond yields were in double-digit territory. I point out to these people, and to everyone else, that the real return on bonds (nominal yield minus inflation) is the same now with ten-year yields at 4 percent and inflation at 2 percent, the real yield is almost the same as when yields were 11 percent and inflation was 8.5 percent. That is, it is 2 percent.

I also point out that when investors buy bonds, they receive a fixed stream of income and a specific date in the future when they receive their principal back. Thus, bonds or fixed-income securities are cornerstones for investment and retirement planning.

What a difference a couple of years makes. I had no idea that the federal government would put an end to the Income Trust IPO bandwagon, but it seems that they had little choice. I decried the fact that IAs and investors alike ignored the fact that these were equity-type investments and also that they were getting their principal returned to them on a regular basis. What a high percentage of investors did do was to treat income trusts as alternatives to bonds—the rest is history. Once again, the value of diversification has been demonstrated. What now?

Many trusts are not waiting, as they find their flexibility is constrained and as they seek international partners. There are a lot of listed convertible bonds issued by various trusts which have remained outstanding after the conversion period. While these issues are unrated, many of them produce above-average yield and have the security of the distributions as security, since interest payments rank ahead of the distributions.

The milk has been spilled. Now it is time to revert to the type of investment planning that leads to good long-term performance: proper asset allocation, high quality securities, and diversification.

With my very positive outlook on Canada and on our real estate market, I believe that REITs and/or their convertibles warrant inclusion in investors' portfolios.

Also, as I indicated, nature abhors a vacuum, and so does Bay Street, and so it did not take very long for the back-room guys to concoct items such as ABCP and subprime mortgages. What could be next? Just remember to say no to something that you cannot understand and which sounds too good to be true!

Investors must understand that trusts are equity-like securities with the attendant risks. They are not a substitute for fixed-income securities.

CHAPTER 11

Attention GIC Shoppers

Canadian investors have a love affair with guaranteed investment certificates (GICs). As of April 30, 2011, they owned $458 billion of GICs, of which $135 billion was in RRSPs. Why is this? For one, they are safe, being issued primarily by Canada's Schedule A chartered banks and other financial intermediaries. For another, the Canadian Deposit and Insurance Corporation (CDIC), a federal Crown corporation, guarantees each GIC of five years or less to maturity up to a maximum of $100,000. This was just raised from $60,000 in the 2005 federal budget, retroactive to February 23, 2005. Investors can buy GICs from different banks to increase this amount. What features do GICs have? They are normally offered in terms from one year to five years, with reasonable, but not great, yields. They are not liquid and so are held to maturity. Again, why are they so popular? Because they are "sold" to investors by their banks. Why do banks issue GICs? To borrow money cheaply to reinvest in higher-yielding securities.

GICs AND RRSPs ARE NOT THE SAME THING

How often have you heard, or how often have you said, "I am going to my bank to buy my RRSPs," or something similar, such as, "My RRSPs were only 5 percent this year"? A whole generation of Canadians is convinced that an RRSP and a GIC are the same thing—as if an RRSP was an actual security or investment itself. Why has this happened? Why does this generation not know that they are subsidizing the issuers of GICs, who merely take your RRSP deposit and lend it out at higher rates? Why not get that higher rate yourself, or at least examine the other investment choices you have that can make your retirement pot that much bigger?

An RRSP is not an individual security or investment. It is a plan; that is what the "P" stands for. It is a plan that provides a medium through which you may choose from a diverse group of securities. One of the prime reasons why Canadians are seduced into the GIC/RRSP trap is the inertia of human nature. It is far easier to "buy" your RRSP from your branch manager than set up a self-administered plan, choose an IA, and select the appropriate securities given your individual needs and objectives. There isn't much at stake here—only your retirement well-being!

To put this in more graphic terms, the size of the GIC market is $458 billion. Assuming an even distribution from one to five years, that equates to approximately $350 million per day! Of this total, an estimated $135 billion is held by RRSP accounts. Assuming that the institutions gathering these deposits are able to reinvest at rates 1 percent higher than they pay for the GICs, all the RRSP/GIC holders together are giving away in excess of $4 billion every year! This money would be better used for their retirement needs.

The astute readers will argue that an individual is unable to lend money in the same markets that the institutions do: the mortgage markets and the personal loan market. This is true. However, there are publicly traded securities that, at different stages of the interest cycle, provide higher yield than do GICs: government bonds, corporate bonds, stripped bonds, and mortgage-backed securities, to name a few. Even investing at an extra one-half of 1 percent would produce an extra $675 million annually for the RRSP holders of GICs and $2.2 billion for all the GIC holders combined.

INTEREST RATE COMPARISONS
As of July 11, 2011 (Annual yield equivalents)

Term/ Years	GICs*	Canada Bonds	Provincial Bonds	Corporate Bonds	Provincial Zero Coupons
1 year	1.42%	1.20%	1.35%	1.47%	1.320%
2 years	1.83%	1.45%	1.55%	2.00%	1.700%
3 years	2.15%	1.70%	2.00%	2.37%	2.150%
4 years	2.40%	1.90%	2.30%	3.35%	2.450%
5 years	2.70%	2.15%	2.64%	4.05%	2.850%
10 years	N/A	2.90%	3.75%	4.83%	4.000%

*Average of 54 issuers

Note that GICs yielded more than all categories of bonds then. Indeed, this has been the case during much of the meltdown and post-meltdown period. The above are averages; it was possible to obtain even higher yields from several issuers. These higher yields for GICs by maturity were:

1 year	2.05%
2 years	2.15%
3 years	2.55%
4 years	2.80%
5 years	3.05%

This was an unusual time in financial history. On November 27, 2008, the Credit Union Deposit Insurance Corporation (CUDIC), a corporation which guarantees all deposits of British Columbia Credit Unions, passed amendments to provide *unlimited* deposit insurance on all deposits in those credit unions. There are a lot of credit unions in B.C and this step not only underscored the safety of the deposits but also removed the ceiling on insurance. The net result is that larger deposits are now insured. These credit unions typically pay higher yields for GIC deposits than do much larger intermediaries.

The point of this is that firms such as Odlum Brown Limited have been able to use GICs more frequently in their portfolios. In particular, with short-term market yields being suppressed by the Bank of Canada, this yield advantage for GICs has allowed us to use them widely in laddered portfolios to offer much needed higher levels of income and yield for our clients.

LADDERS VS. GICs

Assuming a ten-year ladder, as in the previous example, we will demonstrate the long-term advantages accruing to those investors who heretofore have put all their faith in their bank or trust company manager and therefore all their money into GICs. As you know, they are seldom sold with a term greater than five years, which coincides with the longest mortgage term typically available. (Amazing coincidence. Just what do you think they did with your capital? Of course they loan it at much higher rates.) We are trying to get you some of those higher rates and better returns, which will lead to a happier retirement. In the last two economic cycles, you would have earned an additional yield of approximately 100 basis points, which translates into a lot of dollars for a typical investor. An extra 1 percent over 30 years on an annual contribution of $20,000 would produce an extra $129,611. Also, these are all high-quality, marketable instruments.

Even more important, this whole GIC thing flies in the face of proper long-term investment planning. GICs are a narrow asset class, limited as to maturity and marketability, and therefore only suitable for a small percentage of one's portfolio. See the sections on reinvestment risk and laddered portfolios for a more complete analysis.

Providing for one's long-term retirement with short-term assets such as GICs is very risky.

SEPTEMBER 9, 2010

Issuer	Coupon	Maturity	Quantity	Price	YTM	Annual Equiv	Total value
GE Capital	4.75%	May 2, 2011	$ 25,000	$101.80	1.934%	1.944%	$ 25,450.00
Royal Bank	4.53%	May 7, 2012	$ 25,000	$104.20	1.947%	1.956%	$ 26,050.00
Manitoba	4.25%	June 3, 2013	$ 25,000	$106.30	1.874%	1.883%	$ 26,575.00
Royal Bank	4.71%	Dec. 22, 2014	$ 25,000	$107.83	2.759%	2.779%	$ 26,957.50
Telus	5.95%	April 15, 2015	$ 25,000	$110.91	3.369%	3.397%	$ 27.727.50
Nfld Hydro	4.30%	Oct. 3, 2016	$ 25,000	$107.39	2.960%	2.982%	$ 26,847.50
Ontario	4.30%	March 8, 2017	$ 25,000	$107.30	3.053%	3.076%	$ 26,825.00
Suncor	5.80%	May 22, 2018	$ 25,000	$110.87	4.137%	4.179%	$ 27,717.50
Emera	4.83%	Dec. 2, 2019	$ 25,000	$103.00	4.430%	4.479%	$ 25,750.00
B.C.	3.70%	Dec. 18, 2020	$ 25,000	$ 99.74	3.730%	3.765%	$ 24,935.00
			$250,000		**3.019%**	**3.044%**	**$264,835.00**
				Duration 4.54 years			
				Annual Income $10,855.00			

The above portfolio is the same one seen in the chapter on laddered portfolios. The purpose of presenting it again is to point out the extra yield and, therefore, income available by taking advantage of the fact that normally yields at longer maturities are higher than shorter term ones. At the same time, no extra risk is taken since the portfolio is laddered and the average term of this portfolio is almost the same as a five-year GIC except that the average yield is higher than GICs at the time the portfolio was constructed. The yield on five-year GICs on September 9, 2010 was 2 percent. This is not a fluke; it is typical of the yield advantage available from five to ten years.

Ten-year Canadas have averaged 1.15 percent more than five-year GICs since 1997. Substituting higher yielding provincials, corporate bonds, or strips would increase this yield advantage even more. Thus, this makes investment sense and produces significant monetary gains. Of course, the securities are all high quality and marketable so that the portfolio could be altered to suit changing needs or circumstances or to take advantage of better-yielding securities as they become available.

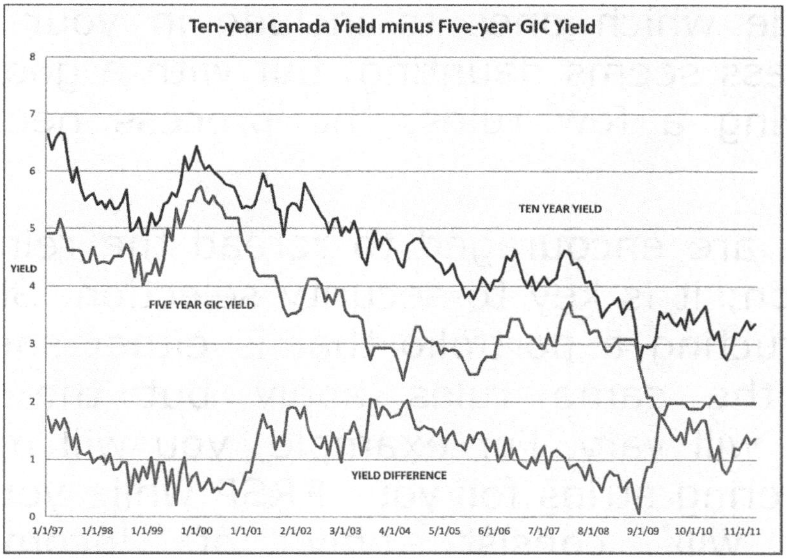

Think of your RRSP as a medium through which you create your retirement nest egg rather than your annual tax deferral that comes dressed up as a GIC. Once you shed the inertia and actually setting up a self-directed retirement savings plan, what then? Stripped bonds or zero coupons frequently offer equal or higher yield than do GICs, have excellent quality and marketability, and are not subject to the $100,000 CDIC limit. Of course, strips are available in maturities as long as 40 years and are totally free of reinvestment risk, allowing for better balance and superior long-term returns.

PORTFOLIO SELECTION

There are thousands of bonds outstanding, issued by a variety of entities with varying features such as coupon, maturity, currency, call features, etc. How do you decide which ones to include in your portfolio? This process seems daunting, but with a good IA, and by following a few rules, the process need not be arduous.

First, you are encouraged to reread the reinvestment risk section; it is key to security selection. Should you be constructing a portfolio that is either sheltered or taxable, the same rules apply but the types of securities will vary. For example, you will most likely be considering strips for your RRSP while your taxable portfolio will consist only of income-bearing instruments.

All right, you have been patiently waiting to find out which securities to buy. Rule number one is what *not* to buy: avoid callable bonds. Individuals poring through weekend bond quotations are drawn to the highest-yielding bonds. These bonds, in almost every instance, contain a feature or features that could result in your investment being called from you. There could be a financial call where the issuer may redeem the bonds and issue them at lower rates. As well, they may be low-quality credits where your capital may be at risk. This is hardly in your best interest and is yet another example of reinvestment risk! There is little point in carefully assembling a laddered portfolio only to have several rungs removed when the purpose of the ladder is to eliminate the possibility of having to reinvest your money when you do not want to (i.e., when rates are low). Some corporate bonds may also be called for sinking fund purposes, where the company buys back a certain percentage of a bond issue every year. In those cases you might not have all your bonds called but you still have a reinvestment decision and your ladder will be all messed up.

Most bonds issued today are either non-callable for their entire life or callable at much narrower spreads than they were issued at. This latter type of call feature is commonly found on corporate issues. Let us consider the Bell Canada 3.65 percent bonds of May 19, 2016, as issued at $99.928 to yield 3.67 percent, 116 basis points over the Canada yield curve. Bell Canada may wish to call these bonds back at some point for corporate reasons. What has evolved in the market is that in order to call these bonds, the issuer would have to pay the higher of $100 or, in this case, at a yield spread of 29 basis points over the Canada yield curve. While the investors would have their principal returned to them prematurely, they would receive a relative improvement of 87 basis points. This would mean a price of $103.94 to yield 2.80 percent, compared with the issue price of $99.928, yielding 3.67 percent. They would still have to reinvest the money, but this is a friendlier call feature than the old style. Of course, your investment advisor will know which issues are callable and which ones are not or the information will be available from your online firm.

Rule number two is to stick to investment-grade securities that are rated BBB or higher. Rating agencies constantly analyze issuers' credit worthiness.

Investing in less than investment-grade bonds is more risky and requires constant research and due diligence.

The prime purpose of this chapter is to underscore the fact that a GIC and an RRSP are two different things. You can obtain greater returns through a number of other investment choices and approaches. In the fixed-income world, zero coupons and laddered portfolios are two such vehicles.

CHAPTER 12

Forecasting Interest Rates

No one has ever been able to accurately forecast the direction and level of interest rates one hundred percent of the time. However, there are a number of tools which can be of great assistance in forecasting; these tools are easily accessible to individual investors and can be maintained on a current basis, as the data is publicly available. Mortgage debt comprises the lions' share of household debt, so it is important to have a view on the direction of interest rates so that decisions to fix a mortgage rate or remain floating can lead to large savings for individuals.

From the chapter about ladders, you know that this approach eschews the need to forecast interest rates and bond yields. Nevertheless, it is useful to go through the various tools for interest rate and bond yield forecasting to get a handle on where things might be going.

THE YIELD CURVE

If there was only one tool to forecast the direction of the economy and interest rates, it would be the yield curve. It has accurately forecast almost every recovery and recession since the Second World War. Created by joining the yields at maturities from three months to 30 years, it is a line, the slope and shape of which tells us a lot about monetary policy and the economic outlook.

When yields are progressively higher from the shortest to the longest maturity, this is a "normal" yield curve as it is logical to expect that the longer the maturity, the higher the yields should be to compensate for the risks in investing in longer dated bonds. The slope of this "normal" is important. Right now, it is considered to be a "steep" yield curve in that the spreads between the various maturity points are wider than "normal."

There are other types of yield curves; the opposite of a normal or positive curve is the inverted yield curve, when the shortest maturities are the highest yielding and thus the slope is downward. This type of curve happens when central banks attempt to rein in inflation and excessive economic expansion by jacking up short-term rates and tightening monetary policy. The opposite is true for the positive yield curve. It reflects stimulative monetary policy by central banks in their efforts to promote economic expansion.

Next, let us look at how the yield curve changes during different times.

The first period shows the shift in the yield curve from 1989 to 1992. The yield curve was inverted in 1989 following an expansion, and inflation was rearing its head. The 1989 curve was forecasting a recession and indeed a recession took place to the extent that the Federal Reserve Board became very stimulative, producing this steep yield curve, which led to the subsequent economic recovery.

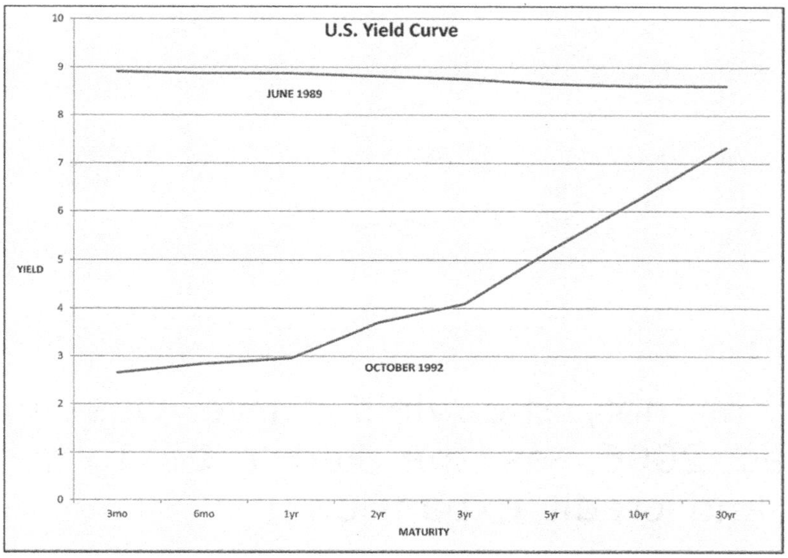

After a long recovery, the Fed had to tighten again in August 2000 and the curve was inverted once again. This was an extraordinary time because, in the midst of this tightening, the markets were witnessing the incredible run-up in the Internet bubble which then burst. This was followed by the horrific events of 9/11. At that point, the Fed threw the floodgates wide open, cutting the Fed Funds Rate 11 times in 2001 alone and the curve became very steep by 2003. It was this development which sowed the seeds for the credit crisis.

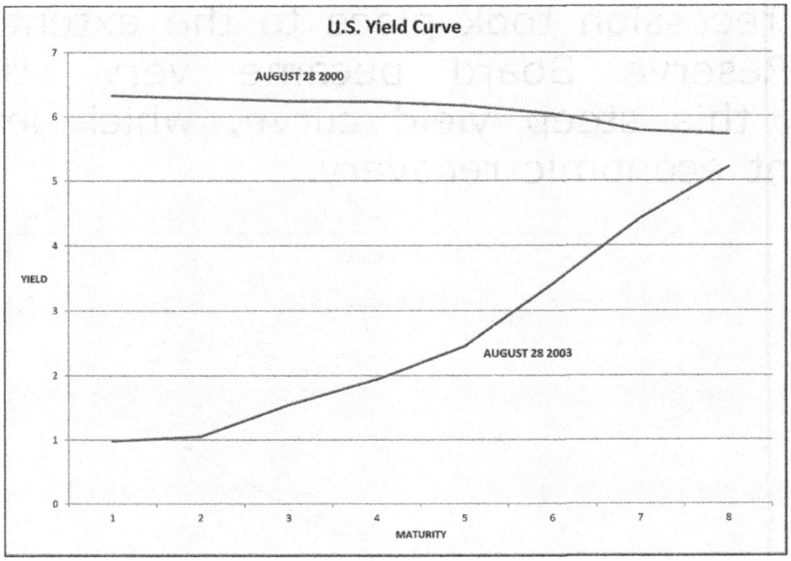

Believe it or not, the yield curve was inverted as recently as 2006, as the Fed tried to rein in the economic and credit expansion.

For good measure, I am including the same chart for Canada for the same period. It is interesting to note that our curve is "flatter" than the U.S. curve, as the Bank of Canada has raised the Bank Rate by 75 basis points, while the Fed has the accelerator to the floor. Short-term interest rates are close to zero in the U.S.

There are many other aspects to analyzing the yield curve. It is dynamic, not static, so it is instructional to monitor it on a regular basis. In Canada, the Bank of Canada (the Bank) influences short-term interest rates directly. Should the Bank begin to move the Bank Rate higher, it will affect the yield on short-term bonds and treasury bills immediately. Investment dealers finance their inventories on margin, such that, if the cost of their funding rises above the yield on their inventories, they will act to sell their inventories, producing higher yields in the process. The Bank`s influence begins to wane past the one-year term as market participants become more influenced by factors such as inflation, yields in other countries, supply and demand for credit, supply of bonds, and economic developments.

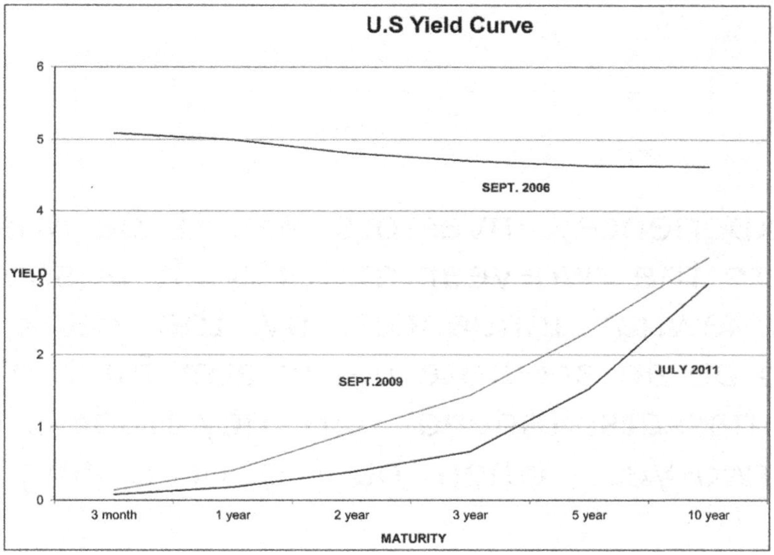

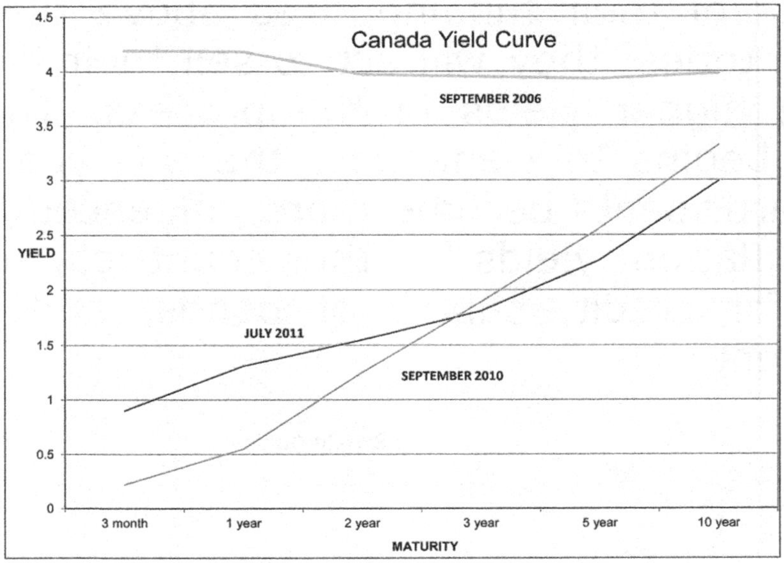

In my experience, investors would be wise to pay attention to the two-year maturity. It is short enough to be somewhat influenced by the Bank but long enough to be an accurate barometer for the bond and currency markets. Indeed, currency traders frequently use the two-year when buying or selling Canadian dollars.

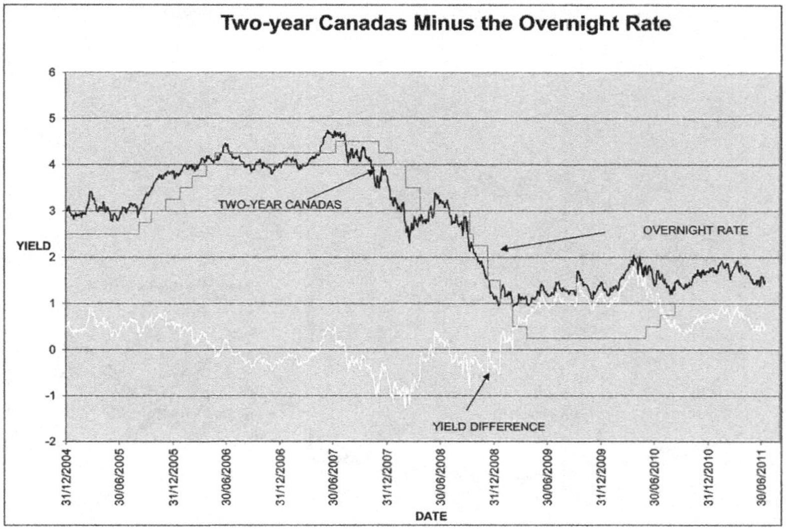

The two-year reflects the market's view of where the Bank Rate is going. In mid-2007, the two-year yield moved below the Bank Rate and the Bank Rate followed quickly. In 2008, this reversed, signalling that the Bank was going to raise rates. It did, with a lag, as you can see. The spread remains comfortably above the Bank Rate; the next move in the Bank Rate will be higher.

The relationship between two-year bond yields and one-year treasury bill yields is also important.

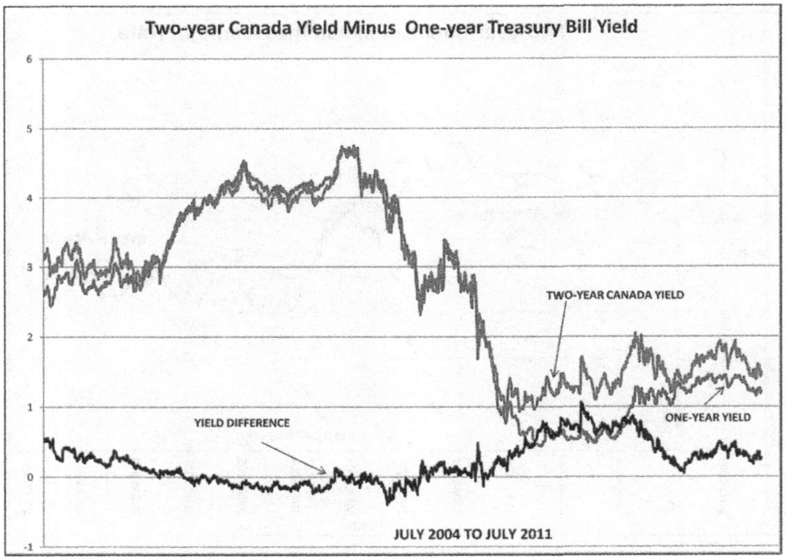

The two-year yielded less than the one-year from November 2005 to May 2007 and then with the monetary ease kicking in, the spread rocketed to over 1 percent positive. The two-year also features prominently for investors when compared to the ten-year yield.

The spread became very wide but has narrowed significantly as the Bank has removed some monetary stimulus, but this spread is still relatively wide.

CURRENT ANALYSIS

The yield curves in North America are steeply positive, signalling an economic recovery; indeed there is a recovery underway but so far it has been somewhat sluggish as the world economy has been facing several headwinds, including the supply chain interruptions following the tsunami in Japan, the events in Egypt and Libya, the ongoing fiscal issues in Europe, plus belt-tightening by governments everywhere.

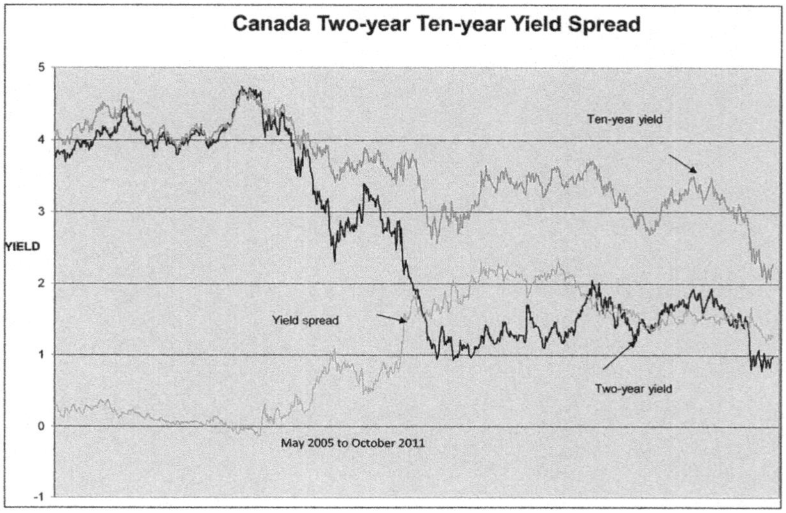

(Source: Bank of Canada)

While growth is subpar, it is growth nonetheless. The yield curves will stay positive indefinitely to promote recovery and growth.

MONEY SUPPLY

> *Inflation is everywhere and anywhere a monetary phenomenon*
>
> —Milton Friedman

Economies cannot grow without growth in the supply of money. Not only must it grow but it must be used. A classic economic equation is: M*V = P*Y. Where *M* is the money supply, *V* is the velocity, *P* is the price level, and *Y* is the quantity of output. Thus P*Y= nominal GDP growth.

Now, let us see what was happening with velocity during the same period.

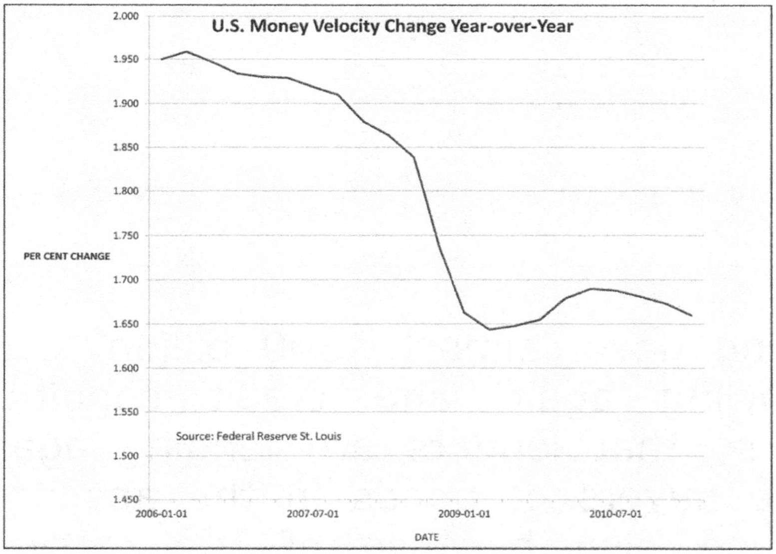

M2 growth is accelerating, while velocity, with a lag, is at least back to unchanged year over year. We can therefore conclude that these charts indicate that the U.S. recovery is taking hold.

CREDIT DEMAND

Credit is the lifeblood of an economy. The credit crisis of 2008 was the worst since the Great Depression. Corporations and consumers alike reacted by trimming their debt levels significantly.

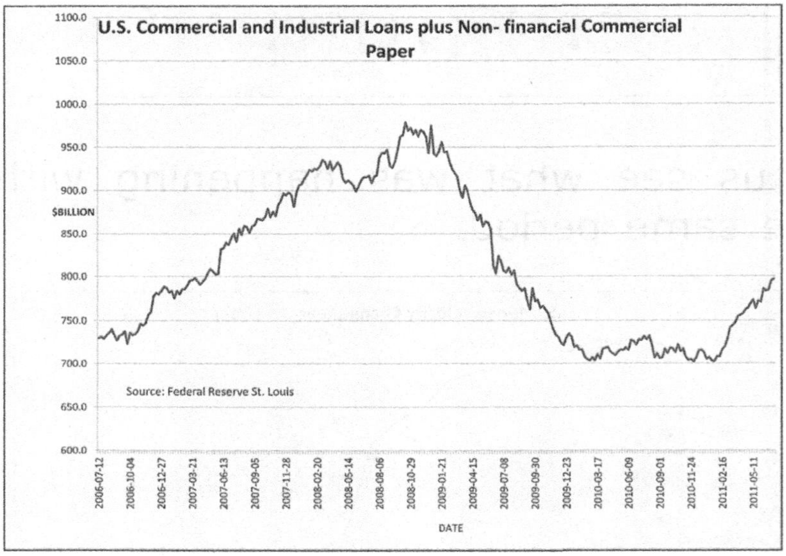

After paying down almost $300 billion, corporations are borrowing again and credit conditions have improved so that lenders are lending again. Banks were large buyers of bonds in the absence of loan demand and also because of the carry profit in borrowing from the Fed at almost nothing and reinvesting the proceeds in higher yielding bonds. As credit demand grows further, eventually banks will begin to sell bonds to fund the loans.

CONSUMER CREDIT

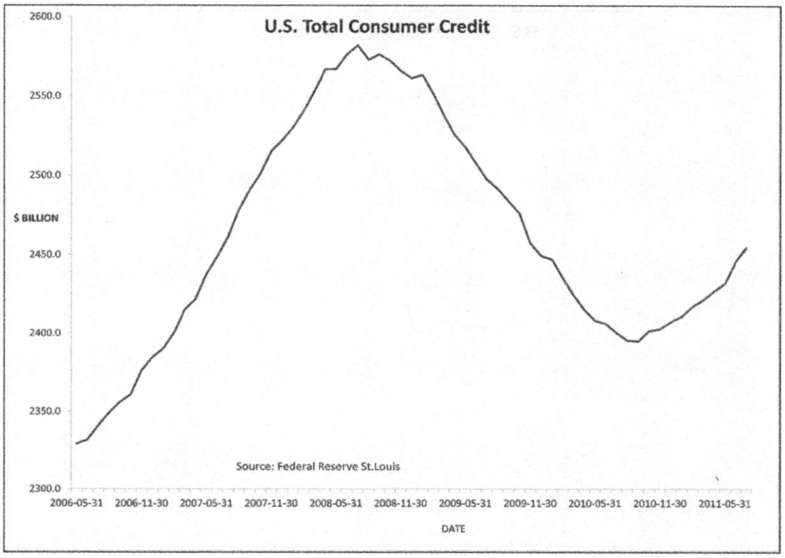

Similarly, the U.S. consumer, shaken by the selloff in real estate values, paid down debt at a furious pace. While the chart depicts a pickup in consumer credit, it masks the fact that U.S. consumers continue to pay down their credit card balances. The pickup in consumer credit has more to do with non-revolving credit such as from buying an asset such as a car or a home appliance. The implication is that overall credit demand is improving, with ultimate pressure on interest rates.

BANK INVESTMENTS

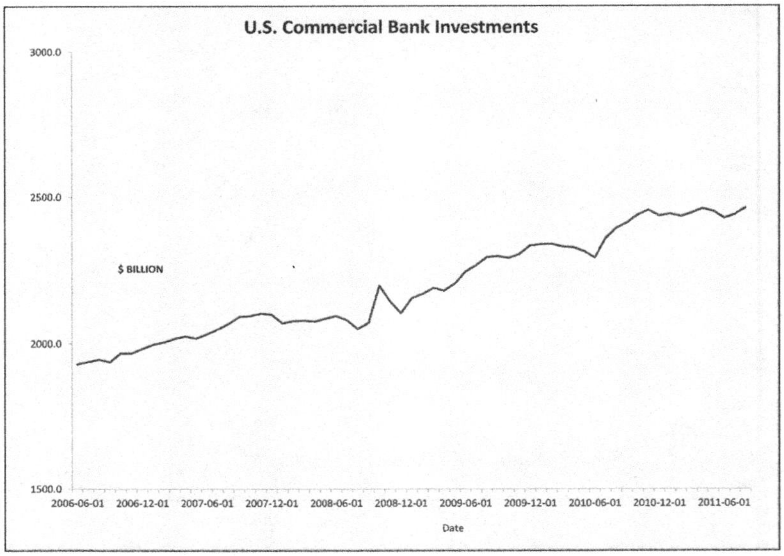

Now it appears that bank investments have plateaued and have begun to fall. This does not augur well for bond yields as the banks will shed bonds for higher yielding loans as demand continues to grow.

CAPACITY UTILIZATION

Another important interest rate tool goes by the name of output gap. It refers to how much an economy is producing compared how much it can produce. The bigger this gap is, the less the pressure on interest rates and, importantly, on the cost of labour. What I have done is chart the industrial production trend and then overlaid it with the unemployment rate. As the output gap shrinks, the unemployment rate falls and the threat of wage-demand increases kicks in.

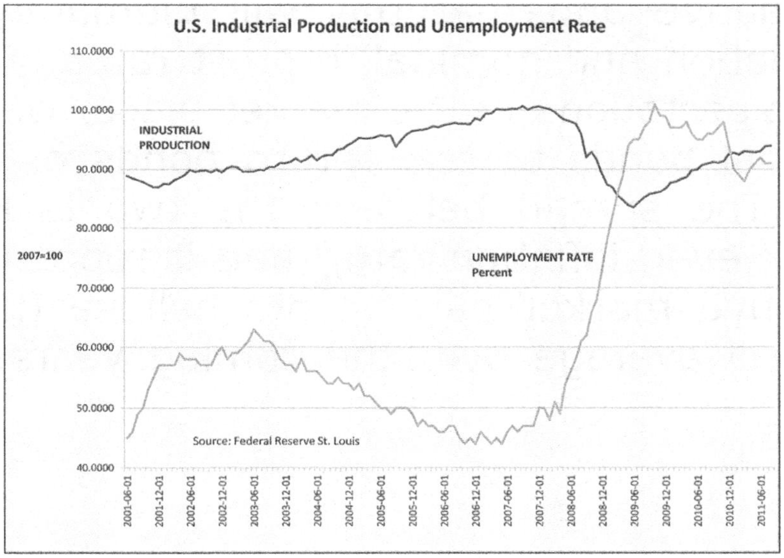

This chart tells a different story. As industrial production recovered from the recessionary lows, unemployment began to fall. Now industrial production has flattened out and the unemployment rate has ticked up, signalling a soft patch for the economy and no upward pressure on wage demands or interest rates.

REAL YIELDS

Another very useful guide to interest rates and market expectations involves real or after-inflation yields. Lenders and savers expect to receive some return net of inflation. The long-term averages indicate that government bonds should return at least 2 percent after inflation. If the yields are well below that level, it is an indication that monetary policy is very accommodative and that this will ultimately lead to higher inflation and nominal interest rates. To capture inflation expectations in the market place, we compare conventional bonds to real return bonds of the same maturity. The spread between the two is known as the "break-even inflation rate," and it represents what the collective market participants believe the rate of inflation will average over the coming years.

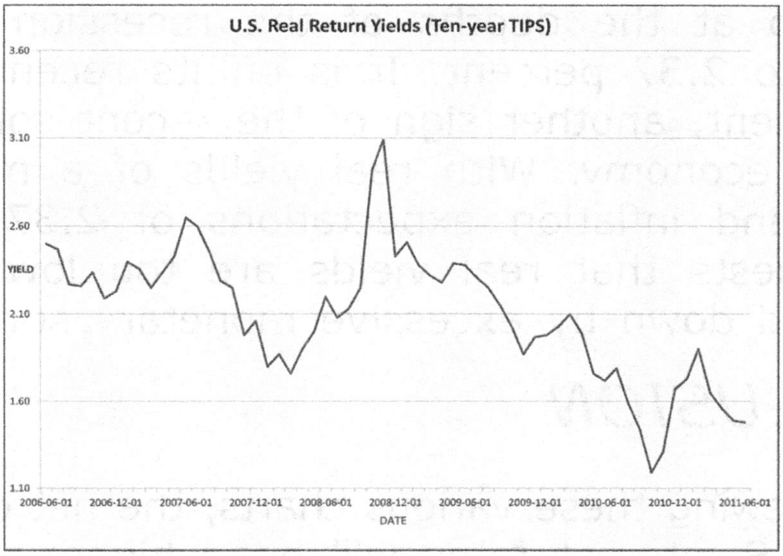

This shows the significant decline in real yields during the past five years. Now let us see what has happened to inflation expectations:

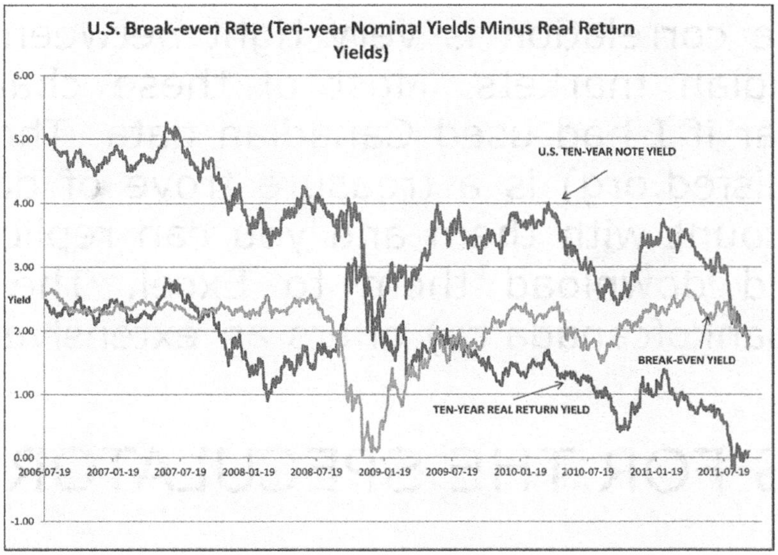

During this extraordinary period, nominal and real yields fell sharply. The break-even yield bottomed out near zero at the depths of the recession and has climbed to 2.37 percent. It is off its recent peak of 2.64 percent, another sign of the recent softening in the U.S. economy. With real yields of a mere 0.54 percent and inflation expectations of 2.37 percent, this suggests that real yields are too low and are being held down by excessive monetary stimulus.

CONCLUSION

After reviewing these various charts, the net conclusion is that U.S interest rates will head higher eventually but, as this is a subdued recovery, so will the rise in bond yields be slower than in previous cycles.

I chose the U.S. market to analyze because it is the most important economy and bond market in the world. The correlation is very tight between the U.S. and Canadian markets. Most of these charts would look similar if I had used Canadian data. The St Louis Fed (stlouisfed.org) is a treasure trove of data. Open a free account with them and you can replicate these charts and download them to Excel. The Bank of Canada (bankofcanada.ca) offers an extensive database also.

BONDS FOR THE SPECULATOR

Bond prices change minute by minute. Daily price fluctuations for longer term bonds (five years and longer) can range from pennies to dollars, with the average daily change approximately 50 cents. The margin rate (the amount you need to put down) can be as low as 4 percent for Canada bonds with a term of three years and longer. You can see that it is possible to make or lose money quickly on 25-times leverage! The margin rate of only 4 percent compares to 50 percent for most equities. Why is it so low? It is because of the very high quality of fixed-income instruments, in addition to their liquidity. Also, bonds pay interest, typically at a higher rate than the cost of borrowing, so they have what we call a "positive" carry (i.e., the interest accruing on the bond exceeds the cost of borrowing on margin).

"Pro" trading, which involves borrowing money for the express purpose of creating capital gains from trading bonds, is confined largely to traders at the largest investment dealers; however, I have dealt with many well-heeled and informed individuals who have enjoyed success trading the bond market on margin. As with the equity markets, there are both fundamental and technical approaches to forecasting the direction of bond prices. Bond traders use both. Often it is relatively easy to observe the general direction of bond prices, but close attention to technical analysis can identify some short-term trading opportunities. The rest of this chapter will deal with technical analysis.

Just to be sure that my message is clear, I am including this chapter for the following reasons: first, the technical analysis of the direction of bond prices is important to investors in general. You now know that bond prices are always changing and can experience dramatic price movements. It is in your best interest to arm yourself with some technical tools to better time your purchases or sales. Using technical analysis can save you a lot of money, or to put it another way, it can add incremental yield to your portfolio. Second, technical analysis for bonds may be used by speculators for capital gains purposes. As I mentioned above, the margin rate for bonds is very low because of their quality, so speculators are able to leverage their investments.

The following section walks you through the process of creating and using your own charts; you can build your own charts in spreadsheets, buy some software, or ask IAs to provide their firms' technical research. Or you can visit the Bank of Canada's wonderful website, which offers a plethora of interest rates and yields.

Again, careful monitoring of bond charts can help in the timing of an investment decision and can add to yield.

The average daily fluctuation of a long-term bond (ten-year and longer) has been approximately half a point for the last ten years. Combine this fact with the very low margin requirements needed to finance bonds and you have a potent combination for astute traders and speculators. Of course, in volatility there is opportunity and risk. There are savvy investors who chart bond prices and familiarize themselves with all the factors that produce short- and medium-term price changes for bonds. This is not for the faint of heart, folks. At a 10 percent margin, for example, leverage works in reverse in a hurry! For the sophisticated investor who is plugged into a bond desk or has a very competent IA, there are plenty of opportunities to employ this leverage for capital gains. Using margin to build a leveraged bond position also multiplies the commission, and since leveraged speculative bond positions are usually actively traded, this leads to repeat business for the IA.

My advice here is not to trade on margin unless you can buy $1 million face value of bonds. While the minimum margin required is only 4 percent for long-term government bonds, most investment dealers will ask for 10 percent margin to allow a cushion against minor price changes; speculators may wish to put down an even higher minimum to avoid margin calls and then maybe run that down to 10 percent as the market (hopefully) rallies. Why $1 million face value? That is the face value at which you can be sure of getting the best dealing price, since it is the minimum trading unit in the massive interdealer bond community. While there is no reason not to trade lesser amounts, and I would not discourage it, you may pay more per transaction since your IA's transfer price from the bond-trading desk may be higher or lower depending on whether you are buying or selling. It also becomes of paramount importance to find the firm (and the IA) that will give you the best service;

you cannot afford to be poorly serviced with bad pricing techniques. In fact, you may bargain for a certain commission rate per transaction, but even then, you will never really know what the transfer price is.

CHARTING THE BOND MARKET

For those determined to trade the bond market aggressively or for those merely looking for information, charting the bond market is a must. Where do you find prices? Which bonds to chart? Your IA's firm may be able to provide you with charts, but they will not likely be what you want. You can build your own charts using pen and paper (squared works best), or (for those with a PC) simple spreadsheets can be built that take some of the drudgery away. First, where to get the prices? Assuming we are charting the Canadian bond market, the *Financial Post* and the *Globe and Mail* both produce bond quotations that represent the closing price levels from the day before, typically at 4:00p.m. So too does Perimeter CBID at www.canadianfixedincome.ca. Since the bond market never really stops trading, participants have to pick a moment every day to declare a closing price. Which bonds do you chart? To speculate in bonds means you should trade the most active and liquid issues. In so doing, you will have a tight bid-ask spread and the assurance that there *will* be a bid and an ask. Therefore, you will be trading and charting the benchmark Government of Canada bonds, the key trading issues in the market at different maturities.

Today, the benchmark maturities are two, three, five, seven, ten, and thirty years. This is true in most global bond markets (although only Canada and the United States have thirty-year benchmark issues). What sets these issues apart from others is the amount of bonds outstanding. Wherever possible, the Bank of Canada will reopen a benchmark issue to provide market participants with increased liquidity at a key maturity. Normally, the bond will have what is called a "current coupon," one that is close to the prevailing interest rate at that maturity. What happens in the real world is that, first, time passes—the former ten-year benchmark is now only eight years, for example, and a new ten-year has to be created—and second, bond prices rise or fall, putting the benchmark price at a large premium or discount. In this case, the central bank may wish to issue a more current coupon.

Since you can find the benchmark issues yourself, you will not have to bother your IA. I would recommend that you chart the two-, five-, ten-, and thirty-year issues. For purposes of this chapter, we will use the Canada 5 percent maturing June 1, 2037, as our chosen benchmark to chart. Even though it is less than thirty years, it is the most actively traded long-term Canada bond. Also, as I mentioned in the chapter on products, it is in your best interest to begin charting the U.S. ten-year benchmark. Also, you might then want to chart the Canadian ten-year.

Since we are intending to speculate, we should be charting the price of the bond, not the yield. You may wish to chart yields also, but what you will have will merely be the inverse of the price chart. Remember the dinosaur?

MOVING AVERAGES

Most serious chartists employ a series of moving averages and momentum to forecast bond prices. There are short-term trading charts, and medium-to long-term as well. I recommend you use the following moving average periods: ten days, thirty days, and two hundred days. For a momentum oscillator, use ten-day minus thirty-day moving averages. What the oscillator does is measure the rate of change between two moving average periods. In moving average terms, you have a buy signal when the spot price is higher than the ten-day and thirty-day moving averages, all three lines are moving up, and the momentum oscillator is moving up and is above zero.

These are all commonly used tools for charting anything, stocks, bonds, gold, etc. If your IA cannot provide you with any price history to begin with, you can get back copies of the newspaper; this is better than starting from scratch since it will be a while before your charts will be complete—and think of all those money-making opportunities that you might miss! The Bank of Canada has extensive yield histories on a very large list of different fixed-income instruments available on their website. Yield charts are merely the inverse of a price chart and are just as useful if you can get your mind around them. You could invert a yield chart to demonstrate what the price action would be like.

What is a moving average? It is an average of a given series of numbers that changes each day as new data is added and old data drops off. Consider the ten daily closes for the Government of Canada 5 percent due June 1, 2037:

August 18, 2011	$136.110
August 19, 2011	$136.031
August 22, 2011	$136.225
August 23, 2011	$134,758
August 24, 2011	$133.257
August 25, 2011	$134.087
August 26, 2011	$134.741
August 29, 2011	$133.641
August 30, 2011	$134.558
August 31, 2011	$132.672
September 1, 2011	$134.044
September 2, 2011	$135.704
September 5, 2011	$135.704
September 6, 2011	$136.340

Now, adding up these ten prices and dividing by ten, you end up with a ten-day average of $134.61. When we add another day, say September 1, the price is now $134.04; the moving average will change as we drop the $136.11 price and add the $134.04 price. The ten-day average is now $134.40, and so on. Since this number changes each day, it is called a "moving average." Averaging smoothes out day-today fluctuations to produce a graph of the price movement. Obviously, the longer the series the less impact a daily price change has. Let us look at our first chart, which tracks the daily price along with the thirty-day moving average.

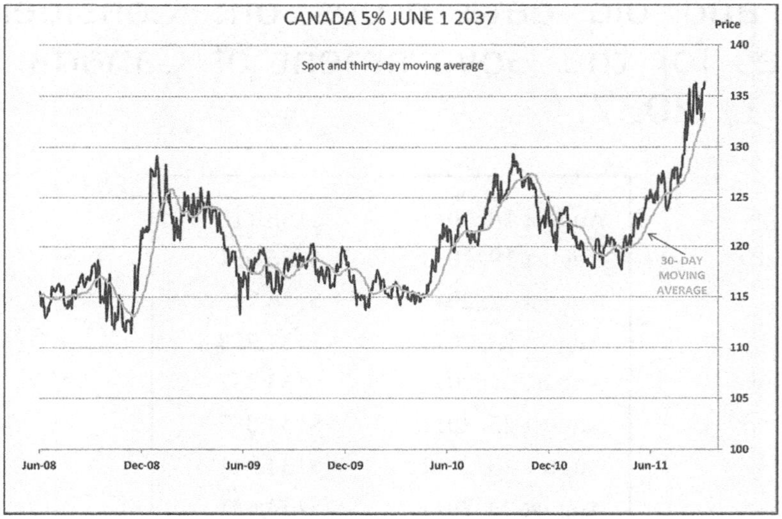

What we see is the two averages moving in an uptrend, but at different speeds. Classic moving average theory indicates that if the price and the two moving averages are moving in one direction, the trend will continue until the daily price starts to move lower and the other two averages eventually follow. As you can see, the gap widens and narrows between the ten-day and thirty-day averages. We chart this gap as an oscillator to be able to spot when the market becomes overbought or oversold on a short-term basis.

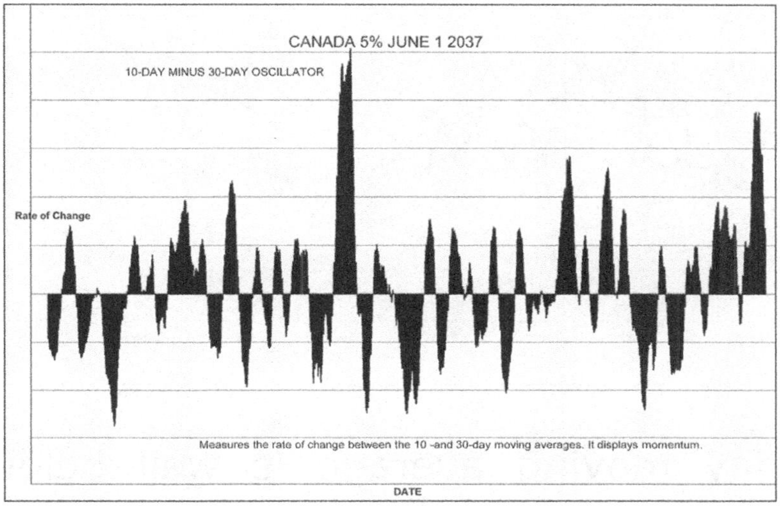

Thus, a speculator would sell (or go short) when the trend was strongly higher but the oscillator had hit an extreme rate of change. In the previous example, the oscillator was at a very high level and, combined with the moving average chart, this represented a selling opportunity—or, to put it another way, a bad time to buy. A more conservative trader would wait for the moving averages to reverse and for the oscillator to move into negative territory. This chart is for short-term trading. Some cyclical perspective is important, since short-term moves against the cyclical trend may not last long. Therefore, we will now add the longer series, which smoothes the data even more.

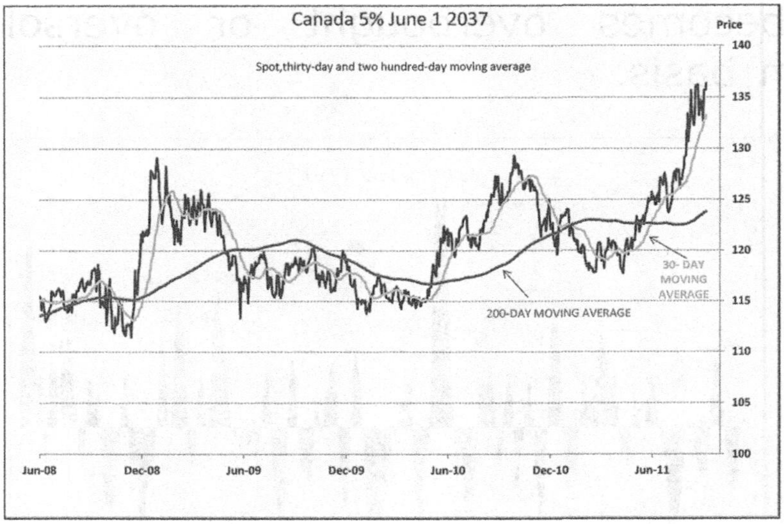

The 200-day moving average is well below current prices, indicating that the long-term trend is still toward higher prices. The oscillator is also well above zero, indicating that this bond is due for a correction.

PRICE MOVING EVENTS

Bond speculators and investors in general should be aware of the constant parade of economic data as well as the issuance of new bonds, otherwise they could be sideswiped. The American and Canadian authorities release a calendar of forthcoming releases, the most important of which for the bond market are the inflation data, the employment market, and the GDP numbers. At different points in the economic cycle, different news may carry more weight. The American calendar is found in Barrons or at, www.bl oomberg.com while the Canadian one is in the weekend *Financial Post* or at one of the major investment dealer websites. BMO research is an excellent site. Your own IA or discount broker will be able to provide such a calendar along with consensus forecasts for the various releases. In any event, large price movements, sometimes irrational, follow the release of key data, providing the nimble trader with opportunity.

AUCTIONS/NEW ISSUES

A feature of the bond market is the constant supply of new issues, as past debt matures and must be rolled over and as the deficit must be funded. Both the American and Canadian federal governments issue bonds via an auction method whereby a group of pre-authorized investment dealers bid for the issues and redistribute them to their client base. The auction schedule is known in advance in both countries. What is important to know for the would-be speculator is that the auction participants are not paid a commission for their role in the auction. What they must do to stay in business is sell the bonds at a slightly higher price than they paid for them. Therefore, there is little incentive to bid up the bond market aggressively before an auction, since that would increase the odds of being stuck with overpriced merchandise. Investment dealers do have an opportunity to pre-sell an auction issue in the "when-issued" (WI) market. As soon as the details of an auction are released, when-issued trading commences. This allows the participants to try and build a book for the auction by pre-selling it, and thus building up a short position with which to bid. This WI period provides opportunities for the nimble, as the auctioned issue may be offered cheaply.

In any event, large new supply can derail a bond market rally. Provincial borrowers do not release their borrowing calendar in advance and can cause some serious disruption to the market with large, surprise issues.

There are other tools that one should arm oneself with.

The Bank of Canada weekly statement is chock full of key numbers, averages, and charts. Phone the Bank of Canada nearest you to get on the list or draw it into your PC. Its website is full of all kinds of useful information.

My website provides updated charts, forthcoming economic and market moving events, and overview commentary.

If you conclude that using technical analysis can at least help save you money or add yield, then it is of value.

CONCLUSION

I have made my case in this book that careful selection of individual fixed-income products is in your best interest, as you can tailor your fixed-income investment portfolio to suit your individual needs. I have attempted to arm you with the appropriate tools and information to augment your well-being. Nothing has happened to alter my opinion that investing in high quality, individual fixed-income securities is the way to follow for individual investors. The investment business is very good at creating products to be sold, with almost no regard for the well-being of the investors. Avoid all of these contrived products and stick to the basics.

The laddered approach is simple enough, but in practice is a very disciplined and effective approach to investing. Zero coupon bonds, combined with the laddered approach, are important investments for retirement planning purposes. Using this approach leads to what I call the sleep at night portfolio, where you will have assembled investments that are most beneficial to you.

As I mentioned in the introduction, when asked how the bond market functions, I blurted out that it was all about relationships. The more I pondered this remark, the more I realized that this was an essential truth. Your relationship with your investment advisor is all-important to your financial well-being, and so I dedicated a chapter in this book discussing how to choose the right IA. Also, you have learned that most fixed-income products trade in relation to something else. A certain bond may be matrix priced to a specific benchmark, to a yield curve, to the Bank Rate, or to the prime lending rate.

From my perspective, after trading over a trillion dollars of fixed-income securities with nary a hitch, my relationships with my traders, my counterparts (the other investment dealers with whom I transact business), my clients (all the IAs and smaller financial organizations that I service), and the rest of my own firm are very important. I owe most of my success to the people who have worked with me and made me look good. These people, many of whom are smarter than I am, have similar strengths. They are all intelligent, hard-working individuals of the highest integrity and possess the most valuable of all traits for my business: tremendous interpersonal skills. They all know how to offer pleasant but excellent service to IAs, they have represented me in the street exceptionally well, and they have maintained strong corporate relationships.

One either has it or one does not. As any manager will say, the hiring process is vitally important, but despite our best efforts, we occasionally make bad hires or exercise bad judgment. In my case, my success ratio is very high. Over the years, a large number of people have approached me to be a bond trader, lured mostly by the glamour and the money.

I have been approached at office parties, in bars, and by phone and email. Some applicants were aggressive; some attempted to pull strings, while others just sent in resumes and then harassed me. It was thus a challenge to separate the glamour seekers from the genuine candidates. The extent that I succeeded is partly owed to the road-less-travelled approach I followed in the investment business.

To help weed out the wannabes, I concocted a simple test to see how they would react to a tiny bit of pressure. I had read the book *Hard Drive* by Bill Gates, in which he described the hiring process that Microsoft used when interviewing. Besides the formal interview process, Microsoft threw in a series of up to twenty random questions to see how the applicants would perform on the spot. This seemed like a good idea to me, so I thought up a couple of what I thought were innocent questions appropriate to my business. What followed was a most educational experience. I would be at a bar or a party and an individual would screw up the courage (or perhaps swallow some liquid courage!) and approach me. Typically, I would know the individual already, but sometimes he or she knew about me but had never met me.

What followed had a predictable outcome. The individuals would tell me why they would make good traders or who they knew. At some point, I would ask how good their math was, and the answer was normally "excellent" or "very good." Then I would quietly ask them to answer a simple question: "What is 1/8 of 1 percent of $100,000?" This was the first of two questions, as this one was so easy I had a backup question. Well, what happened next bordered on the unbelievable! They panicked, froze, guessed, refused to answer, told me it was a stupid question, blurted out different answers, or just stomped off. Very few (maybe 2 percent) actually stopped, thought on their feet, and arrived at the answer. People have accused me of employing an inappropriate question, as my generation learned math without calculators. That may be true, but I was looking for people who could stay cool under pressure and use logic. What I was not looking for were robots! The thought process should go something like this: 10 percent of $100,000 = $10,000, so 1 percent would therefore be $1,000. One-eighth of that is $125.

Almost no one had .125 anywhere in the answer (.125, of course, is 1/8 in decimal form!) Needless to say, those who stayed cool and used logic usually got the job! However, that was only after answering the second question, which was, "What is 1/4 of 1 percent of $250,000?"! These questions and answers were germane to my business, as the results were typical of the small trading profits (or losses) I would frequently make.

There was no typical hire; none of my hires were MBAs or math grads. I have hired chemistry majors, philosophy majors, some who had not finished university, and some who only had secondary school education. I was visited once by the Dean of Business from the University of Toronto, who toured Bay Street asking various managers what they were looking for. I replied that the two most important factors were that a candidate must display excellent interpersonal skills and also be literate! A trading department deals with a multitude of personalities. My traders had to represent me professionally with the street, deal comfortably with all levels of the company, and, most importantly, deal effectively with every kind of human behaviour imaginable in the large number of IAs that we serviced.

Also important were literacy and presentation skills. Raw ability just was not good enough. I often sent my traders to presentation skills development or similar courses to augment their already wonderful traits.

So, relationships are important, and so is integrity.

The investment business has not been without its share of scandals, promotions, hype, and bad IAs. There are only two paths to follow, and I have chosen the high road. By this I mean always conducting my business with honesty and integrity, and transmitting these values to everyone with whom I have had the pleasure of working.

We have only a few tools to work with: computers, the phone, and what is between our ears. What people remember is how they are treated. Thus, one's name is crucial, and I am very proud of the name I have established. As someone who has traded trillions of dollars of fixed-income securities over a span of some thirty-five years on an over-the-counter basis, I can say that I have never had any serious disputes with counterparties. Your word is your bond in this business; once it is given, it is a done deal!

I have had to let traders go who hid transactions from me or who did not represent me professionally. In this business, you are only as good as your weakest link. I have built four trading departments from scratch, each of them successful and each of them full of bright people with a high level of integrity and strong interpersonal skills.

I am pleased to say that, in a male-dominated business, I have always had an above-average ratio of female traders, and this was not lip service, as they are very smart with tremendous interpersonal skills. All of those young women and men who worked for me made me look good and I sincerely hope that I have taught them something and that I helped make them into better people.

In the fixed-income business, billions of dollars of fixed-income securities trade on the basis of a verbal handshake. Admittedly, all our conversations are now taped, but there are almost never any serious trade disputes, as any misunderstandings or differences of opinion are resolved right away. Interestingly, the most serious debates have involved trades between my desk and retail IAs. Sometimes IAs will dispute a trade or a price, convinced that we have somehow done them wrong. As soon as we announce we are going to listen to the tapes, 99 percent of these problems go away! Also, when we review the production records of the IAs in question, they are normally in the bottom 20 percent of commissions, spending too much time on disputes and not enough with their clients. Sometimes I will review the complaint and decide that an IA had a point; however, most of the time, the IA doesn't pass the improved price on to the clients but pockets the difference.

Overall, as I contemplate the next phase of my life, I am proud of my achievements, my conduct, the name I have, and most importantly, of all the wonderful individuals who have made me look good.

In alphabetical order, these people have worked with me since 1988: Mario Addeo, Paulo Alves, Nataly Bozzo, Lucy Brigstocke, Dan Currie, David Falby, Tim Foley, Deborah Gottdenker, Rob Holden, Kevin Landry, Bob Maclean, David Mak, Lesli McCallum, Laura Rubino, Tim Parsons, Jamie Price, and Bill Reid. Since 2009, I have had the pleasure of being associated with David Pearson and Wally Trueman of Odlum Brown Limited.

Of course, there were a few others who did not work out as well, but overall I have always had strong teams of people and I would like to think that it was not all an accident.

As I ponder what to do in my retirement stage, I do know that I will maintain my voice for the individual investor. I do feel lonely at times, but I have had so many heartwarming messages from so many individuals who tell me that they have benefitted from following the principles which I have expressed in this book. It is the ultimate reward for an author to receive such messages.

I hope that you have learned something from reading this book and that you now feel more empowered to enhance your returns. I wrote it in your best interest.

APPENDIX A

List of Websites

www.bankofcanada.ca (excellent)
www.bloomberg.com
www.bmonesbittburns.com/economics
www.bondsonline.com
www.bondtalk.com(excellent)
www.canada.com
www.canadianbondindices.com
www.canadianfixedincome.ca
www.cds.ca
www.dbrs.com
www.fool.com
www.globefund.com
www.globeinvestor.com
www.iiroc.ca
www.independentfinancial.on.ca
www.investinginbonds.com (good Q&A; links to other sites)
www.investopedia.com
www.inyourbestinterest.ca
www.iShares.ca
www.newyorkfed.org
www.osc.ca
www.pimco.com
www.sedar.com
www.smartmoney.com

www.standardandpoors.com
www.stlouisfed.org
www.stockhouse.ca
www.stripbonds.info

APPENDIX B

A Do-It-Yourself Guide to Bond Investing

CASE FOR BONDS

- Certainty—future value known helps planning
- Quality
- Low fees
- Diversity of credit and maturity
- Liquidity
- Performance—ladders get the job done
- Customizable to personalize your portfolio

CASE AGAINST MUTUAL BOND FUNDS

- No certainty as to future value or income
- Very high fees averaging 1.9 percent
- Uneven, unpredictable performance
- Not customizable

RISKS TO BONDS

- Price vulnerable to rise in yields—offset by ladders
- Credit—stick with governments and A-rated or better corporates
- Event
- Yield curve—ladders remove this risk
- Inflation—combine ladders with real return bonds
- Liquidity—very seldom an issue
- Reinvestment—ladders eliminate this
- Maturity—ladders will also eliminate this

HOW DO I DO IT?

- Open an online account with TD Waterhouse or find an IA with fixed-income expertise.
- Add various websites to your favourites. See Appendix A, but add at least mine (inyourbestinte rest.ca) and canadianfixedincome.ca. There is a wealth of information on the Web for fixed-income investors.
- Chart the market—see Forecasting Interest Rates chapter. This helps to time your investments.
- Begin to build ladders; use strips for RRSPs and interest-bearing bonds for taxable accounts.

- Consider RRBs.
- Avoid hybrid or structured products. They were designed to be sold to you and are not in your best interest.

DEVELOP YOUR OWN INVESTMENT STRATEGY

- Minimum/maximum maturities (i.e., from one to ten years)
- Minimum percentage in governments
- Minimum credit rating for corporate (A-rated recommended)
- Maximum percentage in one corporate credit or industry (10 percent suggested)
- Minimum/maximum for RRBs (depends on where real yields are)
- Maximum percentage for other bonds (convertibles, high-yield)

APPENDIX C

Using Excel for Bond Price and Yield Calculations

1. In older versions of Excel, click on Tools, then check the Analysis Tool Pak.
2. In Excel 2010, open a new blank spreadsheet.
3. In any cell, say B2, enter the following: =Today ()+3 This will be the settlement date. The formula may be changed for different settlement dates by changing the number of days.
4. For calculating the price to yield formula you will need the following columns: Coupon Rate, Maturity Date, Price, and Yield.
5. Enter values in the first three columns. Use the Format Cells function to ensure that the values, especially the maturity date, are correct. Let us assume that you have entered the values in D5, E5, and F5.
6. In the yield column (say G5), enter the following formula: =yield (B2, E5, D5, F5,100,2,1) and the yield should appear. Make sure to enter the cell with the maturity date first, then the coupon rate. Also, by using the fixed cell, B2 in this case,

you can copy the formula down to enter more bonds and build a portfolio.

7. For the yield to price formula you use the same cells, but in the price column enter the following: =Price (B2, E5, D5, G5, 100, 2, 1) and the price should appear.

GLOSSARY

ABCP—Asset-backed Commercial Paper were money market notes issued by third-party conduits and backed by assets such as mortgages, car loans, and credit card receivables. Sadly, they also contained subprime mortgages and synthetic derivatives. They were mismatched as to maturity with the assets being in the five-year term and the notes being of thirty-to ninety-day maturities. Liquidity providers backed away when the credit crunch/subprime mess set in.

Accretion— *(see* Amortization)

Accrued interest—Interest that adds up daily between interest payment dates. It is paid to investors on interest payment dates or, if sold between these dates, on the settlement date.

Agency bonds—These bonds are issued by agents of a government. Normally, they are issued with the guarantee of the government, e.g. Canada Housing Trust bonds.

Amortization—From the Latin *a mort,* meaning "to death." This refers to the process where as time passes your fixed-income investment moves inexorably to its face value or maturing value.

Arbitrage—Taking advantage of an anomaly between two or more securities for profit.

Arrears—A company failing to make interest payments or preferred share dividends (on cumulative shares). These arrears must be paid before any other payments can be made, or in the case of a corporate event.

Ask—The price at which a bond trader is willing to sell a certain fixed-income instrument. *Offer* is sometimes used to mean the same thing but can lead to confusion, because if you ask someone to make you an offer, they might think you want a bid. Stick to "ask."

Asset-backed securities (ABS)—These have been around for a long time. They differ from ABCP in that the assets are of much higher quality and the term of the ABS matches the term of the assets.

Balloon—The maturing principal of a bond issue.

Bankers' acceptances (BAs)—Issued by the chartered banks, they are promissory notes issued by companies unable to raise their own short-term money. The banks stamp these notes as guaranteed by them and charge a stamping fee. They are very liquid, being acceptable collateral at the Bank of Canada's window.

Bank of Canada—Canada's central bank. Its responsibilities focus on the goals of low and stable inflation, a safe and secure currency, financial stability, and the efficient management of government funds and the public debt.

Bank Rate—The minimum interest rate at which the Bank of Canada extends short-term loans to members of the Canadian Payments Association. Since February 22, 1996, it is set at the upper limit of the bank's operating band which is 50 basis points wide.

Basis point—How everything gets measured (e.g., so many basis points over Canadas). A basis point is one one-hundredth of 1 percent. Thus, if the Bank Rate falls 25 basis points, that is the same as 25/100=1/4 (0.25) of 1 percent.

Bearer bonds—Bonds that are paid to the "bearer" on demand. They were common but are rare now with the advent of book-based systems.

Bellwether—Essentially the same as benchmark, although its use refers to those issues media and market commentators refer to when describing the bond market's direction. For example, the bellwether long Canada, the 8 percent bond of 2023, rose $1 in active trading. The bellwether is thus a proxy for the market itself. Because of an active crowd of followers and speculators, an issue may remain a bellwether while being replaced as a benchmark! Make sense? For many years the Canada 8 percent bond, due June 1, 2023, was the bellwether issue for the long-term market, even when it rose to $135 when interest rates fell. The major dealers would use it for speculative purposes, to hedge inventories, and to price both other new issues and their own long-term bond inventories. Market commentators would point to this one bond to give an idea of how the market was behaving. Speculators, both individual and institutional, continued to play this issue even after the market had gone up 20 points.

Benchmark—Refers to bonds by which others are valued. The Bank of Canada (and some provinces) issue and reissue bonds at strategic maturity points (typically two, three, five, ten, and thirty years). In so doing, these bonds issues become sizeable enough that they trade freely with tight bid-ask spreads. When issuers bring new bonds to market, the presence of these issues makes pricing easier, since accurate market yields are readily available as references or benchmarks. Retail investors are wise to stick to these benchmark or global issues, as retail desks are more likely to maintain inventory in and have lower transfer prices for such bonds because the turnover is higher.

Of course, old benchmarks are regularly sent to pasture to be replaced by new ones. This is because the passage of time leaves gaps at the key maturities (e.g., a five-year bond becomes a four-year bond one year later). Or interest rates may change significantly, leaving the benchmark issue with too high or too low a coupon for practical use.

BEO—Frequently seen on contracts, it stands for "book entry only," which means that, while the investor does not receive a certificate, a custodian or agent holds one or more global certificates on behalf of the investor.

Bid—What a bond trader is willing to pay for a certain bond.

Bond—A security issued by a government or corporation paying fixed or floating interest payments. There is thus a *bond* between borrower and lender. It is also used in a broader sense to describe the bond market. (*See also* Debentures)

Bond rating—An analysis of the creditworthiness of an issue of bonds.

Bond trader—An individual who makes markets in bonds.

Bonus—What bond traders are paid for skillful trading.

Book—Once you have selected your IA, you become part of his or her "book" of business. This refers to the number of clients the IA has, and the amount of assets in total that the clients have. Ask about an IA's book, and you will discover these facts, as well as their customer turnover rate, number of sales assistants, and other vital information to help you to make an informed decision whether to work with them.

Book-based—Refers to the electronic record keeping of who owns what. The days of physical securities, actual pieces of paper, are almost totally over.

Broker—Terms such as investment advisors (IAs), financial advisors, investment executives (IEs), and financial planners (FPs) have been introduced to give a warm and fuzzy feeling to your investment-making decisions.

Callable—This is important, as this term normally works against you. Suppose you borrow money from your friendly bank when interest rates are at 20 percent. Wouldn't it be nice to be able to refinance the loan when rates fell to 10 percent? Of course. This is referred to as a call feature, where the borrower may prematurely pay off the loan. As a lender, you do not want this to happen. If you call the peak in interest rates accurately, buying long-term bonds at attractive yields for, say, 20 years, the last thing you want is to get your money back in 10 years should rates fall, forcing you to reinvest at the then prevailing lower yields.

Only the borrower may call the issue. Today, most bond issues are non-callable for financial advantage.

Past callable issues still trade and are often quoted in the weekend newspapers. The quoted yield is much higher than other bonds but reflects the fact that they may be called soon. The bigger the gap between the coupon rate on a callable bond and existing market rates, the greater the certainty that the issue will be called and refinanced. Examine your portfolios carefully. Almost all the callable bonds outstanding were issued when rates were much higher than they are today. Sell them and reinvest in a non-callable issue.

Call loan—How investment dealers finance themselves. Also referred to as overnight money. Dealers post their inventory as collateral. This rate is every bit as important as the Bank Rate—ask your IA what the overnight rate is sometime! The Bank of Canada influences money market rates by altering the amount of cash in the system.

Canada call feature—This feature defines how your bond may be called from you. If the bond in question was issued with a spread of 100 basis points over a certain Canada issue, the call feature may say that the issuer may call these bonds from you at a spread of 25 basis points, providing you with yield protection.

Capital Trust Securities—Impossibly complicated securities designed by the banks to qualify as Tier 1 capital. They have to have very long maturities with messy call features that sometimes involve them being convertible into preferred shares.

CARS™—Coupon and Residual Securities—these are corporate strip bonds issued under prospectus

CD—Certificate of deposit—issued by banks, they are an illiquid short-term note.

CDS—Central Depository Service (Clearing and Depository Services Inc.)—an important organization that keeps records of who owns what, maintains CUSIP records, and provides a strip bond service, etc.

Cold-call—A phone call, not solicited by the party being phoned, from an IA; typically, it is a new IA or a junior or someone whose business has fallen. Sales managers give quotas to such IAs and so they interrupt people at work or at home in order to impress upon them that they should move their entire investment portfolio immediately to these starving, but brilliant advisors! Anyone who has to make cold calls is not successful. If it suits you, ask them a few skill-testing questions or for some performance stats!

Collateral—What an issuer offers as security to back up an issue of bonds. The bond holders have first claim to the collateral in the event of dissolution.

Commercial paper—Unsecured short-term promissory notes issued by corporations.

Commissions—What IAs earn on transactions. In the case of equities and exchange traded securities, they are revealed on contracts but in the case of bonds, they are included in the price.

Compound interest—Interest earned by reinvesting interest payments; or interest on interest, to put it another way.

Convertible bonds—Issued with a coupon rate and a maturity date like most bonds, but also carrying a feature which gives investors the right to convert their debt to equity on specific terms.

Convexity—The second derivative of duration.

Corporate bond—A debenture issued by a business entity.

Coupon—The rate of interest set at the time a bond was issued. It is normally fixed at a certain rate for the life of the bond. In Canada, most coupon payments are made twice a year at half of the fixed coupon rate.

Coupon frequency—How often an investor receives an interest payment.

Credit—From the Latin *credere,* "to believe." When you invest in a fixed-income security, you believe that the borrower will pay you back.

Credit card receivables—The monies owed by individuals to credit card companies. They can and are used as collateral for asset-backed securities.

Credit rating—The likelihood that a borrower will pay you back. Credit rating agencies assess the financial strength of issuers. The most well known are Standard & Poor's, Moody's, and Dominion Bond Rating Service.

Current yield—Merely the coupon of a bond divided by its market price.

CUSIP numbers—Uniform securities identification numbers used in Canada and the US.

Dealer—An investment dealer who offers a full range of investment services.

Debenture—A "bond" issued with no specific collateral to back it. Strictly speaking, government bonds are actually debentures.

Default—An event when an issuer declares that it can no longer make interest payments.

Defeasance—Offsetting a future liability with an asset of similar maturity and amount. Strips are commonly used to defease a future debt as they can be invested to a precise future value.

Discount rate—A symbolic rate. Nominally, a rate at which a central bank will advance funds to approved borrowers. It is an instrument of monetary policy; a change in the Discount rate is a signal to the market place that the central bank wants market rates to move in the direction signaled. As well, in the event of emergencies, where a credit crunch is taking place, loans will actually take place at the discount window. Small "d" discount refers to a rate applied to a future sum to arrive at a present value. It also refers to bonds trading at less than their face value or par value. Confused yet?

Dominion Bond Rating Service (DBRS)—An entity which assigns credit ratings to a wide variety of securities.

Doomsday call— *(see* Canada call feature)

Duration—The average life of your fixed-income investment. A ten-year bond is not a ten-year bond. What? All those pesky interest payments shorten the average term. The bigger the interest payments, the shorter the duration. Got it yet? For a zero coupon bond, maturity and duration are the same since there are no cash flows to worry about. Duration is tossed around by bond cognoscenti as a way of measuring risk.

Extendible—A security whose maturity may be extended under certain conditions.

Face value—The stated nominal value of your fixed-income investment. For example, you invest $98,000 in a bond that matures to $100,000. The $100,000 is the face value of the bond. The market price may go above or below that value, but that is what will be returned to you.

Federal Reserve Board—The American equivalent of the Bank of Canada. It is the most important central bank in the world.

First call date—The earliest time at which a security may be called by an issuer. Most securities are non callable for several years.

Fixed—A rate of interest paid by a borrower on a bond that stays constant or *fixed.*

Fixed/Floater—A corporate bond issued by chartered banks. While the stated maturity may be ten years, typically the issuer pays a fixed coupon rate for say, five years, at which point the coupon rate would float at some artificial rate such as Bas plus 100 basis points. They are issued to allow the banks to use them as senior capital.

Flat—A yield curve where yields are the same at all maturities. Also can mean that a bond is trading with no accrued interest, either because the settlement date coincides with the coupon payment date or because the issuer is not able to make interest payments.

Floating—A rate of interest that is adjusted at specific intervals using a specific formula. For example, every three months at three-month treasury bills plus 25 basis points.

Fungible—Interchangeable. One security may be fungible with another one of similar characteristics. The term is most often used when an existing issue is reopened with the new bonds becoming fungible with the existing ones.

Foreign-pay bonds—Bonds that pay their interest in a foreign currency. Many Canadian entities issue them.

GICs—Also pronounced "geeks." These are securities issued by banks so that they can lend your money out at a higher rate.

"Haircut"—What you receive when selling a bond. It is your IA's commission.

Hedge—What bond traders do to protect their inventories from market fluctuation. Typically, it involves selling short benchmark issues against long positions.

Hybrid securities—A security which contains multiple components, most frequently debt and equity. This includes different types of structured products, such as principal-protected notes and step-up bonds.

IIROC—Investment Industry Regulatory Organization of Canada (formerly the IDA). A self-regulatory body for all investment dealer members.

IDB—Interdealer broker. An intermediary who facilitates trade between investment dealers by posting anonymous bids and offerings.

Initial offering price—The price of a bond at the time of issuance.

Institutions—Large financial organizations, namely life insurance, pension funds, mutual funds, governments, and banks, which make up the bulk of bond market activity. They represent the individual investor since they are trading other people's money—your pension, mutual fund units, bank deposits.

Interest—Money paid to investors by borrowers for lending them money. Similar to a landlord/tenant relationship. Interest payments are thus analogous to rent payments.

Inventory—To facilitate the retail and institutional customers, investment dealers maintain inventory of "shelf products," financed with their own capital and offered at (hopefully) competitive prices.

Investment dealers—Organizations that provide a wide range of services to both issuers of securities and those who invest in them. They provide market-making ability in money and bond markets, underwriting capability, and brokerage services.

Investment-grade—Indicates that, according to the credit rating services, a bond is considered safe for investment.

ISIN—International Security Identification Number.

Jobbers—Approved money market dealers who must bid for each week's treasury bill auction. They are Bank Of Montreal, CIBC, Deutsche Bank Securities, HSBC Bank Canada, Laurentian Bank, Merrill Lynch Canada, National Bank Financial, RBC Dominion Securities, Scotia Capital, and Toronto Dominion Bank.

Junk bonds—Bonds issued by companies whose credit ratings have fallen below levels considered safe for investors. Their relative and absolute high yields reflect how risky they are.

Ladder—A portfolio of bonds with evenly staggered maturities.

Leverage—The use of various financial instruments or borrowed capital, such as margin, to increase the potential return of an investment. For example, Long Canadas are marginable at 4 percent for investment dealers and typically 10 percent for individuals. That represents considerable leverage.

Liquidity—The relative ease by which investors may buy or sell bonds.

Listed—A security which trades publicly on an exchange. Most convertible bonds are now listed.

Long position—A bond position owned in inventory by an investment dealer.

Make whole call—A type of call provision allowing the issuer to off any remaining debt under prescribed conditions.

Management fees—What you pay a mutual fund manager to gamble with your money. Also known as management expense ratios, or MERs.

Margin—Money loaned to you by an FI to finance a leveraged position.

Markup—The amount that IAs add to the transfer price from their bond desk in order to get paid.

Matrix—Establishing a price for a bond by linking it to a more actively traded issue in order to provide a quotation.

Maturity—The point in time at which your fixed-income investment comes to an end and your principal or face value is returned to you.

Monetary policy—Carried out by the Bank of Canada, it refers to policy that either stimulates or restricts money supply growth by either lowering or raising interest rates or by expanding or contracting bank reserves.

Money market—Fixed-income securities issued with a term to maturity of one year or less. It is also applied to those bonds issued with a maturity date longer than one year but whose maturities have now reached less than one year owing to the passage of time.

Mortgage-backed securities—Issued as marketable bonds; they are backed by first mortgages on real estate. Investors receive a blended monthly payment of interest and principal.

Mutual funds—Entities that take your money and mingle it with a whole lot of other people's money and pay themselves handsomely in the process.

Net amount—In a bond transaction, the total amount owed on a bond purchase, including the accrued interest.

New issues—Also called Primary Issues, these are brand new securities. In the world of government bonds, some new issues are identical, or fungible, with existing issues.

Non callable—The issuer has no right to call the securities away from the investor before maturity.

Note—An unsecured short-term instrument.

Offer *(see also* Ask)—Opposite of a bid. It is the price at which a trader is willing to sell a bond.

Off the run—A bond issue that is not a benchmark issue. It may have a very high or low coupon; it may be a small, illiquid issue; its ownership may be concentrated in few hands or it may have a feature or features that make it unattractive to trade—the bid-ask spread will be wider for such an issue, as dealers either do not wish to hold them in inventory, or if they do, find it difficult to sell them quickly. This sometimes works in the favour of the client, but not often, as the transfer price is typically higher than it would be if the issue was "on the run."

On the run—An actively traded bond whose coupon rate is close to current yield levels so that its price is close to par.

Over-the-counter—Something that is "not centralized." Unlike the equity market, which has a recognizable physical location to trade stocks, the bond market is decentralized, with no one meeting place; transactions occur verbally or electronically between market participants. Bonds trade on a principal basis. Unlike equities, where buyers and sellers meet to trade a stock and charge each client a commission, bonds trade on a net basis—dealers maintain inventories of fixed-income products, financing them with their own capital and attempting to sell them at slightly higher prices than they paid. At the retail level, it is similar to a store. The dealers maintain "shelf product," marking up from wholesale to compensate for risk, cost of capital, etc. They must maintain competitive pricing since they are selling the same line of goods as their principal competitors.

Packages—The fixed-income answer to annuities. By removing or stripping several years of interest payments from a bond, one can create a deferred annuity.

Par—A price of $100. Bonds mature at par, or 100 percent of their face value.

Performance—What your investments return.

Present value—What an amount of money due in the future is worth today after applying a discount rate.

Primary dealers—Those investment dealers chosen by the Bank of Canada to bid for new issues and to make orderly secondary markets for Government of Canada issues. At present there are 11 primary dealers: BMO Nesbitt Burns, Casgrain and Co., CIBC World Markets, Desjardins Securities Inc., Deutsche Bank Securities, Merrill Lynch Canada, Laurentian Bank Securities, National Bank Financial, RBC Dominion Securities, Scotia Capital, and Toronto Dominion Bank.

Positive—Refers to a "normal" yield curve, one where the longer the term to maturity, the higher the yield. Also known as upward-sloping.

Principal—What you lend. It is returned to you at maturity date.

Private placement—An issue not made available to the investing public. Such an issue is sold to a few institutional clients.

Reconstitution—The reverse of stripping: putting a bond back together again.

Redeemable—Similar to callable bonds but with one HUGE difference. Normally issued by corporations, a redeemable bond may be "called" by the issuer but NOT for financial advantage. In other words, the issue may not be redone at a lower coupon rate. Rather, should a company have surplus cash, or in the event of a corporate development (e.g. a takeover), the bond issue may be retired prematurely.

Reinvestment risk—There are two basic risks. First, the yield to maturity quoted on a bond may not be realized, since interest payments never get reinvested at the same rate. Second, having your entire portfolio mature at the same time is a financial version of Russian roulette. Rates may have fallen dramatically, leaving you much poorer.

Residuals—The principal portion left over after all the interest payments have been stripped away. (We do not call them *principals* because that would be too easy to understand!)

Registered Retirement Savings Plan (RRSP)—A plan that allows individuals to defer tax until retirement.

Retirement Savings Bond (RSB)—A partly stripped bond. It is analogous to an annuity, as the payments begin at a prescribed time in the future. They can be customized to individuals' needs.

Retractable—A bond or preferred issue whose maturity may be shortened. Opposite of extendible.

Semi-annual—For bonds, twice a year. Most bonds pay interest on a semi-annual basis. Do not be tricked into buying any biennial pay bonds!

Short-selling—Selling a security that one does not own. Typically used by investment dealers to hedge their long positions, to accommodate client demands, or to speculate on falling bond prices.

Sinking fund—There are two types of sinking funds. The first is found on older corporate bonds: it is a feature that says that a company must redeem a certain percentage of an issue each year before maturity. This feature reduces the burden of paying an entire issue off at one date and also reduces the debt in proportion to the depreciation of the asset built or purchased with the proceeds. It also provides for liquidity, since the issuing company provides bids for the bonds; however, should interest rates fall, the company redeems the bonds at par or face value, again not a welcome development for the lender, since the bonds should trade at a premium! In the good old days when there was a thriving corporate bond market, with all these features attached, institutional bond jockeys would play the "sinking fund game," corralling large blocks in an attempt to get the sinker to pay a higher price than justified by the credit. Those days are, sadly, no more. Steadily declining rates in the last 12 years have brought home to many the negative side of these features, which may lead to their investment being prematurely terminated.

A second type of sinking fund is a general sinking fund. Normally issued by provinces, this feature indicates that the borrower must set aside a certain percentage of money every year but does not have to buy that specific one. This adds to liquidity and allows the issuer to invest in bonds (frequently stripped bonds) to allow for the orderly repayment of the bond issue at maturity.

Spread—The difference between the bid side and the offered side of a bond quotation. The shorter the bond and the higher the quality of the bond, the closer or "tighter" the bid-ask spread. Benchmark issues trade tighter than other bonds. Small corporate bond issues with little float may not even have a two-sided market. The spread thus incorporates a trader's feel for how quickly a bond may be sold.

Strips—Zero coupon bonds that pay no interest. Zeros, residuals, TIGRs, Sentinels, and Cougars are all the same. They are excellent for retirement planning, as they trade at a discount from par or maturing value; the size of the discount will depend on the amount of time to maturity and the yield to maturity.

Stripping—Separating the components of a bond—interest payments and the principal—and selling them all as separate zero coupon securities.

Subject—A bid or an offering that may be changed or cancelled before a transaction.

Switches—Transactions or trades where one bond is exchanged or traded for another for any one of a number of reasons—to shorten term, extend term, pick up yield, or improve quality.

Transfer price—The price at which the bond-trading desk transfers a bond to an IA. In other words, the salesperson's cost. To make a living, the salesperson must add a commission to this cost. The client does not see this since bonds are quoted on a "net" or "all-in" basis. Therefore, there are two factors at work here. The transfer price will vary from one investment dealer to another and is a function of the philosophy and structure of that organization. This is why it is important to ask about a firm's philosophy as to whether or not the retail desk is master of its own destiny or has to pay the wholesale desk something. Clearly, the lower the transfer price, the lower the cost to the client; an FA with the lowest transfer price will increase his business over competitors with higher transfer prices (assuming the same markup). Word spreads when a broker has the best prices around. The corollary is that a broker facing a higher transfer price may have to reduce the mark-up in order to remain competitive and thus face lower earnings.

Transparency—The ease with which one can view bond quotes and transactions. The Canadian bond market is more opaque than transparent.

Unit holder—One who owns units in a mutual fund.

Volatility—How much the price of a bond changes for a given movement in yield.

Yield—Current, to maturity. Basically, what an investment returns. Current yield of a bond is the coupon rate divided by the price. This is also known as "running yield." However, it is misleading, as bonds have a maturity date, and the difference between the market price and the value at maturity must be factored into the yield.

Yield curve—A line drawn joining yields at different maturity dates.

Zero coupon bonds— *(See* Strips)

Of Related Interest

Business and Retirement Guide to Belize
Bob Dhillon with Fred Langan

An introduction to living, working, and retiring in Belize, as well as owning property there. Dhillon introduces the reader to the country, its beauty and friendly people, and its economic attractions. One of the world's undiscovered secrets, Belize is a retirement haven and a safe place to park your money.

BACK COVER MATERIAL

"WISE, JUSTIFIABLY OPINIONATED, AND CLEARLY WRITTEN—ACCESSIBLE TO THE ORDINARY INVESTER."

—Tom Kierans, former president of Scotia McLeod Inc.

***

With more than one trillion dollars in bonds outstanding, the Canadian fixed-income market is enormous. In fact, its daily trading volume is almost !ve times that of the equity markets. Yet investors and even many financial advisors know little about it.

In Your Best Interest demystifies the retail fixed-income market, from the basics of a bond to the various products available and a full discussion of the mathematics of bonds and the bond market. It also provides useful tips on selecting the right advisor. "is third edition of *In Your Best Interest* gives you the tools to meet your income and retirement needs by making the retail fixed-income market less expensive, more accessible, and more efficient.

***

HANK CUNNINGHAM has more than forty years of experience in fixed-income markets. He has been a trader, institutional salesman, portfolio manager, and zero coupon specialist. Since 1988, he has specialized in the retail aspect of the investment business, building and managing three di8erent retail fixed-income trading desks. He is currently the fixed-income strategist for Odlum Brown Limited. He maintains a website, inyourbestinterest.ca, and is a frequent guest on the Business News Network and a regular contributor to the business print media.

H

I

J

L

M

N

O

P

Q

R

S

T

U

Made in the USA
Monee, IL
08 November 2026

68091701R00197